NICHOLAS PARSONS

With Just a Touch of Hesitation, Repetition and Deviation

My Life in Comedy

MAINSTREAM
PUBLISHING

EDINBURGH AND LONDON

This edition, 2011

First published in Great Britain in 2010 by
MAINSTREAM PUBLISHING COMPANY
(EDINBURGH) LTD
7 Albany Street
Edinburgh EH1 3UG

ISBN 9781845967123

A catalogue record for this book is available
from the British Library

Printed in Great Britain by
CPI Cox and Wyman Reading RG1 8EX

1 3 5 7 9 10 8 6 4 2

Nicholas Parsons

With Just a Touch of Hesitation,
Repetition and Deviation

My Life in Comedy

Nicholas Parsons was born in Grantham and moved to London with his family at the age of eight. In 1940, he travelled to Glasgow and served a full engineering apprenticeship with a pump firm in the harsh world of Clydeside. After the war, he became a professional actor and has rarely been unemployed since. He has worked in almost every branch of show business, as a serious actor, comedy performer, solo cabaret artist and stand-up comedian. He has performed for fifteen years at the Edinburgh Festival, with three different shows. His longest-running professional role has been as the chairman of *Just a Minute*, which he took on in 1967 and continues to this day.

He actively supports a number of children's charities, including the Lord's Taverners, of which he was president for two years. He was rector of St Andrews University and was given an honorary degree of LLD for his work. In 2004, he was awarded an OBE for his services to drama and broadcasting.

To Annie, whose love, tolerance
and support have been invaluable.

CONTENTS

PREFACE

My autobiography was published in 1994, 16 years ago. I found the writing a struggle; I would rather go on stage and express myself verbally. It was made worthwhile when my daughter said to me how thrilled she was that I had completed it because my grandchildren would know about their grandfather.

A lot has happened in my life since the publication of that book, both professionally and personally, and as a result I decided to write these memoirs, revealing some of my more recent experiences and the humorous incidents to which they gave rise. I also look back at the influences of the past that have a bearing or connection to what has happened to me in my later years. In my first book, I covered every aspect of my personal life, but it was never my intention to go over all the same ground here. Instead, I have chosen to focus on my long and varied professional career. Where appropriate, to understand the decisions I made or why I accepted the opportunities that came my way, I have adapted and reprised certain areas of activity from my autobiography.

When you reach your 80s and continue to be employed in the amazing and unpredictable world that we call show business, you achieve a status that is very flattering. You find yourself being introduced as an icon of British entertainment, probably because people are surprised that you are still actively working in a profession that is very insensitive to age and rapidly casts elderly performers aside. Employers are always looking for new talent and new faces, and yet these are the same people who say they need a 'name' to sell the show.

People often ask me if I am going to retire. My answer is very simple: 'I am in a profession that retires you.' There is no truer statement in show business than 'You are only as good as your last job.' One indifferent performance and you are not asked again. You always have to be on top of your game, giving your best, or you will not be re-engaged.

What has sustained and kept me going all these years? Not the professional successes I have experienced. I have enjoyed them, certainly. They have been wonderful, but they are ephemeral and no guarantee of future work in our crazy profession. It is undoubtedly my family, the true constant in my life. The day my daughter, Suzy, was born and then two and a half years later my son, Justin, were the two most joyous events of my life, and to be involved in every stage of their growing up and development has been such a happy time. The unconditional love that a child gives to its parent is something to be treasured. Now, between them they have given me four grandchildren, and this has been a double blessing. Someone asked when I first became a grandparent, 'Didn't it make you suddenly feel old?' On the contrary, it made me feel young again, and being with any of the four of them is very special.

When my wife, Annie, came into my life, besides the love and support she brought, there was the bonus of the fact that she had two children approximately the same ages as mine. Now we have nine grandchildren between us, and we find time in our busy lives to see all of them.

The one occasion I became sad and depressed was when my first wife, Denise, and I separated. There was no acrimony; we just developed in different ways and drifted apart. She has made a new life for herself and seems happy, and we have remained good friends. When it happened, I felt I had failed. Perhaps I had, but the comfort and attention I receive from Annie has filled that void.

A preface is no place to suddenly bear your soul, but when I started writing about myself I began to think about what was important and what has helped me handle the ups and downs that life and show business have thrown at me. At times, it has felt as if I was writing a very long obituary, and it is certain there will not be another autobiographical book after this one. I hope you find what I have written interesting and entertaining. I have been candid and, I hope, not critical. I have huge respect for my profession and all those who struggle to make a living within it.

Let me finish this preface by thanking David Wilson, who was seconded to me from Mainstream Publishing to be my editor. He showed understanding and forbearance when I missed my delivery date for the manuscript and helped in the assembly of the text into the chapters here. Finally, my thanks to Bill Campbell and everyone at Mainstream for the faith they have shown in commissioning this book. I hope it justifies their hopes and delivers what we all wish.

Nicholas Parsons

FIRST IMPRESSIONS

It was the elephants. The sight of four of them walking in single file down the high street, each holding in its trunk the tail of the one in front, is a moment from more than eighty years ago that I remember as clearly as if it happened yesterday. I was five years old, and the travelling circus was parading through Grantham, the town where I was born and lived until the age of eight. As I watched spellbound, I was drawn in particular to the clowns in their garish costumes and funny make-up, mingling and laughing with the townspeople, and stared in disbelief as the acrobats performed simple gymnastics on a decorated float.

Later that week, my mother took me and my six-year-old brother, John, and three-year-old sister, Patricia, to see the show. I was fascinated by the animals, awestruck by the trapeze artists and thrilled by the acrobats, particularly when two of them jumped on and off a horse and performed tricks whilst balancing on the animal's back as it cantered around the ring. As someone who was agile and a natural tumbler, I think that is what I most wanted to do. If someone had whisked me away to join the circus at that moment, I would have been blissfully happy. It was then, I believe, that I was first imbued with the desire to be a performer.

When we returned home, I immediately started taking off the clowns and trying in a clumsy way to emulate the acrobats. Later, John and I put together our own version of the circus show in the nursery and invited our parents and other relations to watch. John, being the more authoritative personality, was naturally the ringmaster. Patricia and I appeared as the show horses, scampering around on our hands and knees in response to our brother's orders. I did some kind of tumbling act on a mattress, and Patricia was then instructed to be a trapeze artist, which, in a flood of tears, she quite rightly said was impossible. We compromised and let her go on as a solo horse. John and I then changed our clothes and came out as the clowns we had seen, who had called themselves Cuckoo and Sparrow. We tried to reproduce their routine, which mostly consisted of me, as Cuckoo, the more outrageous of the two, appealing to Sparrow in a cooing voice, 'Cuckoo . . . Sparrow.' For weeks, the house echoed to the sound of me calling out, 'Cuckoo . . . Sparrow,' until my mother, bored with the repetition, told me to stop being a clown and behaving in such a stupid way or I would be confined to my bedroom. A seed had been sown, however, that was to continue growing for the rest of my life.

My father was one of three doctors in a partnership in the town. My mother, a staff nurse, had trained at University College Hospital in London, where she met my Cambridge-educated father. He came from a well-connected family whose Scottish ancestors were landed gentry in Dumfriesshire and whose English ancestors owned tracts of land in Oxfordshire. Rumour has it that the English ancestors drank their inheritance away and the Calvinist Scottish ones gave it away. My grandfather on my father's side died young, leaving my father, his brother and mother little money but a magnificent family crest, a deep Christian faith and a dedication to the service of others. I sensed sometimes that my mother felt her family were socially inferior to my father's, when she had every reason to be proud of them. Her father was an extremely successful businessman, Walter Maggs, who, with his brother, had built up the large Bristol store B. Maggs and Co. to its eminence in the '30s. My mother's attitude was perhaps understandable. In those days, there was still a rigid class system, and people in business were regarded as *in trade*. Nowadays, business people are among the most admired in society.

The first school I attended was Kesteven and Grantham High School for Girls. I went there for the simple reason that its kindergarten took both boys and girls. A young Margaret Roberts was a pupil at the same school, and my father attended her when her own doctor was not available. In time, she would go on to marry Denis Thatcher and make quite a name for herself. After kindergarten, I was enrolled at King's School for Boys in Grantham, but I was there only a term before my parents decided that I should join my brother at Tenterden Hall, a boarding prep school in north London. In fact, the whole family moved south, as my father bought a practice on the edge of Clapham Common. Their decision to send me to Tenterden was obviously made in my best interests, but I was miserable there. The conditions and regime could be described only as Dickensian. The real ogre of the place was the matron, who seemed to have no understanding, nor even liking, of children. Her name was Mrs Blanche. We called her 'Blancmange'. She dressed in the full regalia of a hospital matron of the '30s, with starched apron, starched headdress and starched cuffs. She was a forbidding figure, and I was terrified of her. It did not help that she also had her favourites and I was not one of them. The masters, an unhappy mix of First World War veterans, were not unkind but were very strict, and the cane or slipper was used frequently. It was almost part of the ethos of the school. Matron would report me to the housemaster for the slightest misdemeanour, and the punishment I received was usually quite severe. I never spoke to my parents about my distress or discomfort. I suppose I assumed it was all part of the normal school regime and they must have experienced the same in their youth. It was just another aspect of growing up that had to be endured.

Not for the last time in my life, comedy saved me. I survived because I found I could make my chums laugh either by playing the fool or by mimicking the masters. This policy was not without its risks. On one occasion, one of our teachers, Mr Stavitsky, was late for a lesson, so I left my desk, took his gown off the back of the door and put it on. With the gown trailing around my ankles, I proceeded to try to impersonate his military way of speaking and limped about, aping his walk, which was a result, we had been told, of bullets still lodged in his leg. I was going magnificently. I had the audience in the palm of my hand. I loved it. Then suddenly it went quiet. Like a true professional, I tried harder. Why had I lost my audience? Was my material not good enough? A second later, I discovered the real reason. Standing just behind me was Mr Stavitsky, looking distinctly displeased. I tried a nine year old's joke: 'You were late, sir, so I thought I would help by talking to the class.'

Mr Stavitsky was not amused and barked out, 'Parsons, you have mocked me; you have mocked my infirmities. You have made an exhibition of yourself, and now I will make an exhibition of you in front of the whole class. Take off my gown and bend over.' Six of the best quickly followed. I can still feel the pain, the indignity and the unfairness. My triumph was turned to ashes, but deep down the seed had sprouted more roots. I had enjoyed my moment while it had lasted. What I say in my one-man comedy show is that back then I was caned for getting laughs but now I am paid for it.

Eventually, my parents realised how unhappy I was at Tenterden Hall and moved both my brother and me to Colet Court, the preparatory day school for St Paul's. I enjoyed my time there, particularly the games, and even won cups and medals for boxing. I moved up to the main school in 1938, the same year my father bought a new medical practice, as well as an expensive house, in Hampstead. The following year proved to be a great one for me, even as the international situation deteriorated swiftly. I was barely 15, aware of what was unfolding in Europe, but never dreamed the worst could happen. I was awarded my colours for rugby and cricket, playing for the under-16 colts, and academically I was top of my form.

Throughout this period, my desire to perform never left me. My mother did not approve, but she did say that if I wanted to act I should do so as an amateur, like one of my father's patients, Lila Henderson. 'That is the way you do it,' she told me. 'As a hobby, like Lila. They have such fun doing their little plays.' Lila did arrange for me to have a part in one of the productions her group, the Stock Exchange Players, was putting on. I appeared as a schoolboy in *Housemaster* by Ian Hay. I adored it. We rehearsed in the evenings and played at two country houses outside London, followed by three nights at the little Cripplegate Theatre, near the Barbican, which is now a library. It was tremendous fun, and I felt in my natural element when acting on the stage.

That year, I was also cast in a school play. The reaction to my performance was very positive, and I was promised a leading role the following year. It began to dawn on my parents that I was serious about acting. My mother was appalled. She may have encouraged me to play and perform in my nursery, and even pushed me in the direction of Lila and her am-dram, but talk of an acting career was altogether different: 'If you want to keep on with amateur dramatics, that is fine. But you must not do it as a profession. All actors are in some way debauched. Someone like you, Nicholas, will just end up as an alcoholic or some kind of pervert. That is not going to happen to my son.'

I think my mother thought I would be incapable of resisting the 'dreadful temptations' of show business. She looked upon me as being weak and ineffectual. There were reasons my mother felt this way. I am dyslexic, although in those days that was not a recognised condition, and she couldn't understand why I had trouble reading. She thought I was slow. My dyslexia has proved to be both a burden and a benefit to me. As is common with many sufferers, I have very good recall. People with dyslexia have to rely on their memory in order to achieve things. I did so at school and excelled in my exams, because I worked hard at remembering facts, figures and information. Developing my memory has proved invaluable in my profession, especially when I worked in repertory, where you have to learn a whole new part during the week while playing another in the evening. It was also crucial during my time presenting *Sale of the Century*, where I did not work with an autocue. Anglia Television found I could run the show without it and never bothered to invest in the technology. Also, when we record *Just a Minute*, I have to listen carefully and remember every word that is said in order to adjudicate on challenges, particularly for repetition. There have also been tremendous drawbacks. I read slowly and have not consumed as many books as my appetite has demanded. I would dearly love to have read much more, as I enjoy acquiring knowledge. Perhaps that is part of my Scottish heritage, a passion to acquire knowledge for its own sake.

Not only was I regarded as being slow, but I also stammered. That was partly down to my mother's actions, not that she, or anyone else, could have known it at the time. My mother was a great traditionalist, and in the '30s it was considered wrong to be left-handed. She was horrified when I started to write and took up the pen in my left hand. I remember her saying to a friend that when she saw this she snatched the pen away and forced it into my right hand. I have subsequently been told by academics that this can create a disturbance in the mind, because one part of the brain controls your actions on the left, and another the right. If this is forcibly disrupted, it can result in difficulties in speech. This caused me great problems socially until I found a way to control my stuttering. Strangely, it has rarely caused difficulties professionally.

My mother saw all this and, perhaps not unreasonably, thought I was far from an ideal person to become an actor. My cause was not helped by her discovery that I had acquired the nickname 'Shirley' at Colet Court. My good friend John Treacher had asked me what I wanted to do when I left school. I told him I wanted to be an actor. The only acting John knew was the cinema, and at the time Shirley Temple was a big star. The name stuck for a while, and I embraced it, as it helped me to feel closer to the profession I hoped to join when I grew up. For my mother, however, it only confirmed her worst fears. I think, genuinely, she did her best to stop me becoming an actor because she thought it would be a disaster. My father supported her. He was less hands-on with the children, but he was a professional man, and, as far as he was concerned, you did not go into the weird world of show business unless you were born to it.

On 3 September 1939, we were all glued to our wireless sets when Prime Minister Neville Chamberlain addressed the nation, during which he uttered the fateful words '. . . this country is at war with Germany'. My world came to a stop. Yet it need not have done. My father was badly affected by the outbreak of hostilities, and while he and my mother could have sent me away with St Paul's, which had been evacuated to Crowthorne in Berkshire, they decided instead that I was a non-achiever and pulled me out. I had been blissfully happy at St Paul's, almost invariably being the last to leave the grounds at the end of the day. The education I received there has formed the basis of any learning I now possess. I have enormous affection for the school, and I am still involved in fundraising activities to support their renovation projects at the site they now occupy near Barnes, in south-west London.

My brother, John, who was about to leave school, had already been offered a training course with Rolls-Royce, and soon he went to Derby, where he worked very hard and later became a successful businessman. Patricia went with her school to Berkhamsted. As for me, my parents put their decision down to their parlous financial situation, brought on by my father's wealthy patients in Hampstead moving away from the capital almost overnight, and sent me to the only educational establishment that was open in north London, Clark's College, in Finchley. I was born in an age when you did not necessarily do what you wanted; you did what you were told. I was upset but accepted everything with depressed resignation. I think I was in shock. All the joy of the last two years at school and the prospects I had dreamed about had been shattered.

This was the period known as the 'Phoney War', with no fighting, no bombing, just an eerie foreboding. I was lonely, all my friends had left London, the cinemas were shut and there were no games at Clark's. I had nothing to do every night but go down to the public library and study for my exams. I soon discovered, thanks to the high quality of teaching at St Paul's, that I knew more in some subjects than the masters at my new school. I worked hard and took my exams in December. I came through with flying colours and matriculated. At the age of sixteen and two months, I was qualified to go to university.

When my parents asked me what I wanted to do next, I told them I wanted to be an actor and if that was not possible, because of the war, I would like to continue with my schooling. Their response was to the point: 'Let's be sensible. You have got to think about getting a job. A proper job.'

I do not know what was going through their minds. I was barely 16 and not ready for a 'proper' job. It was then that my uncle Hugh, my father's brother, to whom I was close and very fond of, took a hand. He pointed out that I was very capable at making and repairing things, such as old clocks. Why not become an engineer? I did enjoy working with my hands, but only as a hobby. By that stage, however, I was already in a somewhat depressed state from the impact of the war, from being taken out of a school that I loved and from being asked to make a decision about my future. I was just drifting. If I was not going to become an actor, I did not give a damn what I did. Uncle Hugh took further action. He contacted close friends in Scotland who in turn spoke on his behalf to their relations who ran a pump and turbine firm on Clydebank called Drysdale's. The next thing I knew, I had been accepted for an engineering apprenticeship by the company and was on a train to Glasgow to begin a new life on my own.

This was a culture shock. Suddenly this 16-year-old boy from an English public school and professional middle-class family was transplanted to the hard, harsh and challenging environment of Clydebank. On arrival in Glasgow, I stayed with our family friends the McClaurens for a couple of days, then found my way to the YMCA, arranged some lodgings, got myself a boiler suit, and on the Monday morning I was on a tramcar trundling down to Yoker on Clydebank. The snow was on the ground; it was 8 a.m. and dark. I walked down Ferry Road to Drysdale's and heard all these characters talking in broad, guttural Glaswegian. It seemed they were speaking a different language. I thought I had entered another world, and to my amazement I discovered they were using as adjectives words that I had only ever seen written on lavatory walls. I warily moved closer to a couple of them to check if I had heard correctly.

The firm had been very kind, taking me on immediately and offering me a comprehensive apprenticeship. I was to spend six months in each department, starting with the tool room, where the machine tools were forged and ground. The foreman, or gaffer, was Alex Woods, a gentle man who treated me with great tolerance. I found the hours terribly demanding. I had never before stood for nearly nine hours with only one break, and my back ached. Sitting down was forbidden, except in the lunch break, and to begin with I found it so difficult that I would sneak off for a little rest, and the only sanctuary in which this was possible was the lavatories. That was a sophisticated word for the place that was commonly referred to in far baser terms.

All that could be said in favour of the 'lavvies' was that they served their basic purpose. In fact, they had been very practically designed to that end but with no thought for privacy. There was one central building in the middle of the works that was used by everyone on the shop floor. The entrance was through a swing door, and to the left was a wall for urination – no urinals. To the right were two facing rows of white china toilets with no seats, each separated by a low partition. At the entrance was an elderly man in a little wooden cubicle with a shelf in front of him, who gave you a ring with a metal counter that had a number on it, which entitled you to a seven-minute session. The man's name was Sam, known to everyone, inevitably, as 'S***house Sam'. He ran the place like a boating pond, keeping a close eye on proceedings, regularly announcing, 'Number five, your time is up, come on oot,' or, 'Number three, thirty seconds to go.' He smoked a combination of what was described to me as 'thick black and old shag', which slightly relieved the other pungent odours. Once you received your metal disc, you knew there was a vacant seat. You had to remember to take a newspaper: toilet paper was unheard of. You went to the empty pan and joined the nine other men squatting in a row with their boiler suits round their ankles, arms on knees, holding copies of the *Daily Mirror* or *Daily Record*. Opposite was another row of men doing exactly the same.

Hygiene was maintained by an automatic flushing system, which was activated every two minutes, beginning at one end and rushing down the line. It generated a fair amount of power, so if you did not rise at the crucial moment you could get very wet. The system, though effective, was pretty antiquated, and every flush would be heralded by a rumbling in the pipes. It was customary, therefore, for the man nearest the start of the flush, on hearing the warning noise, to shout down the line, 'It's on its way, lads. Arses up.' Ten naked bums of different shapes and sizes would then rise in unison to avoid a soaking. It may have been basic, but you can get used to anything if there is no alternative. My only real embarrassment was during one of my escapes to relieve my aching back muscles. The gaffer had eagle eyes, and he had spotted me leaving my bench. Estimating that I had overstayed my seven minutes, and while I was still studying the sports pages of my newspaper, he burst in and dragged me away, announcing at the top of his voice that my time was up and that it was also my second visit that day. It is difficult to maintain any poise with your trousers and boiler suit round your ankles. Any awkward moments I have encountered in show business since have been nothing compared with the embarrassment that I felt then in front of that audience.

The fact that I survived my time in Clydebank, and indeed prospered, is one of the things I am most proud of in my life. How I did it, I am not entirely sure, but I do know that it gave me a grounding that has stayed with me to this day. I was recently interviewed by Steve Wright on his Radio 2 show, and he asked me how I had managed to keep myself together throughout my career when so many others of my generation had fallen apart, turned to drink or just disappeared. I told him that I thought it was probably because I went through this incredibly tough time on Clydebank and found a way to cope. Show business is full of upsets, disappointments, frustrations and insults, but after what I went through on Clydebank nothing could be so daunting or difficult again. In retrospect, I was lucky to have had such a challenging experience.

Something else I had to adjust to was the noise generated by the engines. It stopped only at lunchtime, and the relief was indescribable. We would hungrily devour our sandwiches – or 'pieces' as they are called, presumably because they are two pieces of bread with something in the middle – with the grimy hands that had worked the machines. Only the offices had washing facilities. They also had the canteen, which was used more by the office staff than the shop-floor workers. There was a marked division between those who wore a jacket and a collar and tie and those who wore a boiler suit. The two rarely mixed. In those days, headgear was fairly traditional: nothing in the offices, peaked caps for the workers, usually a bowler hat for the foreman and always a bowler hat for the works manager. I wore a beret, which I still have.

Perhaps I survived by instinct. One thing I have learned is that, if you are always yourself and accept others as they are, people will accept you. They may not always warm to you, but they will accept you. It is also possible to embrace people from different backgrounds who have different attitudes and behaviours if you can find how to relate to them. Once again, my way was humour. I did impersonations and took off the different foremen, which endeared me to my fellow apprentices and made them smile. Slowly, I found a way to build a rapport. I even became known as 'Big Nick', because I was taller than most. It was a term of endearment and a compliment.

I remember one of the lads came up to me one day and said, 'Nick, I got te tell ye. I mean, ye're OK, but ye came here with that "Woah-Woah" accent and yer right proper manners, with nae clue what livin' is all aboot. Well, this is livin', Nick. This is what it's all aboot. We've showed ye how to get yer effin' haunds dirty. Ye mucked in, and we like ye, in spite of yer right English way of talking. Working here will make a man of ye.' He was right. Clydebank was the greatest learning for life anyone could have.

While I was learning to be an engineer, I was also determined to learn to be an actor. Away from the disapproving eye of my parents, I sought out every opportunity I could. Glasgow has a wonderful feeling for the theatre and the arts, and I was going to take full advantage of that. In their attempts to steer me away from performing, my parents had done me a favour by sending me to Scotland. I contacted the local amateur dramatic society, the Transport Players, who were delighted to hear from me. They were desperate to find young men who had not been called up.

I performed in a play called *Paddy the Next Best Thing* at the Lyric Theatre, which was owned by the YMCA and housed in the same building. I was a 16 year old in the role of a young man in his 20s who romanced a young woman, played by an actress who was 30. We made an odd pair, but I was delighted to perform in my first adult role. As I hoped to be a serious actor, I used my actual first initial as well as my more usual name and called myself C. (for Christopher) Nicholas Parsons. It had a ring to it when spoken but looked pompous in print. The habit did not last long.

There were many anti-aircraft sites and small barracks around the west of Scotland, and concert parties were always welcome to entertain the troops. They were organised by a group called Scottish Command Troop Entertainments, run by Archie McCulloch, a serving officer who understood show business. I saw an advert in the *Evening Times* for volunteer performers, applied and was made welcome. It was somewhat rough and ready but great experience and good fun. I usually compèred the shows and did impersonations of current radio and cinema stars, plus a comedy routine. I had no knowledge of comedy writing, so I reproduced material I had heard on the wireless and elsewhere. The style was immature, but my instincts to make people laugh seemed to be well received. Working on the assumption that you had to look funny to be funny, I wore large baggy trousers, a colourful waistcoat and a comical hat. That did not last long either.

After I had been at Drysdale's for a short while, Charlie Drysdale, who ran the 'outside squad', a highly skilled group of engineers who fitted and repaired the pumps manufactured by the works, called me to his office. Weir's of Cathcart had recently taken over the engineering yard, but the Drysdale family continued to run it. Charlie took a fatherly interest in me and suggested that, if I was going to be an engineer, I should go to university to study for a degree and become fully qualified. I wondered why my parents had not shown the same interest. I was in Clydebank only to please them, after all. I applied to the University of Glasgow but was informed that, with the subjects I had studied for my matriculation exams, I could enter any faculty except engineering and science. The only way I could be admitted to the engineering course was if I obtained Higher Mathematics, which meant taking a correspondence course with Glasgow Polytechnic, studying at night and passing the exam in six, not twelve, months. This was a lot to ask, given how tough I found the work during the day, and my increasing theatrical commitments, but I decided to take it on. I passed the exam in the summer of 1940 and was enrolled at the university that autumn on a sandwich course: six months' studying in the winter and six months' apprenticeship in the summer with an engineering firm. In my case, that would continue to be at Drysdale's.

Throughout my two years at Glasgow University, I found the academic side challenging. My school education had been based in

Classics rather than science, and, as my heart was never really in engineering, it was a struggle to pass the various exams. I did, however, become actively involved in the social life, performing for the Dramatic Society and playing loose-head prop for the First XV rugby team. I actually played for the university for three years, continuing for a season after I ceased to be a student, and was fairly successful. I was selected for the East versus West game at Murrayfield, which was in effect a trial for the Scottish team. I had a decent game but was not picked to represent the country. It is surprising to think now that at 12 and a half stone I was one of the heavier forwards in the university team. Today, that would be light for a back. I enjoyed my rugby and was good at the game, and it is possible that if I had decided to pursue it as a serious sport I might have achieved something significant.

When I enrolled in my course, I moved out of the YMCA and into accommodation nearer the university, off Byres Road, which also happened to be nearer the main BBC studios in Glasgow. I ventured up there, asked if I could have an audition and was invited back to read some scripts. I also did some of my impersonations, which went down well, and I was cast in a small part as a straight actor.

I loved the quiet, relaxed atmosphere of the studios and nonchalant professionalism of the experienced broadcasters. It was another world, a world to which I wanted to belong, and I suspect my enthusiasm was a little overwhelming. The producer was a very able man called Moultrie R. Kelsall, from whom I learned a great deal. Moultrie went on to have a distinguished acting career thoughout the '50s, appearing in films such as *The Lavender Hill Mob* and *The Inn of the Sixth Happiness*. I met him many years later and was pleased to be able to tell him how I remembered my first professional job in a play and how much I owed him.

Being at university, I had a break at Christmas, so I went home to London, where the bombing had now started in earnest. There was one particular evening, 29 December 1940, when the sirens had gone off as usual, a dreaded noise that never failed to send a chill through you. Soon, a distant drone of planes could be heard, accompanied by the reassuring barrage from the anti-aircraft guns. The whistling noise of descending bombs was then followed by a 'crunch', as somewhere in the distance the frightening onslaught from the skies rained down. It used to be said that it was the bomb that you could not hear that would drop on or near you. On that evening, however, there appeared to be none of those dreaded 'crunch' noises. It did not seem like a normal raid. In the darkness because of the blackout, I pulled back the curtain to look out. The sky glowed red in the distance, and there was more light than there had been at dusk. I told my father, and we decided to investigate. We walked up to Hampstead Heath, which was only about half a mile from our house, for a better view. At the Whitestone Pond, the highest point on the Heath, from where on a clear day you can just about make out the skyline of the City of London, there was already a small group of people. We stared in disbelief towards the city. It was lit up by innumerable fires, the intensity of which was turning night back into day for miles around. The entire area looked as if it was ablaze, a vast red and yellow fireball. Right in the centre was St Paul's, illuminated as no floodlights could possibly achieve. There were no explosions, only firebombs. This was what became known as the 'Second Great Fire of London', intended to destroy the heart of London not by explosion but by incendiaries. Incredible damage was inflicted, but for some reason the Germans never repeated the tactic.

To this day, I become choked when talking about this distressing event. I recently recorded an archive programme for radio in which various people recounted their memories of the Blitz. As I described the scene my father and I witnessed, I could not keep the emotion out of my voice. I had to stop the recording, compose myself and begin again. My overriding feeling, as we stood on Hampstead Heath that evening watching the dreadful destruction of the great City of London, was that the world we knew was coming to an end.

The next morning, we went down to see what help we could give, and with many others handed out hot drinks to the weary firemen who were still fighting the remains of the numerous blazes. The destruction the Germans had wrought was vast and shocking but not complete. Alone, surrounded by gutted buildings, ruined churches and rubble-strewn streets, stood St Paul's Cathedral, majestic, almost unscathed. An unforgettable image of hope.

The Luftwaffe's attack on Clydebank in March 1941 had a different feel to it but was no less devastating. It was carnage over two nights on a scale never seen before. This was not incendiary but mass destruction designed to flatten the town and the shipyards. Over a thousand bombs were dropped, and hundreds lost their lives. I am embarrassed to admit that my university friend Ross Belch and I slept through the first night of the attack. Together we had taken on the role of fire-watchers for a large building near Glasgow city centre. Our duties were simple. We arrived at 6 p.m. and stayed until 7 a.m. We had camp beds on which to sleep, and our main responsibility came in the event of an air raid. When the sirens sounded, we were to put on our tin hats, take up positions on the roof with stirrup pumps, be on hand to deal with any incendiary bombs and generally help prevent the building burning down. Up until that devastating raid, we had rarely been disturbed, and, as we were both studying hard, and I was continuing to perform, we were exhausted and slept through the Clydebank bombing, some 17 miles away. It is amazing to what you can become accustomed.

When we discovered the extent of the attack, we volunteered, along with many others, to help the emergency services in the worst-hit areas. It was grim. The tenement buildings might have been constructed as solid, practical housing, but when subjected to heavy bombardment they caused more damage and injury than less robust structures. Some of them had only partially collapsed, crushing people inside. We concentrated our energies on helping clear a way for the ambulance and first-aid services to reach the injured and dying.

After the 1940 Christmas break, I returned to Glasgow and continued to study and look for theatre work. In the '40s, there was a very successful Canadian showman called Carroll Levis. His great claim to fame was his 'discoveries' stage show, in which he presented unknown and aspiring performers whom he had found and introduced them as the great new stars of the future. Searching out new talent was nothing original, but Carroll Levis was probably the first to make a successful business out of it. His show toured the top variety theatres, and the public loved it. He had a good eye for talent, but it was not infallible. By the '50s, his show had migrated to television, and in June 1957 he was looking for acts to appear on his next broadcast. A group calling themselves the Quarrymen auditioned but lost out to another band based on the results of an audience clap-o-meter. The guitarist and lead singer of the group was John Lennon, and the band was soon to feature Paul McCartney and, later, George Harrison.

When Carroll Levis came to the Empire Theatre in Glasgow in 1941, I plucked up courage, went backstage one evening, tried my best to control my stutter and nervously asked if I could see Mr Levis. His manager was pleasant, put me at my ease, asked what I did as an act and invited me to an audition session later in the week.

The actual audition was not nearly as stressful. I had some material that had gone well in the concert-party shows and did two of my best impersonations: Jimmy Stewart and Charles Boyer. Carroll liked them and asked who else I could do. Encouraged, I gave him Robb Wilton, Max Miller, W.C. Fields, Tommy Trinder and a radio star of the time, Oliver Wakefield, who was banned from the BBC as a result of the double entendres hidden in his distinctive hesitant delivery. Carroll was impressed. I could not believe it. To be granted an audition had been the height of my ambition, and now he was offering me work. Could I travel to London in six weeks' time and be the discovery in an edition of his new radio series? My answer was an immediate yes.

I was due some leave from Drysdale's, so I took it to coincide with the show. All radio transmissions were live then, and the broadcast came from the Paris Cinema in Lower Regent Street, which the BBC had converted into a radio studio. (Since it was at basement level in a large building, it was safer than places above ground if there was any bombing.) Light-entertainment shows in the '40s, and even the '50s, could afford a full orchestra as well as a singer and a number of well-known artists. This broadcast was one in a series called *Carroll Levis Carries On* and comprised a guest star and a resident singer and orchestra, as well as special items, including the patriotic 'Worker of the Week'. The whole programme, which was devised and compèred by Carroll himself, was described in the *Radio Times* as 'dedicated to the workers and Forces of Great Britain'. I was introduced as his latest discovery and given four minutes, during which I did three impersonations. The transmission time was 12.30 p.m., a popular slot during the war for comedy shows. Our audience consisted of any members of the military who were passing through London and civilians who were working nearby. My parents did not come. Uncle Hugh, though, whose office was not far away – he ran a business that designed and made ties – did and, when he took me out to lunch afterwards, told me he was very impressed.

Carroll had talked of some more broadcasts in his next series, and he was as good as his word. The following winter, I was asked to appear in three broadcasts for his new show, *Happy-Go-Lucky Hour*. He had an item in each programme called 'Radio Deceivers', in which two of his discoveries, Diane Darling and myself, did an impression. The BBC had decided it was too dangerous in London to transmit evening broadcasts with an audience, so they had moved their light-entertainment operation to a place as far as possible from London and the bombs yet which was still accessible by train. This turned out to be Bangor, in north-west Wales, which was a long way from Glasgow just for a two-minute impersonation.

Travelling by train was no pleasure then. There were no refreshments and strict blackout rules: dimmed lights in the carriages and blinds tightly drawn. Nor were there signs at any stations. Every signpost in the country, as well as station names, had been removed so that if the Germans landed they would have no idea where they were. I do not think the authorities had worked out that everyone else in the country would be equally confused. You had to shout to anyone standing on a platform when a train stopped to establish the name of the town. Sometimes, people refused to answer for fear you were a spy, following the slogan printed everywhere, 'Careless Talk Costs Lives'. With the bombings, rail travel had become even more hazardous, as lines would be hit and trains diverted or forced to a standstill if approaching a town during an air raid.

These problems paled into insignificance for me. I was too excited at the prospect of the job and of staying in a hotel for the first time. I did two broadcasts. It was another small step in the direction I wanted to go.

I failed two of my exams in my first year at university but was still young enough to be allowed to resit. I got through those exams at the second attempt but realised that academically I was not going to be able to complete the course. I wondered then if I would do better to volunteer to be accepted into the Merchant Navy and start a full, professional career in show business after the war ended. I was already officially registered for military service, but as my apprenticeship was an important reserve occupation I was instructed to continue with that.

Around this time, I had my first experience as a professional stage actor. There was an excellent theatrical company in Glasgow, run by Wilson Barrett, which performed a weekly repertory of plays at the lovely Alhambra Theatre. This was a fine building, with huge pillars outside and ornate plasterwork inside, that was pulled down in the '60s, when provincial theatre was struggling against the impact of television. The smaller Theatre Royal and the King's Theatre were saved, but the loss of the Alhambra was a tragedy for Glasgow.

I visited Wilson Barrett and asked if he would see me. He did, and I was immediately offered a job. He was about to revive *Mr Wu*, an early '20s play with a Chinese setting, and I was given a tiny role as an English officer on a Chinese ship. It required minimal rehearsal, so I could fit it around my work at Drysdale's. I was greatly excited about being in a professional company, on a huge stage, before a packed audience every night. The production went well, and Wilson Barrett offered me parts in the last two shows of his season at the Alhambra. I could not take both of them because of my apprenticeship, but since the rehearsals for the first play coincided with the summer-holiday break I was able to accept that role. It was in *The Silver King*, a well-known play from the turn of the century by Henry Arthur Jones and Henry Herman.

The Silver King was written at a time when asides to the audience were still employed, and the revival was performed in the true spirit of the original. As a consequence, I learned a theatrical lesson that I tried to take to heart when working as a professional actor many years later.

I had a small part as a clerk who had done something dubious but was inspired by Wilson Barrett's character to mend his ways. At the end of the short scene with him, I turned to the audience and spoke an old-fashioned, corny line, which I delivered with great passion: 'He is wonderful. From this day on, I will lead a new life.' The timing must have been right, because it not only got a big laugh but received a round of applause. I was also mentioned in the brief review that appeared in the newspaper. A small-part guest actor, who in this instance was not even a professional, does not steal the limelight from the main lead. I might have endeared myself to the audience but not to the star actor, who also happened to be my employer. He gave me a stern look and gently suggested that I should not dwell on the line and should leave the stage more quickly.

There existed on the outskirts of Glasgow, in Rutherglen, a tiny theatre run by an exceptional woman, Molly S. Urquhart, who later became known nationally as Molly Urquhart. She was a distinguished Scottish actress married to an inspector of police, a marvellous man called William MacIntosh. Molly had taken a disused church hall, turned it into a theatre and used her initials for the name. The MSU became very successful in Rutherglen and also well known in Glasgow. She rehearsed every evening one week and played every evening the next, so you could hold down your day job and still accept an engagement. She presented about ten shows a year and paid £2 for each play in which you appeared.

I first came to her attention when she persuaded a friend of hers, Paul Vincent Carroll, a distinguished Irish author living in Glasgow, to allow her to present his new play, *The Strings, My Lord, Are False*, about the Clydebank Blitz. Molly rang me on a Thursday in the winter of 1942 and asked if I could learn lines quickly. The play opened on the Monday. I accepted happily, assuring her I was a quick study and assuming the character must be someone young, as actors for such parts were impossible to find during the war. I arrived in Rutherglen the following evening to discover that I had been cast as a middle-aged, mid-European Jewish refugee, Louis Liebens, who had settled in Glasgow and was shell-shocked and traumatised by the Blitz. Not exactly typecasting. I thought my career as an actor could only move upwards from there, or perhaps it would finish the following Monday. I learned the part, and while I am sure I overacted I remembered my lines and must have impressed Molly, because she seemed keen to employ me again. She gave me the chance to play some very good parts and took me under her wing. I was made to feel like a member of her family. In many ways, she became a surrogate mother, and I owe her and her husband, Willie, a great deal.

I met some wonderful characters at MSU, like Guy Muir, who kept a sweet shop, Bert Ross, who worked on the railways, and Rosina McCulloch, who had a reputation for chasing anything presentable in trousers. There was also a marvellous woman, Mrs McGuinness, who cleaned the theatre. An Irish Glaswegian with a broad accent and a gift for colourful language, she received a new lease of life through the MSU and worshipped Molly. In 1943, Molly became pregnant, much to everyone's surprise, as she was 37 years old, which was late in those days to be having a child. She told everyone, with endearing naivety, that it was a miracle, since she and Willie had not been intimate for ages. We all took this with a pinch of salt, but Mrs McGuinness believed every word Molly told her without question. When the baby was on its way, Mrs McGuinness rang the hospital to enquire after Molly and instructed the nursing staff to take special care, as only one other child in Christendom had been conceived this way.

Working with Molly, I also met a schoolmaster called John Macrae, who was a fine actor and performed regularly at the MSU. I learned a great deal from him about acting. He talked about economy of gesture, demonstrated the use of the dramatic pause and said it was essential to be aware of the contours of your face, which helped greatly when making yourself up for a character role. Above all, he was a man of integrity who possessed high standards that he never compromised but who was nevertheless very tolerant of others. He later gave up teaching and became a full-time professional actor when the Citizens Theatre opened in 1943. I had two small parts in that company's first production, when it was still based at the seldom-used Athenaeum Theatre. It was only later that it moved to the Gorbals. John changed his name to Duncan Macrae when he joined the Citizens and never looked back. He gave some fine performances and eventually moved to London, where his ability to play unusual or eccentric characters brought him solid work. I particularly remember him in Joe Orton's *Loot*, though he is probably best remembered for his part in the film *Whisky Galore!* Tired of the pressures and the insecurities he found in London, he returned to his beloved Scotland, where he formed his own company and toured, taking quality theatre to places that might not normally see good plays. In many ways, John was my theatrical hero, and I was delighted, many years later, when I was Rector of St Andrews University, to meet a member of the University Court who was married to John's daughter. Reforging my connection with John was important to me.

Molly, too, enjoyed presenting quality plays, and she had a gift for persuading people to appear at her theatre. The fine Scottish actor Gordon Jackson had achieved some fame at a young age by starring with Tommy Trinder in the film *The Foreman Went to France*. When he was back in Glasgow for a spell, he appeared for Molly in the Scottish play *Marigold*. Gordon played Lt Archie Forsyth, and I was his army friend Bobbie Townsend. In any MSU show, performed after little rehearsal, things could always go wrong, mostly owing to forgotten lines or mistaken moves. In *Marigold*, it was the set that let us down.

In one scene, Archie is alone with Marigold and she is worried because she does not have a chaperone. Archie is keen to put her mind at rest, so he tells her in his refined Kelvinside accent, 'Don't worry, Marigold. My friend Bobbie Townsend will be here any moment. In fact, I think I hear him at the door. Is that you, Bobbie?' I was meant to walk on stage, but the door through which I was to make my entrance wouldn't budge an inch. It had jammed tight.

'Archie,' I called, 'I am terribly sorry. The door, it seems to be jammed.'

'Well, put your shoulder into it.' I did exactly as suggested. 'No, no, Bobbie,' Gordon shouted suddenly. 'Stop that. The whole wall is moving!'

We were stuck. There seemed to be no other way for me to get onto the stage. Then I remembered that the set included a large baronial mantelpiece with a fake fire in the hearth. I could duck down behind that. 'Archie,' I called, in my similarly cultured Glasgow accent, 'carry on conversing with Marigold. I think I have found a way I can join you.' Gordon continued to ad-lib, and the next thing the audience saw was a pair of legs appearing behind the fire. I ducked under the mantelpiece and stepped over the blazing fire, artificial, of course, for which I received a round of applause. I then said, 'Hello there, it seems to be Christmas.' Another big laugh, and then we had to try to get the play back on track. We were just about managing this, but all the time we could hear someone scraping away at the door. Eventually, it swung open and our stage manager burst through, wearing modern clothing.

'Right,' he said. 'I've got it open now. You can come and go whenever you like. Oh my God, I shouldn't be here.' With that, he rushed offstage to the biggest round of applause of the evening, and he never knew why.

Gordon was always fun to work with, and we remained good friends. He appeared as a guest on *This Is Your Life* when I was the surprised subject and told Eamonn Andrews the *Marigold* story.

Having left university in 1943, I was pursuing my apprenticeship with as much energy as I could. During that year, I had been moved to the pattern shop, where wooden patterns of the pumps were made, which were then sent to the foundry to be cast. Pattern-making was highly skilled and one of the best-paid jobs in the industry. It was also interesting and creative work, which I enjoyed, but most of all I loved working with wood. If I had not possessed such a strong desire to perform, I think I would have been quite content as a cabinetmaker or a furniture designer.

The foreman of the pattern shop was an unforgettable character called Jock Cunningham. He had a small, raised office with glass all round at one end of the large working area, which consisted of a long workbench down each side and various machines in the centre. Most of these were highly dangerous, particularly the sawing and planing machines. More than one worker had a finger or a half-finger missing. Jock could survey the whole of his domain from his office and keep an eye on each worker at his apportioned section of the bench. He decided

I was a troublemaker, principally because he could not make me out, and put me at the end of the bench nearest to his office so that he could watch me more closely. He was a tough character with a temper on a short fuse, but he was not particularly frightening; it was mostly bluster. I was more nervous of him than anything else. The reason he did not command complete respect was owing, I think, to his dentures. Like many Scots of his generation, he had false teeth, which the Glaswegians blamed on their soft water. Jock's dentures did not fit properly, and he never bothered to have them fixed. You could see them sliding around his mouth when he spoke, and it made his speech sound rather slurred. In fact, when he became very angry and was struggling to get his words out, he had been known to spit his dentures into his hand so that he could swear more freely.

Smoking was strictly forbidden in the pattern shop because of the wood all around. There were two small lavatories at the rear of the buildings, which were often used by one or two apprentices sneaking off to have a smoke or, as they called it, a 'wee drag'. On one occasion when I went out to the loos, I opened the door of the first one to find three of my fellow apprentices puffing away. I said, 'Oh, I'll go next door.'

They replied, 'No, no, come in, Nick. Quick, shut the door. D'ye wanna fag?'

'No, I want a piss.'

'Well, go ahead. Don't mind us. Next door's busy.' It is difficult enough to relieve yourself comfortably with three people closely watching, but it is made worse by one of them suddenly saying, 'Hey, Nick, gi' us one of yer impersonations. Gi' us Charles Boyer.'

It was a ridiculous situation. I was standing there trying to have a pee while putting on the deep voice and French accent of the great cinema heart-throb, speaking the words he delivered in an emotional farewell scene with Bette Davis in the film *All This, and Heaven Too*: 'No, no, my darling. Don't move. As I see you standing there, with the light on your hair and your image in the mirror behind, this is how I want to remember you . . .' I finished, did up my fly buttons and made to leave.

'Hey, Nick, that was great. Come on now, gi' us yer Jimmy Stewart.' They would not let me go. Squashed between the three of them, I did a passage from *Mr Smith Goes to Washington*. I then had to give them their favourite, W.C. Fields. They were an appreciative audience, so I moved on to William Bendix, Max Miller and had just launched into an impromptu script in Winston Churchill's voice about being closeted in an outside loo with three young characters discussing the war effort when there was this almighty banging on the door. It was forced open, and there stood an irate Jock Cunningham, minus teeth, purple with rage at this unforgivable waste of the firm's time. He rounded off an almost continuous string of expletives with 'Get back to yer bench, ye big impersonator. Ye're here to make patterns not to make yon buggers laugh.'

While I was working at the pattern shop, Carroll Levis brought his show to the Glasgow Empire. He had written to me asking if I would like to be included as one of his discoveries for the week. I was delighted but concerned that, as I was working in a reserved occupation, I might be contravening some official rule if I accepted. I was also worried that Drysdale's might think I was not taking my work seriously and stop my apprenticeship, with all the embarrassment that would create. To ease my worries, I arranged to be excused overtime, which I would make up by working on Saturday, accepted the engagement and changed my name to Nick Marlowe. I have no idea why I chose such an unoriginal name – perhaps I had read too many Raymond Chandler novels.

It was a memorable week, appearing on the stage of the famous Glasgow Empire, playing to a huge, packed audience. I was billed as 'Glasgow's BBC Impressionist' and was given a marvellous reception, helped, I am sure, by the fact that Carroll Levis billed me as a local lad. One memorable night, a party of workmates from Drysdale's came to support me. In spite of my efforts not to advertise my appearance at the theatre, it seemed to be common knowledge around the firm. I was touched when, after a couple of days of performing, one of the men in the pattern shop came up to me and said, 'Here, Nick, I see ye're on at the Empire.'

'Yes, I am,' I replied, 'but I am trying to keep quiet about it.'

He ignored me. 'If one of oor mates is working somewhere, we've gotta come along and gi' him a big haund. I'll tell ye what, second hoose, Friday. I'll go and do a wee round robin and find out how many seats we want.' He tracked me down after lunch. 'Get 45 for a start . . .'

By the time of the second house on Friday, I had forgotten about the Drysdale's contingent – until I stepped out on stage and received a rapturous reception, particularly from the upper circle. My act was going down better than I could ever have hoped. The Glasgow Empire is notorious for being the graveyard of many comedians, especially those with an English accent. For me, however, it holds nothing but happy memories. I used to finish with an impersonation of Winston Churchill: 'Now, for my final item I would like to dedicate this to all my friends on Clydebank.'

They erupted and started to shout out requests: 'Nick, gi' us Jock Cunningham.'

'No, do Davy Mitchell.'

A chorus of Drysdale names was rained down on me. The audience in the stalls were looking perplexed; the stage manager was looking annoyed. I was in danger of overrunning. Suddenly, a voice called out, 'Hey, Nick, gi' us wee Willy McGinty!'

Immediately, a high-pitched, excited voice came back, 'Ye're no gonna impersonate me, no on that stage. If ye do, I'll come roond and put one in yer teeth.' This broke up the whole audience, and they roared with laughter. They now seemed to realise what was going on, which was more than the stage manager did.

Carroll walked on stage and brought my act to an abrupt close: 'Ladies and gentlemen, a round of applause for Nick Marlowe.'

A rough voice came back, 'He hasna finished, ye big Jessie. Let the kid do his last number.'

'All right,' said a rather shaken Carroll. You do not argue with a Glasgow Empire audience. 'Winston Churchill in 30 seconds.' I launched into the impersonation, Carroll started the applause, the orchestra struck up loudly and I walked offstage, still doing my routine.

In 1944, I did apply to join the Merchant Navy, as a junior engineer. I was young for such a position but had almost the full qualifications from my apprenticeship work, and there was a great shortage of personnel. The losses in this branch of the services were higher than in any other, because so many of our merchant fleet had been sunk by German U-boats.

I had experienced the atmosphere of a large merchant ship from working on one during sea trials and thought that I would find the service preferable to the vigorous discipline of the Royal Navy. I was very keen to join the Canadian Pacific Company, which had some magnificent ships in its fleet, including the *Empress of Russia*, which was in dock. I could have stayed on as a qualified engineer at Drysdale's when my apprenticeship finished, but I felt that was wrong. My heart was in show business, and I had proved to myself, if not my family, that I could succeed in the theatre. In letters exchanged with my parents around this time, I was still being persuaded to follow a proper career and to forget the 'play-acting nonsense'. I knew that I could not start an acting career in 1944, and perhaps there was a certain aggression in my wish to join a service in which, statistically, the risks were highest and the chances of survival lowest. My uncle Hugh approved, which was some consolation. He and Aunt Gladys had lost their son, Basil, at the battle of El Alamein, and they were pleased to see a relation taking such a positive step in the war.

My Merchant Navy service did not last long. In fact, I probably hold the record for the shortest stay: no more than a few days. I am not even sure if I was officially in the service. I had indicated my interest in taking a position on the *Empress of Russia*, and the Canadian Pacific told me to continue working until a vacancy came up, which could be in a week or two. I was accepted but had no ship. In the meantime, the pressures of work and other activities took their toll. For a long time, I had been rushing back to my digs after a day's work, cleaning up, jumping on the tram, perhaps to Rutherglen and the MSU, or to another engagement, working in a play, taking the last tram home, getting to bed late and then getting up at 6.30 a.m. to start all over again in Clydebank. I was exhausted, on top of which we were experiencing severe rationing. I felt dreadful but put it down to a bout of the flu – until I collapsed. I managed to stagger back home to my accommodation and took to my bed. There was a mature student there, Dr Munro, who was qualified and undertaking research. He examined me, said it was my lungs and told me that I should go straight to hospital.

I had recently signed a contract for the best part I had so far been offered at the BBC and was looking forward to doing it the following week, before I went to the Merchant Navy. I was to play the student Augustus Raby in James Bridie's *The Anatomist*, with Alastair Sim playing the lead. I pleaded that I would surely be all right after a few days in bed. Dr Munro explained that pleurisy was serious and without proper treatment it could develop into something worse. I spoke to my father, who insisted that I do exactly as Dr Munro had advised. With great sadness, I cancelled my appearance in the radio play. An ambulance was called, and the next thing I knew I was in the Victoria Infirmary.

My condition deteriorated rapidly. In 1944, the necessary antibiotics did not exist to fight pleurisy. My right lung was worst, and fluid had to be drawn off, which was painful. There was also always the risk of tuberculosis. I just wanted to sleep, which I did continually for about three weeks. The condition was aggravated by a deep depression, a result, no doubt, of letting go after working too hard for too long. While I was at the Victoria Infirmary, the two young men with whom I shared a room both died. My brother, who was on company business in the city, visited me there. My parents were unable to travel up to Scotland, so John reported back on my condition. He apparently gave me a 50–50 chance of survival. After the fourth week, I was moved to a branch of the hospital called Philipshill, based at East Kilbride, outside Glasgow. Philipshill was primarily an orthopaedic hospital, but the move was the tonic I required. Surrounded by a mixed group of men of all ages, who were on the whole cheerful, my spirits soon lifted and I was on the road to recovery.

I was in hospital for five months, then spent two weeks at a convalescent home in Largs. During my stay, D-Day came and went. The end of the war in Europe seemed in sight, though it would take another year – and even longer in the Far East. In late October, I was finally discharged and was free to return to London and my parents, whom I had not seen for nearly a year. Before I did so, I visited Drysdale's to say goodbye. I collected what was known as my 'lines', which detailed my work experience and confirmed that I had completed a full apprenticeship. It was good to feel that I had some qualifications for all the long hours and hard work. I said goodbye to as many men as I could. I then returned to Charlie Drysdale's office for my final farewells, and he asked if I had paid my respects to Matthew Russell, the works manager, a dour martinet of a man who ran the whole shop floor with aggressive efficiency. I was truly scared of him – it was principally because of Mr Russell that I had changed my name when appearing at the Glasgow Empire. I had spent pretty much my entire time at Drysdale's living in fear of this man discovering that I was spending my spare time trying to become an actor and entertainer.

I told Charlie that I had not said goodbye as I hardly had any dealings with Mr Russell. Charlie suggested that it would be courteous. I went to his office, knocked on the door and received a brusque 'Come in.' I explained why I had come, adding tactfully that I was not sure what I was going to do next. He was his usual taciturn self but pleasant and surprisingly complimentary about my work for the firm. He wished me luck and shook my hand, and I started to leave. I reached the door, and he suddenly said, 'By the way, if you ever come back to the Empire, you will let us know? I certainly enjoyed your act the last time.'

I was sad to leave Glasgow. I had made many good friends there and had grown to love the city and its people. I had been given the most wonderful opportunities to act and perform as a solo artist. It was the end of probably the most important chapter in my life and the one, I now realise, that left the deepest impression. That feeling has never left me and was rekindled recently when I retraced my steps for a BBC Radio 4 show I devised called *Doon the Watta*, a title that reflects the sailings of the famous steamers down the Clyde, past the incredible industry that used to exist there, to the mouth of the river and the stunning scenery beyond. I visited the site of Drysdale's and met one of the apprentices with whom I had worked. I also spoke to characters who shared similar experiences to mine, such as Jimmy Reid, the great activist, and Johnny Beattie, the wonderful comedian and actor, who had served an apprenticeship similar to mine. Throughout the three programmes, I was not surprised to discover that the Glasgow I knew had physically changed beyond all recognition, but I was delighted to confirm that its heart, soul and love of the arts remain constant and as powerful as ever.

The three months in London after I left Glasgow were extremely difficult. I was still convalescing, regularly visiting a chest specialist and forbidden to go any place people congregated for fear of infection, principally TB. It was also a challenge learning to live with my parents once again. Except for brief visits, I had not been home since I was 16. I am sure they found the adjustment equally difficult. It was a troubling time to be in the capital. In addition to the air raids, about which Londoners and my parents had become fatalistic, there was a new threat: the silent doodlebugs and V-2 rockets. One minute, you would be going about your life, and then suddenly there would be a huge explosion. At least previously the sirens gave you a warning of the impending Luftwaffe attacks. This new menace was more unsettling to the city and its inhabitants.

My days were spent taking fresh air and exercise, on doctor's orders, every morning on Hampstead Heath, usually accompanied by the family dog, a Bedlington terrier called Polly. I rested a lot, visited the library and wrote letters to the BBC requesting auditions for radio plays: the specialist had agreed that I could work in a studio if an engagement was offered.

I was called before a medical board to see if I might be fit to return to the Merchant Navy. Anyone with a dodgy lung was too great a risk, however, and I was discharged from all further national service. The year 1945 arrived, and I was growing stronger by the day. The time had come for my parents to ask the question that had been looming over us all since my return from Glasgow: 'You are a mechanical engineer. What are you going to do with your qualification?'

My response was unequivocal: 'I am going to forget it. I qualified to please you. Now I am going to follow the path I have always wanted. I am going to become a professional actor.'

NOW FULLY PROFESSIONAL

The stutter I had as a boy was not acute but was sufficient that it might have ended my acting career before it had even begun. My stutter has not been cured, but I have found a way to control it and have now been performing for almost 70 years.

When I was younger, my stutter was more pronounced. In later years, I developed breathing techniques that have helped me manage it, but when I was at school and working in Clydebank I had no idea that this might be possible. I would stutter at home, in class and at work, but the moment I walked on stage in front of an audience my stutter disappeared, because I was at ease with myself. I would be nervous, with my heart racing, but physically I would relax and was able to speak without any hindrance. This confirmed to me what I wanted to do for the rest of my life.

After I announced to my parents in early 1945 that I would not be pursuing a career in engineering, my father made one last attempt to try to dissuade me from my chosen profession. He had a patient, a literary agent called Joan Ling, who, he felt sure, would spell out in graphic detail the folly of my ways. He called Joan and explained that his son was a qualified engineer but had the mad idea of becoming an actor. Joan understood the issue: 'Don't worry. I know the profession. I'll put him off. Send him down to see me. With no contacts here in London to open doors, he has no hope of making it in acting.' I had no idea this conversation had taken place.

Joan did not live far away from our family home, and on a pretext my father sent me to see her: 'Will you go and deliver this parcel for me?' I arrived and was invited in. Joan and I started talking, and she asked me what I had been doing. I told her about my experiences in Glasgow and the concert parties and my impersonations and silly jokes and also about being a Carroll Levis discovery. As we chatted together, I acted out some of the material I had been performing in Glasgow and told a few of my favourite gags. Joan's elderly mother, who lived with her, was listening to our conversation, apparently in fits of laughter.

When Joan later called my father to report back, she did not deliver the message he had been expecting: 'I met your son,' she told him. 'I am not going to dissuade Nicholas from becoming an actor. I am going to encourage him. He has got talent.'

Joan immediately set about arranging an interview with Firth Shepherd Management, who produced successful West End shows. They saw me, and I was invited to audition for *Chicken Every Sunday*, which they were presenting in the spring at the Savoy Theatre. After the audition, I was asked to understudy the two young men in the play. It was my first West End job, and I had the excitement of making a few appearances on stage when one of the other actors was sick. I had no agent, so I had asked Joan to negotiate the contract and paid her commission. I received £15 per week, which seemed a fortune at the time. Joan became a very good friend, and we always kept in touch, meeting up with each other from time to time. She was like an adoptive godmother, and her advice on occasions has been invaluable.

Angela Baddeley and Frank Leighton starred in *Chicken Every Sunday*, which was extremely American in style and content. It had been successful on Broadway, but it was not to be in the West End. The reviews were terrible, and we were all soon taking cuts in salary to keep the play running. That did not worry me, however: I was on the first rung of the professional entertainment ladder.

Having failed in his attempt to steer me away from what he regarded as a terribly insecure career path, and having realised that I was indeed totally serious about becoming a professional actor, my father accepted the inevitable and offered some advice. 'Nicholas,' he said to me one day, 'if you are going to take acting seriously, it may be worth considering going to a dramatic academy first. For some formal training.'

From those early days in the classroom, I had always felt I was an instinctive performer. It came naturally to me, even back then, and my experiences in Glasgow had cemented that feeling. I said to my father, 'Thank you, but no, I have thought about it, and I know I can act. I have proved that. Academies can help you if you are just starting. What I need is some help with voice production. I am going to find somebody who can help me produce my voice correctly in order to project it in the theatre.'

I made some enquiries and discovered an amazing voice woman called Iris Warren, the top person in the industry at that time. I went to see her and had a number of lessons. She explained that to project your voice in a way that you can be heard properly, and to be able to reproduce that night after night on the stage, requires correct breathing, using the diaphragm. This is the same technique that singers employ on stage, or used to employ before the arrival of the sophisticated microphones they use today. I found Iris tremendously helpful. I still use some of her exercises now to keep my voice in shape and to control my stutter on a day-to-day basis. Logically, when you stutter, your muscles seize up and you cannot get the words out, and in order for your voice to project you must relax and breathe properly. I soon realised that if I could produce my voice in the correct way I would not stutter. Over the years, I have learned to keep my impediment in check, apart from the rare occasion when my brain gets ahead of my speech. If I jump in to interject in *Just a Minute* and forget to breathe in the way Iris taught me, my stutter can resurface. Nowadays, it is called a stammer, and I am a patron of the British Stammering Association.

While I was at the Savoy in *Chicken Every Sunday*, VE Day arrived, 8 May 1945. I was determined to enjoy myself on this day of national celebration, with the church bells ringing out for the first time since the war had started and bonnets being thrown over the proverbial windmill. After the show finished, an Irish friend who was in the play, Dermot MacDowell, and I made our way to Trafalgar Square. It was already packed with people. There was some singing and jollity, but where was the abandon? It was flat and dreary. Perhaps everyone was too tired after nearly six years of conflict. Also, there was still fighting in the Far East, and perhaps that had a sobering effect. My hopes of finding lots of girls who wanted to be kissed, of perhaps finishing up in bed with some pretty creature, of enjoying a night of abandoned lovemaking as we looked forward to a new life now the horrors of the war were over were just fantasies inspired by too many Hollywood films. Dermot and I were soon bored, tired, completely unkissed and somewhat subdued. I decided to catch the last Tube home and wondered what I would say if I had children one day who asked, 'Daddy, what did you do on the day the war stopped?' I would have to reply, 'Nothing, I went home.'

It was around this time that I read in *The Stage* that Firth Shepherd was going to present *The Hasty Heart* by John Patrick, which had been a huge success on Broadway. It was set in a hospital ward behind the lines in Burma, and the cast consisted of eight men of different nationalities and one woman, a nursing sister. I felt there must be a part I could play, so I did something that required considerable determination and cheeky persistence. In retrospect, I am amazed that I saw it through.

I went to Firth Shepherd's offices in Charing Cross Road and entered the outer reception area on the second floor, which was connected by a door to an inner office that had one of those old-fashioned sliding panels, behind which sat a receptionist. The panel was drawn back, and through the small aperture I asked if I could see Mr Laurence Green, the assistant production manager. The receptionist asked my business, and, trying to control my stutter, I said that I wanted to read for the new play, *The Hasty Heart*. The sliding panel was closed. I could hear mutterings on the internal phone, then the panel was drawn back and the part of the face that was visible informed me that Mr Green was busy. I said that I would wait until he was free, and took a seat in the reception area.

After about an hour, I tapped on the sliding panel. It was drawn back, and I asked if Mr Green was free yet. The panel was closed, there were more internal mutterings and the panel was pulled back again. The receptionist said that Mr Green had asked her to say that he was going to be busy all morning and, anyway, there was no point in reading for the new play, since I was already working at the Savoy

Theatre, which they knew because Firth Shepherd was also presenting *Chicken Every Sunday*. I was determined not to be put off. I said that I would still like to see Mr Green and would return in the afternoon. This I duly did. We went through the sliding-panel routine, and I made the same request. A very resigned young lady said that she would ask him but did not hold out much hope. There were more mutterings on the internal phone, and then back came the sliding panel: 'Mr Green says he is too busy to see you this afternoon, and he has asked me to repeat what he said this morning.'

Before she could finish, I said, 'All right, I'll wait until he is free. I've nothing else to do.' I sat down. The sliding panel was closed again. I picked up my newspaper. After an hour, I tried again. Mr Green was still busy. After two hours, the panel was drawn back again and the half-face – I never did see more – informed me that Mr Green had left the office on business. I did not believe her, since he would have had to pass the door to the reception area. I told her that I would come back the next day.

Next morning, 10 a.m., up the stairs, into the reception area, knock on the panel. It was slid back, the same mouth and nose on the other side. The same request from me: 'Could I see Mr Green, please?' Back went the panel, phone mutterings, much briefer this time, same message relayed, much more forcibly expressed. I said that I would wait. After an hour, a gentle knock on the panel. It was slid back. 'Excuse me, is Mr Green free yet?' No response this time, just the panel returned and silence. After a few seconds, the panel opened again and I was informed that Mr Green would be busy all day. I said that I would try again in the afternoon in the hope that he might be free. I had started something, and I had to see it through. I felt that, if I could be given the chance to read at an audition, it would be a step forward. Getting another job now seemed entirely secondary.

I came back that afternoon and went through the routine again, except that the half-face was now becoming extremely bored. I kept this up for two more days, and by the Thursday the reaction behind the panel had become resigned: 'Oh, it's you. Yes, I know. You want to see Mr Green. You know he's busy but you'll wait.' Words had now become unnecessary on my part. I sat down and hoped and did begin to wonder if I was making a complete fool of myself.

On the Friday morning, I made one last attempt. I thought that the half-face was now a little sorry for me. I said that I would leave; I had failed. I walked towards the exit. She must have been watching me through the sliding panel and, when I was out of sight, presumably told Mr Green that I had given up and left. I reached the stairs and paused. Something made me go back for one last try. I did not approach the sliding panel but just sat in the reception area. Within a few minutes, Laurie Green walked through reception. I could not believe it. I leaped up. The stutter returned: 'M-m-mister G-g-green, can I c-c-come and r-r-read for the Hay-hay-hay . . .'

I never got the title out. He interrupted, 'Oh, for goodness sake. Come to the Aldwych Theatre at 3 p.m. this afternoon. We're auditioning.'

Auditions are daunting occasions, and in those days they were far more impersonal than they are now. Today, the artist being auditioned is usually sent the script in advance. In those days, you walked onto an empty stage, which was fully lit, and there would be one man standing in the centre with two scripts. On this occasion, it was Laurie Green. You looked out at a darkened auditorium, and, while you could see nothing, you knew that sitting somewhere were representatives of the management and the director of the play. You were asked to announce yourself then handed a script and told to open it at a certain page. As I did this on that memorable Friday, Laurie Green said to me, 'Will you please read the part of Digger, the Australian.' I stuttered that I could not do an Australian accent and asked if I could read it as a cockney. This was acceptable, and I must have been reasonable, because the director then asked me what I had been doing.

At this point, a voice from the stalls interrupted. It was Firth Shepherd's production manager, Danny O'Neil, an experienced theatre man and a real character with a high-pitched voice and cockney accent. He shouted, 'What's that young man doing up on the stage, Laurie? He's working along at the Savoy.'

Laurie Green replied, 'He's pestered the life out of me all week; this is the only way I could get rid of him. He says he's a Scot and would like to read the Scot's part.' I did not know at the time that the Scot in the play was the leading role.

Danny O'Neil's voice came back from the empty darkness, 'All right, while he's up there, let him have his fun. Read the ruddy Scot's part.' As the Glasgow dialect was second nature to me, and it is easier to read a character part unseen than it is a straight role, I did much better at this second reading. The director thanked me and asked where I could be contacted, at which point Danny O'Neil's voice came back, 'It's all right, we know where to find him.' I left the stage feeling content. I had been given my audition, and I thought I had impressed them. It would be a good investment for the future. I thought no more about it.

That night, I was called to the stage door at the Savoy Theatre, where I was greeted by Laurie Green. He said, 'I had to see you in private, because no one else in the cast knows that this play is about to come off. They liked your reading. They want you to play the New Zealander.' There are times when you need some good fortune to help you on your way, and I certainly received a slice here. Even though *Chicken Every Sunday* was destined to close early, I would probably not have been released from that engagement before its demise had both productions not been run by the same management company. As it was, they were, and I secured the part. I could not believe it. I did not add that I could not do a New Zealand accent. There was time to acquire one. I was sworn to secrecy, as rehearsals were to start soon and they did not want to undermine the confidence of the cast at the Savoy, who might well have put two and two together if they had learned I had been given a part in a new play.

Before rehearsals began, however, I had to learn to speak as a New Zealander. Fortunately, at that time the ANZAC Club was in existence, which catered for military personnel from New Zealand and Australia. I had to be inventive. I went up there and said, 'I've come here because I would like to talk to some people from New Zealand. I am thinking of emigrating and would like to get a flavour of the country.' I was made very welcome. People will always happily talk about their home town and country, and I just sat and listened, absorbing the intonation and accent, noticing the subtle but definite difference between the New Zealand and the Australian accents, the latter of which has a harsher sound, more nasal. It was essential that I got the distinction correct, because I had heard that Frank Leighton, an Australian, was to play Digger in the production. I could not sound the same as him.

The Hasty Heart was well cast. Margaretta Scott played the leading role of the nursing sister. She was always a beautiful and radiant actress, but in nursing uniform she was enchanting. I was, however, far too young and shy to talk to her easily. Much later she became well known for playing Mrs Pumphrey in *All Creatures Great and Small* on television, alongside the irascible Tricky Woo. I was more confident with the men, except Emrys Jones, who played Lachie, the Scotsman. He was very unsure of himself. He was extremely good-looking and had a great deal of charm but had no idea how to cope with the star status he had achieved. The part he played was 'actor-proof', that is, it was so well written and drew such sympathy from the audience that one would have had to be an awfully bad actor to fail in it. Emrys was Welsh, and his Scottish accent was not bad, but it never sounded quite authentic, since the inflections and cadences were those of a Welshman.

The play was launched in Glasgow. It seemed like an omen, returning so quickly to the city where I had first struggled to become an actor. The production was well received when it opened in London, with universally good reviews, except from James Agate, that doyen of drama critics who was then writing for the *Sunday Times*. The West End was still very different from Broadway, where a bad review from a leading critic could kill a show overnight. Mr Agate was widely read and respected, but his opinions did not destroy plays that the public liked, and they enjoyed *The Hasty Heart*. We ran for over a year and then had a successful 13-week tour.

While *The Hasty Heart* was on at the Aldwych, the Joseph Kesselring play *Arsenic and Old Lace* was enjoying a run at the next-door theatre, the Strand. I went to see a matinee performance and enjoyed it thoroughly, in particular Naunton Wayne's portrayal of the lead character, Mortimer Brewster. Naunton Wayne was a wonderful actor, perhaps best known as one of the cricket-mad English gents in the film

The Lady Vanishes, alongside Basil Radford. In *Arsenic and Old Lace*, he played the nephew of two sweet, lovable, elderly aunts who feel it is their mission in life to bump off lonely old men by poisoning them with their amazing home-made wine. The corpses are then buried in the cellar of the family home. Mortimer has two brothers, who are as crazy as the aunts. One of them has undergone plastic surgery in order to resemble Boris Karloff, who actually played the part in the original Broadway production, and the other thinks he is Teddy Roosevelt and is happy to bury the bodies for the aunts. With such madness rife in his family, Mortimer must decide whether he should go ahead with his proposed marriage.

This set-up leads to a famous moment in the theatre of the '40s, and Naunton played it perfectly when I saw him in the part. It is towards end of the play, and one of the aunts says to Mortimer, 'Darling, there is something we have to tell you. We have kept it from you all this time, but we think perhaps you should know. You are not actually legitimate. No, we adopted you. We found you as a little foundling.'

On hearing this news, Mortimer turns excitedly to his fiancée and says, 'Elaine, do you understand what this means? I am a bastard!' In a similar way to when George Bernard Shaw used the word 'bloody' in *Pygmalion*, the use of 'bastard' caused quite a stir, and it always received the biggest laugh in the play. In fact, it almost stopped the show every time.

Shortly after *The Hasty Heart* came to the end of its run, I landed the part of Mortimer in a tour of *Arsenic and Old Lace* that Firth Shepherd was producing. We played twice nightly in variety theatres, rather than in traditional venues, which was quite a surprising thing to do, and they had to cut the play down to the bare bones to be able to fit in the two performances. It was wonderful experience, but, unlike Naunton Wayne, I did not have the professional skill to make the most of that character. I got away with it but only because it is such a great comedy role.

As part of the tour, we visited Belfast – one of the first shows to do so since the war had ended. We played at the Opera House to fantastically enthusiastic audiences, perhaps because they had been deprived of productions from London for such a long time. They enjoyed the performance hugely, apart from the one famous line. It was the first night, and I knew the line was coming up. I gave it my all, expecting the inevitable response. How wrong I was. Instead of the usual fantastic laugh, there was a horrified gasp. The Belfast audience were clearly far more prudish than their London counterparts. I was so horrified at the reaction that I just grabbed Elaine's hand and rushed off the stage. Fortunately, it was my exit cue anyway. After that first experience, I knew what was coming and delivered the line more gently. If I was not going to receive the customary laugh, at least I was able to produce a more measured response from the audience.

Before I set out with *Arsenic and Old Lace*, I still had one week's involvement in *The Hasty Heart* to fulfil. It proved to be an important week in my career. When our production had ended its London run and provincial tour, the repertory companies across the country began to present it as one of their weekly offerings. Ronald Kerr, a supremely gifted director, especially in weekly rep, was at that time directing at the Intimate Theatre, Palmers Green, and he decided to produce *The Hasty Heart*. Ronnie was looking for someone to play the American, and a friend of mine, Mac Picton, who had understudied during the London run, said to him, 'Nicholas can play the part for you.' Ronnie found me via the actors directory, *The Spotlight*, and offered me the role. I was delighted to accept, as the Intimate Theatre was well regarded. I was doubly pleased some two years later when Ronnie contacted me again, asking me to come to Bromley, where he was now running the repertory theatre. He wanted me to play an American in another play.

Following *Arsenic and Old Lace*, I toured for what seemed like an eternity in the farce *Charley's Aunt*. We were not a starry cast, but we had one great attraction: Cecil Beaton's costumes and sets, which were magnificent. This was the first revival of the play in the costumes of the period, and it was well received. Business was good, and consequently new dates were constantly being added, which was, of course, good news, but it was exhausting.

Prior to the tour, I had spent most of my savings on a car. It was my pride and joy. There were only a few second-hand vehicles around at the time, since no new ones had been built during the war. The one I found had been renovated by a mechanic who ran a small mews garage in Kensington. It was one of the early box-shaped Fords built in the '30s, an open car with a dilapidated roof. I paid £164, which was a lot of money then, but for me it was worth it, as I had always dreamed of owning my own car.

In those days, you had to get permission to travel by car on tour, rather than join the Sunday train call. I remember the remarks of the production manager when he first saw my Ford. He turned to the company manager and said, 'What have we done? It's held together with string and sealing wax. Will he ever arrive?' I did arrive, just, but the car soon became unreliable and I was forced to join the rest of the cast on the train, heading third-class on a Sunday to whichever town or city in which we were performing.

The continuing success of the tour gave us all hope that we might secure a West End theatre, but as the weeks went by with no news it seemed we were destined to play to audiences outside the capital. Finally, after three months on the road, we received the wonderful news that we were going to open just before Christmas at the Palace Theatre, London.

The season at the Palace Theatre was very successful. We were even honoured by a visit from Queen Mary, resplendent in her famous toque, sitting in the royal box. The cast were presented in the second interval, and, as I had not been briefed about royal protocol nor told not to speak unless I had been addressed, I made an awful gaffe. I thought at one point the Queen was struggling for something to say and tried to help out. She seemed unperturbed and took it in her stride, but the cast fully expected me to be taken off to the Tower after the final curtain.

Queen Mary's visit was certainly a highlight of that Christmas period, but for me what was particularly remarkable was our opening night, when my whole family came to see me. By that stage, my parents had accepted that this was the career I had chosen, but my performance in *Charley's Aunt* at the Palace was probably the first time my father had seen me in anything significant. They all came backstage afterwards, and my parents were clearly happy and proud of what their son had achieved. I was pleased to have them there, but I worried my father looked rather tense. 'Dad, is there anything worrying you?' I asked.

'Well, actually there is something,' he replied. 'As I came through that stage door, I remembered it was the very door my mother pointed out to me many years ago when I was a boy and we had come up to London to do some shopping. She said to me, pointing at the door, "My son, beyond there lies a den of iniquity. If ever you go through those portals, you will be taking the first step towards everlasting damnation." So I was just wondering whether or not I should go to church on Sunday and offer up a special prayer. Just in case she was right all along.'

My father did not come to see me in many productions, but only because he was not a great theatre-goer. My mother, on the other hand, enjoyed the theatre and would often come to see me on stage, in particular when I was later in the Bromley Rep, which was very loyal of her seeing as it was quite a drive.

After the London season of *Charley's Aunt* came to an end, we were off on tour again in the spring – more train calls and more digs with an assortment of landladies who would look after us, disapprove of us, be forward to some of us or be nosey about all of us. Then, in early summer, it was all over.

It might have seemed to some that I had 'made it' by then. I had appeared in the West End in two shows and had successfully toured the country in a variety of well-regarded roles. This was show business, however. I certainly had not made it. I was only beginning. I was enjoying having a little money for the first time, as well as the chance to spend it. Part of me was making up for the freedom I had missed as a teenager. Deep down, though, I knew I still had a lot to learn.

Following the extended *Charley's Aunt* tour, I was completely exhausted both physically and emotionally and could hardly move. I was not ill but had no energy for anything. The therapy of work in our profession is, however, amazing. I made a rapid recovery following Ronnie Kerr's phone call asking me to go to Bromley and play the American in Terence Rattigan's wartime comedy *While the Sun Shines*. Once again, my ability to speak in different dialects had proved crucial:

he had been impressed enough with my week-long appearance in *The Hasty Heart* at the Intimate Theatre to remember me.

Terence Rattigan was a master craftsman. His comedies are stylish and witty, his characters beautifully drawn. In *While the Sun Shines*, the American is a larger-than-life, rather ingenious person, and I enjoyed every minute of the week's engagement. The greatest pleasure, however, was working with a producer who gave you positive direction and encouragement. The confidence you exude in those circumstances communicates itself to the audience, and the play was a big success. It was just the tonic I needed.

Ronnie was very complimentary and asked if I would like to stay on as one of the resident company. I was reluctant to go back to repertory after working in the West End, but Ronnie was persuasive. I thought about it and realised that was what I should do. I was not yet a name. I had no reason to get carried away with my success. I still had to develop my craft, and playing a different part in a different play every week could help achieve that. Ronnie said to me, 'I think you will learn a lot down here.' He was quite correct.

I did not know at the time that he had been a teacher at RADA, the Royal Academy of Dramatic Art. As a theatre director, or producer, he had a gift not only for managing to stage and direct a play in a week but also for giving you limited but sufficient guidance about the character you were playing. For those who were prepared to work hard, it was therefore possible, with little rehearsal time, to give a real performance rather than simply walk through the play speaking the lines you had somehow crammed into your head.

In rep, you are all working against time, learning against time, rehearsing against time, and the set goes up against time. It all begins on a Monday, with dress rehearsals all day for the production opening that night – sometimes while they are still putting the finishing touches to the stage design and lighting. Tuesday morning, you meet to read through the play that will open the following week, and the moves are marked out at the same time. Tuesday afternoon, you have some time to learn the lines of the new play before the evening performance of the current one. Wednesday morning, you rehearse the first act of the forthcoming play. Wednesday afternoon, you run through the second act and learn more lines. Thursday morning, you rehearse the second act. In the afternoon, it is once through the third act with, you hope, more time to learn lines. Friday morning, you rehearse the third act – if it is a two-act play, it is broken down into three segments for rehearsal. On Friday afternoon, you go through the whole play, and on Saturday morning you do the same again, hopefully with words and moves now in your head. Saturday afternoon and evening, you perform the last two performances of the current production. Sunday is free, and for the conscientious there is time to become completely conversant with the lines of the new play. On Monday, the whole process begins again.

I worked hard at each role every week. By listening to Ronnie's guidance, and by spending all day Sunday repeatedly going over the part until I had absorbed the words and the character, I was able to give a fluent performance on the Monday night, when the critic from the local paper would be in the audience.

The experience I gained at Bromley was invaluable. We did almost every kind of play imaginable, from Restoration comedy to modern drama, all of which required a different style and approach. We performed at least one Shakespeare every year, which was wonderful. I remember being terrible in my first Shakespearean part, but I was learning. I played many kinds of roles and quite soon found out my weaknesses as well as my strengths. I was not very good at playing romantic roles. My forte was character acting and comedy.

I was contracted initially to stay at the New Theatre in Bromley for 12 weeks. I then stayed on without a contract for nearly 15 months and not only enjoyed it but was grateful for the opportunities Ronnie gave me to play many different roles. I was paid £12 a week, a good rep salary in those days. From that I had to find money for my lodgings – which was three guineas, including meals, at the little Hackwood Hotel in Widmore Road – for extra food and for clothes. Every actor in repertory was expected to have two lounge suits and one evening suit, as well as shirts and shoes. The management supplied only period clothes. There was also make-up, laundry, petrol and fares for the occasional trip to London.

I was now running a dilapidated Hillman Minx. It was a drophead, a type I have always loved. Once again, it cost me all my savings to buy and any extra cash from my earnings to keep on the road, but it was worth it. I enjoy cars, and over the years I have owned quite a variety. In the '60s, I had a succession of Alvis cars, one of the finest British vehicles on the road, with a beautiful, classic line. In fact, I owned one of the last cars Alvis made before they were taken over by Rover. I wish I had kept it as an investment: as a vintage car, it is now worth a lot of money.

The New Theatre, which was later destroyed by fire, rebuilt in 1978 and named the Churchill Theatre, had not been running as a repertory theatre for long when I joined it, but we soon created a loyal and faithful following. In time, Ronnie mounted more ambitious productions, such as *The Barretts of Wimpole Street* and Sheridan's *The School for Scandal*, with the resident company augmented by extra actors. Kenneth Williams appeared in *The School for Scandal*, playing a comparatively small and entirely straight role. He had guested the previous week in a thriller, *The Shop at Sly Corner*, in which he played an eccentric young teenager who worked in the jeweller's shop of the title. He was an original even then, but for some reason Ronnie did not warm to him and found him difficult to cast. The more conventional, regular members of the cast could not cope with him at all, finding him odd and overbearing. I enjoyed his theatrical, camp stories but would never have predicted that he would become the cult comedian that he did.

I persuaded Ronnie to let me photograph the shows, so there were pictures in the foyer every week. I had been interested in photography ever since my father gave me my first camera, a Box Brownie, at the age of eight. I wish I had used it during the war. My father had always been an excellent photographer with an artist's eye for composition. He even did his own enlarging. He had given me his trusted Rolleiflex, which he had used for years, and this was the camera with which I photographed the Bromley shows. It was quite a challenge, as I had just half an hour after the dress rehearsal to set up, bring in extra lights and compose the pictures. After the opening performance, I delivered the single roll of

12 photographs to a local photographer. He would have them developed by 9.30 a.m. on the Tuesday, when I would drop in, look at the negatives, choose the best and have prints on display in the theatre foyer by evening. The theatre management, however, were reluctant to part with extra money to an actor. In addition, as business was good, a promotional exercise to increase box-office returns was deemed unimportant. They eventually gave me a modest £2 a week and the cost of the films and prints. Ronnie also seemed insensitive to the situation, saying simply, 'Just think of the experience you are getting as a photographer.' All through my career, I have noticed an unwillingness on the part of employers to admit that an actor could have any special talent, let alone an extra talent, for which he should be rewarded. It is almost as if they want us to feel that we are still strolling players, the vagabonds of society, lucky to be accepted. It is a British trait not to praise anyone for fear it might make them swollen-headed or, worse still, prompt the agent to ask for more money.

Ronnie inspired great loyalty, but he was by no means an easy man with whom to work. There was a mildly sadistic streak in him. For instance, he had a habit of sneaking up on stage during rehearsals and singeing the back of your hair with his lighted cigarette. He did this only to people he liked and knew well, and usually to young, male members of the cast to whom he was clearly attracted. I had learned by this time how to deal with unwarranted attention from my own sex – not that Ronnie ever made any actual advances to me. The nearest was the hair singeing. Once, I was so angry that I lifted him bodily off his feet and manhandled him into a chair in the wings. The thing was, he enjoyed it. It was just the kind of reaction for which he was hoping.

One of the greatest lessons about acting I learned from Ronnie is the value of good diction. I have the impression that it is not something that is given much attention in drama school now. The vogue of naturalistic acting, which you see most vividly displayed in the cinema and to a great extent on television, where the desire to sound real at all costs, whether or not the words can be understood, seems to have developed into a cult. If you cannot understand the words, how can you follow the plot? Just because people in real life may speak in a sloppy, incoherent way, it does not mean they have to be imitated. A character has to be drawn from life, and the accent has to be genuine, but if the diction is poor, clarity is lost and you lose the audience concentration. I worked hard on my diction and was able to project thanks to the advice and techniques given to me by Iris Warren.

When I eventually left Bromley, I hoped my experience might have put me in a strong position to challenge for some good West End roles. In those days, however, they cast according to type. This was not ideal for me, as I was now a character actor and most of the plays in the West End at the time were what were known as 'drawing-room comedies', where the young juvenile lead bursts through the French windows and says, 'Hello, anyone for tennis?' My face may have said 'wet romantic' to directors, but they were not the roles I was particularly good at playing.

I found it very frustrating that I was not being considered for parts that I had proved to myself I could play. The kitchen-sink dramas of John Osborne and others had not yet arrived, and while Rattigan was writing great plays they were based more on middle-class characters, which my face again did not fit. I realised I had to prove once more that I had a broader talent than might be judged by my features. I also needed to earn some money. So I set out on a challenging course of action: I decided to put a cabaret act together.

I had met Joan Ling's nephew, Peter Ling, who wanted to become a scriptwriter once he had completed his national service. (He later became well known as the creator of *Crossroads*.) I had the idea to take off the popular films from Europe and Japan by acting out scenes in gibberish, keeping the music of the language but not speaking a coherent word. This concept was something I reprised ten years later for a series of award-winning television commercials that my own production company made. Peter helped me put together a routine, for which I paid him £9.

A chance to try out this material came when the Under Thirties Theatre Club, of which I was a member and whose aims were to promote the work of those starting in show business by putting on plays for Sunday-night audiences, required a cabaret for a party they were having in a London club and I volunteered. I realised, however, that I needed music for some of my other material and spoke to another member of the club, a talented young actor called Leslie Crowther. An accomplished musician, he was very helpful, and we struck up what was to become a long-lasting friendship.

I was extremely nervous on the night. I had never performed a cabaret act before, and the material was all entirely new. In fact, it was to a great extent thanks to Leslie's reassurance my material was funny that I had the confidence to stand up and perform. It went surprisingly well for a first attempt, and I was encouraged to write to a man called Frank Shaw, who ran an exclusive club called the Cavalero. It was exclusive and intimate, catering particularly for the young people who moved in smart circles – the men tended to be members of the Brigade of Guards; their girlfriends, invariably debutantes, would often appear in the pages of *Tatler*.

Frank Shaw booked me a number of times, both at the Cavalero and then, later, at his new club, the Caballero. It was while working there that I had the idea for what was to be one of my most successful 'point' numbers, which was written by a clever lyricist-composer friend, John Hurst. It was called 'Up Guards and At 'Em' and was an affectionate send-up of the typical officer of the Brigade of Guards who patronised the club. They were distinguishable in civilian life by their rolled-up umbrellas and their bowler hats with a slightly enlarged crown, worn at a rakish angle over their eyes. Suitably attired, I performed the number, which was always well received, particularly by the audience at whom it was poking fun. Of all the material I performed, the Guards number most reflected the social climate of the '50s, and it seems very dated in today's more egalitarian society.

One evening, Princess Margaret was at the Caballero with a group of friends, some of whom had a distinctly military air. Frank Shaw came up to me with a worried expression: 'Nicholas, I think you should drop the Guards number, since there seems to be a Guards officer in Princess Margaret's party.' Knowing the capacity of the British for laughing at themselves, I thought he was being oversensitive. I asked the restaurant manager if he could tactfully find out to which regiment the officer belonged. He said he thought it was the Blues and Royals. So I made out that the character I was portraying was a member of the Coldstream Guards. There is a natural rivalry between the different regiments, and whether I got it right or wrong the number went down well.

Working in cabaret, and regularly returning home in the early hours of the morning, you see the other side of life in any large city. Certain parts of London were known as areas where sex could be bought from prostitutes on the street, and apparently the price varied from place to place depending on the standard of service on offer. Jermyn Street was smart, Shepherd's Market was noted for kinky sex, Gerrard Street in Soho was middle-of-the-road, Lisle Street, also in Soho, near Leicester Square, was where you found what were described as 'cheap tarts' and Bayswater Road was even more downmarket.

I discovered a great deal of this when I struck up a conversation with a prostitute one night after she had accosted me. I told her that I was not interested in paying for sex but that I was interested to know why she was prepared to sell herself in this way. The girl turned out to be a former nurse. She told me, 'I got fed up looking after the needs of men who were lying in bed. I thought I'd get into bed myself and look after their needs that way – and make a much better living.' She was knowledgeable about the problems of walking the street, of the hazards of working alone and not having what she called a 'manager'. It was a glimpse into another world. Nowadays, we have a smoking ban in offices and public buildings, and it is not uncommon to see young women standing on the street having a crafty cigarette. The only women you saw smoking on the street when I was younger were those in the sex industry looking for business. It is something I still find difficult to which to become accustomed.

My work flourished. A variety of places featured cabaret, some consisting of only a single act, others a full floor show. There were clubs with an exclusive membership; nightclubs, which charged an entrance fee; and restaurants, where there was also dancing. In the late '50s, Al Burnett, who ran the Stork Club, opened the Pigalle in Piccadilly and presented glamorous shows of more than an hour's entertainment featuring a star name. I performed there as the comedy attraction in the big floor show starring the exotic singer Yana.

One of the most prestigious venues in the '50s was Quaglino's, and my first engagement there was certainly a step up the cabaret ladder. Based on my performances at the Caballero and other, less fashionable, restaurants, I was booked to appear at Quaglino's for a month in August 1954. This was the quiet time when less well-known artists were engaged. The room was not easy to work, as it was rectangular and the artist stood in front of the band, with the diners mostly on either side and only a solitary row of tables facing you. If you played to one side of the room at any time, those on the opposite side had only your back view. The audience were always appreciative, if a little quiet on occasions, but then I was young and unknown and had to win them over. The cabaret act at Quaglino's always doubled with the little Allegro Room downstairs: 11.15 p.m. at Quag's; midnight in the Allegro, where the audience were more my age and related spontaneously to my material. The atmosphere there was similar to the Caballero and often attracted the same audience.

I had one unfortunate incident at Quaglino's. I used to do an encore if the act had gone well, which consisted of Winston Churchill, one of my most successful impersonations, giving a talk on cooking – a subject that had suddenly become popular on television – and describing how he made a 'cabinet pudding'. He was then prime minister, and all the ingredients were facetious comments about various members of the government, especially those in the public eye. It was political satire at a time when it was not usual to send up leading politicians, let alone impersonate respected public figures. It usually went well, particularly with the young crowd. On this occasion, I returned to a warm reception, introduced the item and launched into the impersonation. Instead of the usual ripple of applause that greeted the opening, a man with a powerful, military-sounding voice suddenly shouted from the gloom, 'How dare you! How dare you, sir!'

The audience went quiet. I stopped and turned to face the dark area from where the voice came. 'I beg your pardon?' I said, which was pretty tame, but I could think of nothing else.

The voice came back, even louder: 'How dare you impersonate the Prime Minister!'

Having regained some composure, I asked, 'Why? Can you impersonate him better?'

This only incensed him further: 'If you carry on, you impudent toad, I will come up there and knock your block off.' The audience were now deathly quiet – the British always become embarrassed if anyone makes a scene. I could not change my act just because one individual did not like it. I turned my back on him and tried to carry on, but my legs were shaking. There was a scuffling behind me. The bluff had failed. The irate, possibly drunk, man was storming towards me. The orchestra leader shouted a warning, and I swung round to find a very tall gentleman making a lunge at me.

My early boxing training had not been in vain. I parried his fist and swayed, and the slippery dance floor saved me. As I fended off his attack, he lost his balance and slid to the ground. He was up immediately, but further embarrassment was saved by his lady companion, who, with another friend, dragged him back to their table. What amazed me was that nobody from the audience said a word. They simply returned to their food or pretended the whole thing had not happened. It was typical of the British. No one wants to be involved. In America, they would have shouted, in France they would have taken sides, in Italy they probably would have joined in and in South America they would have started a riot.

My problem now was to finish and make my final exit. Today, I would probably ask if there was anyone else who wished to express an opinion; then, I was too inexperienced. I tried a couple of throwaway jokes, but the audience were completely withdrawn. I walked off to polite applause, which was followed the next day by a request from the management not to aggravate the customers. The joys of show business.

One restaurant to which I returned frequently was the Royal Court Theatre Club, which was on the top floor of the Royal Court Theatre in Sloane Square and was owned and run by Clement Freud. A trained cook who had served his apprenticeship in the kitchens of the Dorchester, he was an expert in the culinary arts as well as a shrewd businessman. He also found time to be a sporting journalist.

When he started his club at the Royal Court in 1952, he was not a speaker in the raconteur sense and probably had no aspirations to be one. When I first worked there in 1954, he used to step forward onto the small dance floor at midnight and simply say, 'In cabaret tonight, we have Nicholas Parsons.' By my second visit, he had stretched this introduction to, 'Before I introduce the cabaret tonight, I thought I would tell you a story.' Then, with his head slightly to one side, a deadpan expression and a somewhat lugubrious delivery, he would tell a rather suggestive joke. The audience enjoyed it, and he gained confidence. By my next visit, he was telling two or three stories and they were getting broader. So it continued until he was almost doing a comedy routine before introducing the cabaret.

I would return frequently to Clement's club. It was a marvellous venue to try out new material. There was a nucleus of young entertainers that Clement called upon: Rolf Harris, Thelma Ruby, Lance Percival, Jimmy Thompson, Noel Harrison, and Peter Reeves with Bryan Blackburn. David Frost, then a researcher at Associated-Rediffusion, did some of his first cabarets at the club. Dudley Moore and Jonathan Miller also worked there. Jonathan Miller's act was particularly esoteric. I remember Clement saying to me, 'He wasn't really right for this audience. And it is difficult to respond to someone who walks out to entertain in his bare feet.'

An engagement from Clement always began with a telephone call and a kind enquiry as to my availability in two weeks' time or, sometimes, the following week. If I was free, I would say yes. Money was never discussed: it was always £10 a week, which was quite good in those days. There was never any need for a contract or letter. It was all done as show business used to be conducted – on trust – and you were paid in full on your last Saturday. There was no nagging for payment a few weeks later.

By the late '50s, Clement had become so assured in his storytelling that it became difficult to follow him. His clientele were used to his style and expected some outrageous stories. One evening, before he introduced me, he finished by telling a long and dreadfully coarse story that I had last heard from my workmates in Clydebank. After he delivered the crude pay-off line, through the laughter he said, 'Would you now welcome Nicholas Parsons.' I went out to try to make the audience laugh with some gentle, subtle material. It was almost impossible, and I asked Clement if he could tone down his routine before introducing me. He was understanding. From then on, he engaged me only when he was taking a holiday.

The success of any restaurant or club is entirely dependent on the personality of the individual running it. He or she needs to be a first-class host with shrewd business acumen and a strong personality. Clement was all of those and made a huge success of his club, and it was sad when the theatre failed to renew his lease in 1962, saying that they wanted the room for experimental theatre work. On the last evening, he got nearly everyone he had ever employed to do a show for free. We did about 15 minutes each. It was a fantastic night. Everyone was there. None of the performers would have missed it for the world. The wine was flowing – Clement was clearing out his stock at cut prices – and the atmosphere was incredible. I understand that Clement made a tape of the evening, but I have no idea what happened to it. It would be wonderful if it was ever found and restored. It was a one-off occasion that could never be repeated.

Some people patronised the club for the atmosphere, some for the cuisine and some because they enjoyed the personality of the owner, whose agile brain and quick eye never missed a thing. He was always courteous but would not suffer fools and was never afraid to be candid in a subtle way with those he found unpleasant. On one occasion, a difficult customer complained to the waiter about the wine. The waiter reported it to Clement, who immediately went up to the man's table and politely said, 'You have a complaint?'

'Yes,' said the man. 'This wine is disgusting. It tastes like vinegar.'

'I'm sorry,' said Clement. 'I'll bring you something else.' He took the bottle and the man's glass and returned with another glass, full to the brim. 'Would you like to try this?' he asked in a concerned manner.

The man accepted the glass and took a large gulp. Immediately, he spluttered his mouthful over the table: 'Good God, what was that?'

'That was vinegar,' said Clement with a wry smile. The man never returned, and Clement was perfectly happy.

I reached what seemed to be a peak in my cabaret career in 1956. The finest cabaret room in London, the Café de Paris, on a corner of Leicester Square, had received a direct hit from a bomb during the war, but was refurbished and opened again in 1955 to much publicity. Mecca, the leisure group, had bought the premises with the idea that, even if the costs were not justified by the returns, any losses could be set against profits elsewhere, and they had the laudable aim of bringing back to the West End this wonderful venue and recapturing the style and sophistication for which the club had been famous.

No room could have been better designed for cabaret. Of reasonable size, it had a small dance area in front of the bandstand, and dining tables on three sides. There was a magnificent balcony with a wrought-iron balustrade and tables all round. To reach the dance floor, you walked down one of the curved staircases on either side. This was also the staircase down which the cabaret artist came to perform. What a magnificent entrance it afforded.

There was a glamorous opening night, and thereafter the very best performers were engaged. Noël Coward did a season there, as did Marlene Dietrich, Maurice Chevalier, Jack Buchanan, Danny Kaye, Liberace, Hermione Gingold and Hermione Baddeley. It was intended that the cabaret would be the main attraction, as it had been in the past. People would book a table because they wanted to see the artist, not simply because they wanted a meal out with entertainment attached. It was soon discovered, unfortunately, that the costs of running such an expensive restaurant did not cover the fees name artists could command, and the public for this kind of entertainment had dwindled since the war with the rise in popularity of television. They might pack the restaurant for Coward, Dietrich or Chevalier, but other names did not have the pulling power, especially at the prices the restaurant was asking.

The management came up with an idea to attract custom and keep the costs down. They announced that they were going to have a season of fresh, young performers. I was booked on the strength of my previous work, principally at Quaglino's, and went along to see the room and absorb the atmosphere. The first in this season of new talent was a young Shirley Bassey, who had been discovered in her home town of Cardiff and had recently appeared at the Adelphi Theatre in the West End in a show introducing new artists. She was performing the night I visited the Café de Paris. She had what can only be described as raw talent. While her style was immature, there was no doubt that she would go places. Her singing at the time reminded me of Eartha Kitt, possibly because her big number had a rather suggestive lyric about burning her candle at both ends. The style of Shirley Bassey today is very different from that of the talented newcomer I saw.

I was engaged at the Café de Paris for two weeks. It could have been intimidating, but there was something about the magnificent room that inspired confidence. Working there was one of my biggest show-business successes to date, and it seemed as if it could be the springboard to greater things as a solo performer. Little did I realise that I was witnessing the beginning of the end of an era. Shortly after the season of young cabaret artists, the Café de Paris closed. Mecca turned the room into a dance hall, and so it has remained for many years, a sad end to one of the most elegant rooms in London.

To a large extent, I believe it was television that put paid to cabaret as a popular form of entertainment in this country. The full blame, however, cannot be placed at the door of what was then a new medium, because Britain had never really had a tradition of cabaret. Even though there was a vibrant scene in the '50s and into the early '60s, its hold on the public was tenuous, and while popular venues still exist today, they are few and far between. In Britain, we have a tradition of music hall, which is in contrast to the continent, where cabaret has deep roots. The differences in attitude are still noticeable now but were even more pronounced back in the '50s. If you perform in Paris, then everything stops when the show begins. The audience treat it as a performance. They clap, laugh and are repsectful. When the show is over, it is back to the food. In this country, there will be people who have gone primarily to dine and do not want any entertainment, but as it is there on the menu they will heckle and talk. As the performer, your task is to try to gain control and convince them you have something to which it is worth listening. It is tough, but it is a satisfying experience.

As more and more people acquired television sets and the programmes became increasingly popular, attitudes towards entertainment changed a great deal. Where there used to be two distinct areas of live performance – variety or music-hall theatre, which delivered broad humour; and the legitimate theatre, with serious comedies and sophisticated revue material – television brought accessibility to both, and slowly the audiences merged. Those who only ever went to variety suddenly saw plays on television and thought, 'Oh, I enjoyed that,' and started to visit the legitimate theatre. Those who would go to a theatre only to see a play were entertained by variety shows and other performers on television and discovered they were funny. In time, plays, variety and musicals attracted the audiences, while smart comedy, including cabaret, was squeezed out and its popularity dwindled dramatically.

The early '60s was probably the true peak of my cabaret career. I had the material that the late-night diners enjoyed, and there was a style and sophistication in the entertainment that was popular in the West End, which had reached its height at the turn of the decade. I was engaged to work at the Savoy Hotel, which had always featured cabaret in its restaurant. The entertainment consisted of a mini floor show with a dancer, a singer and a name artist.

I bought a new number for this engagement, written by Alan Reeve-Jones, a gifted writer of monologues. It was all about Lady Chatterley, a topical subject given the recent obscenity trial over the book's publication. The monologue was witty but also suggestive. The management of the Savoy were horrified, and after the first performance I was told to drop it or I might find myself dropped. They said that the number was lewd, and a witty pay-off line that ran, 'The sign on the box at the end of the drive said "For Letters",' was, to them, positively obscene. The four-letter word had yet to be uttered in any form of entertainment, and even a subtle reference brought the Savoy management to apoplexy. Naturally, I complied with their request, but what a waste of effort, because of a management who were out of touch with changing attitudes.

A hotel audience is very different from that in a restaurant, and the management has to take this into account. I found out just how different when a party of Americans, who were staying in the hotel, took a table near the dance floor. They talked loudly all through my act, and with them sitting so near to me it was difficult to compete. They were not only ruining my timing but also inhibiting the rest of the audience. I paused and politely asked them if they would stop talking while the cabaret was on, as it was spoiling other people's enjoyment. This received a round of sympathetic applause from some of the other diners. The Americans, however, became aggressive. 'Listen, buddy,' one of them said in a loud voice, 'we're guests here, and we didn't come here to listen to you. You're part of the service, and we can take you or we can leave you.'

'I think we'd all be happy if you left us,' I replied, arousing more applause from the rest of the audience.

Another member of the group then piped up in a strong southern drawl, 'Hey, kid, you got it wrong. We ain't goin'. We're just leavin' you to get on with that rubbish you're dishin' out.'

'Perhaps you don't understand English,' I responded.

'We don't understand your accent,' said another.

'Then why did you answer me?'

'Oh, ignore him, Horace. Get the waiter. We need more wine,' said a third.

'You'll have no luck. He only speaks English,' I replied. I was roused now, and the rest of the audience were clearly on my side, which helped. I then came out with a remark that created an uproar: 'What a pity, when we colonised America, that we didn't teach them manners.'

The place erupted, and a man on the other side of the room stood up and said, 'I am an American, sir. I hope I know what manners are, and I want to say I am enjoying your act and I hope you won't judge Americans by that uncouth lot over there.'

Everyone applauded, and I said, 'Thank you. I love America, and I am touched by what you said. Every country has a few bad eggs that let the side down.' I thought some other Americans in the audience were going to break into 'The Star-Spangled Banner' and quickly asked everyone if they wanted me to continue. They responded enthusiastically, but after that kind of incident it is difficult to coax an audience back into a mood to laugh.

After the show, I expected the management to compliment me on the way I handled a difficult situation. Instead, they took me to task for insulting some of their customers, adding, 'They've paid their money and have a right to respond as they wish.' Once more, the joys of show business.

One of the most unusual venues at which I performed cabaret was the 21 Club, in Chesterfield Gardens, Mayfair. It was smart, luxurious and probably extremely expensive. To me, however, it was just work and more experience.

The 21 Club was owned and run by an engaging character called Bertie Meadows. He only ever booked a single act, as opposed to a full floor show, and the exclusive audience were always most attentive and usually appreciative. I found it difficult to understand how the club could be so successful, as it was never full, not downstairs that is. After a while, I realised that there were rooms upstairs that were used for private, discreet functions, where guests could spend the night if they wished.

Bertie, who dressed immaculately, sported expensive jewellery and always seemed to be surrounded by pretty girls, was a charming host to all his customers. He seemed to enjoy my cabaret material immensely and was always extremely complimentary. He paid me £20 a week and occasionally gave me a little extra when he asked me to repeat my act for some small party he had organised for special guests in one of the rooms upstairs. I was naive at the time, having recently married and started a family. I did not think about the audiences for whom I was performing, exclusive gatherings where attractive girls seemed plentiful and contacts were made and secrets swapped. I cannot say for sure who might have been there at some of these private performances, but I do know that the criminal world overlapped into the nightclub world. I never enquired into the personalities who were there, and no one ever offered the information. I would do my act and head home, happy in my ignorance but enjoying the glimpses of an intimate, exotic world far removed from the gentle domestic life I was enjoying.

In complete contrast to the 21 Club – in fact, in complete contrast to any club I had worked in London – I accepted a seven-night engagement in March 1962 at a small club in Wakefield, Yorkshire, called the Kon-Tiki. I arrived at the club on the Sunday afternoon. The air was full of the stench of stale cigarettes, and the floor and tables were covered with beer dregs and other debris from the night before. I was greeted by a man whom I assumed was the restaurant manager, a bluff, down-to-earth, abrasive type with a strong Yorkshire accent. He greeted me with the rhetorical question 'Oh, you got here, did you? Have you got your dots?' He was referring to my music. He motioned towards the back of the dance area, which had a single naked light bulb hanging above it, to where three musicians sat idly, two of them strumming their instruments. This was the trio, led by the drummer Phil Langton, that was available to play any music I might have in my act.

'The lads are waiting to play for you.' I explained that I did not use any music, except for a play-on and a play-off. He looked mystified. 'What d'you do, then? A sort of straight-man act?'

I shook my head.

'You're not a ventriloqual are you? You got a dummy?'

'No,' I replied.

He looked even more confused. 'It's not magic is it?'

I shook my head again.

'Well, I know you don't sing, so what the heck do you do?'

I was beginning to lose confidence at this barrage of questions. I said that I did a comedy act. He came straight back: 'What? Patter?'

'I suppose you could call it that.'

He paused for a moment, then, with a wealth of meaning, said, 'Well, don't expect to get a laugh here on Friday.'

'Why not?'

He said, almost with a half-smile, 'No bugger's had a laugh here yet on a Friday. He can't be heard. They get up at the bar there, and they've had that much to drink. You're lucky if you can shout 'em down.'

'What happens on Saturday?'

His answer was succinct: 'Pandemonium.'

I was beginning to think I had made a mistake. I asked, with as much tact as I could, 'Why do you pay a lot of money to have artists come up from London and elsewhere if nobody is going to listen to them?'

'I'll have you know,' he replied, emphasising his point by prodding me in the chest, 'we've had some of the best acts in show business die here.'

The problem with the Kon-Tiki was that the club's management had tried to attract diners as well as drinkers by filling the room with tables where people could sit and eat. Those who wanted only to drink had to stay at the large bar at the back. As there were not too many diners, the tables were mostly empty and there was a huge, noisy crush at the bar, which made it difficult for the cabaret artist to be heard. On the Monday night, I asked for a long flex on my hand-held microphone so that I could go across the room and harangue the customers at the bar who were not listening. I was living dangerously, and it was an effort, but I survived, even if I did not enjoy it.

I reached the dreaded Friday night without disaster and was still on my feet at the end of a gruelling performance. I was just catching my breath when a well-dressed character approached and invited me to join him for a drink. He asked my opinion of the club. I told him in no uncertain terms what the problem was. They did not know whether they wanted a dining club or a drinking club. Until they made up their minds, the place was doomed.

'Oh,' he said. 'I am the owner.'

I said, 'Really? So I am not working here again?'

'No, you're in Yorkshire, lad. We respect people who speak their minds. I get your drift. What you want is a bit of hush, a bit of quiet so you can get your patter over, is that it? I'll tell you what I'll do. I'll get someone to give you a right proper introduction, get them quiet for you.' I thanked him and hoped that my last performance would not be as difficult as the others had been.

Saturday night arrived, and as promised the owner had found someone to introduce me. When it was time for me to start my act, the chap went out ahead, faced the audience and boomed in a broad Yorkshire accent, 'Now, I want a bit of hush. Tonight we have an *arteest* who is very good. He's got real class. The best-dressed act we've had for some time. He wants a bit of quiet so you can hear his patter. You won't laugh at his gags if you can't hear them. Now, before I introduce him, there's just one thing I want to say to all the men. It's about the new toilets. We've had them built; they are working, flushes and all. The sign's up there. It says "Gents". You can read it. We want you to follow the arrow and bloody well use them. We're fed up of all this pissing in the car park. Here he is, Nicholas Parsons.'

It was the most bizarre and impossible introduction I have ever received in all my life in show business. The audience were so overwhelmed that, for the first time, there was no noise during the beginning of my act. Unfortunately, neither were there any laughs. It took me quite some time to get them going. I did not perform in many working men's clubs after that.

From that first performance for the Under Thirties Theatre Club, my cabaret work went well, but at no point had I given up on my acting career. I knew I had continually to extend my experience if I was to win the straight acting roles I so enjoyed. In the '40s and early '50s, BBC Radio was producing some wonderful, creative plays, with some of the best talent in the country, and I realised that this could offer me a great opportunity to play a broad sweep of roles. My first jobs had been on the radio, thanks to Carroll Levis and BBC Scotland in Glasgow, and I loved the medium – I still do – so decided to apply to join the BBC Drama Repertory Company.

The Rep had existed for a short while in the '30s but had been disbanded until the outbreak of war, when the BBC re-formed it. The Rep consisted of a group of actors and actresses who were put under contract and were available to appear in any production on the 'wireless' for which a producer cared to book them. They received a regular salary and a modest amount extra if any programme in which they appeared was repeated. Producers could always employ performers on a freelance basis, but as the members of the Rep were all talented they were in constant demand. Some of the performers in the '40s who became household names through their work in the Rep were Marjorie Westbury, Gladys Young, Laidman Browne, Norman Shelley, Deryck Guyler, Grizelda Hervey, Richard Williams, James McKechnie, Gladys Spencer and Carleton Hobbs. Others who joined later became equally well known: Anthony Jacobs, Denise Bryer, Patricia Hayes, Duncan McIntyre and Richard Hurndall. These were the popular stars in the early '50s, unseen faces whose pictures only occasionally appeared in magazines but who were known to millions by their voices alone.

In 1951, BBC radio decided it was time to bring in some fresh blood to the Rep. The established players would still be employed on a freelance basis, but a number who had been around for many years were not to have their contracts renewed. It must have come as quite a shock to those who thought that, because of their standing in the public eye, or rather ear, they had a job for life. Suddenly, there were places to fill. Exhaustive auditions were held, and this prompted me to fill in the forms, stating all my experience, which looked quite impressive in print. I was called for the audition, at which I was asked to perform a piece of Shakespeare, a character role, a comedy item and any other pieces that would illustrate my range and experience.

Standing in front of a solitary microphone with no one else in sight and a group of producers listening in a control room is a forbidding way to audition, perhaps even more so than standing up in a theatre. At least there you are performing to a small group on the other side of the footlights. As I entered the cold, uninviting studio, a voice came over the intercom: 'Go to the microphone, announce your name and your agent's name, if any, introduce each item clearly, continue for your allotted time. At which point, announce your name again and remain in the studio for any questions we may wish to ask.' What a congenial atmosphere in which to declaim a piece from *Macbeth*; become angry and then sentimental, with an American accent, in an excerpt from *Ah, Wilderness!*; play a piece of high comedy from *The School for Scandal*; and display my ability with dialects and comedy in two other extracts, one of which was a speech from *The Cure for Love*.

I finished, gave my name again and said I had no agent. A deathly pause. Had they gone to sleep? Had they gone home? Were they waiting for me to go, too embarrassed to say anything? Eventually, the unseen voice said, 'Thank you, Mr Parsons.' No comment, no encouragement, no indication of success or failure. I stood there, not knowing what to do. I thought they might be discussing me. I began to feel like an object in an antique shop, with the customers debating whether I had enough class to blend in with their other possessions. At last, the voice came back, 'Mr Parsons. What have you done recently?' This was a hopeful sign.

I told them and then asked, 'Do you want to hear anything else? I have more prepared.'

'No, thank you, Mr Parsons. That will be all. We'll call and let you know.'

They did telephone, and I had the job. Beginning in the New Year, I would be a member of the BBC Drama Repertory Company. Unfortunately, 1952 was not a good time to join. The producers had money to spare in their budgets and were not obliged to cast contract players and quite frequently employed freelance performers. Most of those who had left the Drama Rep were still engaged to perform, which was natural, as producers knew their worth, and some of them made more money than they had under contract. The new intake had to work hard to earn their positions in the Rep.

I found it all hugely frustrating. My greatest joy was working for the producer Raymond Raikes, who during his time at the BBC created some of the most brilliant radio productions, particularly of the classics. He had a unique policy with newcomers. He cast them in principal parts in the early read-throughs and rehearsals of his major productions, which had longer rehearsal times, before the arrival of the star actor he had engaged. This served three purposes: he could iron out technical problems without boring his main players, save money on their fees and discover the newcomers' abilities. I enjoyed these 'audition' performances. They gave me the chance to play some magnificent roles that I might not have been offered on the stage, and they also paid off professionally, as Raymond later cast me in some excellent parts in his productions, long after I had left the Rep.

One of my first engagements after joining was in a Wednesday matinee, a short play, which was a regular feature at the time on the old Home Service – now Radio 4. In this particular production, I played one half of an engaged couple opposite one of the young stars of the Rep at the time, Denise Bryer. She was charming, attractive and popular with everyone. I could never have imagined what a significant role she was soon to play in my life.

My hope when I joined the Rep had been to broaden my experience in straight and character roles, but unfortunately this proved not to be the case. It was a lovely place to work, and the atmosphere was wonderful, but I was not being given many exciting opportunities. Nor was I making much of a living. Most of the productions in which I appeared were not repeated, and you made a reasonable living in the Rep only if you received repeat fees. On my audition sheet, I can only imagine that someone had written 'Good at dialects', because most of my parts during the first few months were supporting roles, playing characters of different nationalities. At various times, I played an Italian waiter, a Greek seaman, an Egyptian camel-herder, a Scottish gillie, a Welsh miner, a Yorkshire farmer, a Chinese coolie, a Croatian freedom fighter, a London taxi driver and an Indian immigrant, amongst others. Breaking free from professional pigeonholing was proving difficult.

After nine months of playing these roles, I resigned from the Rep. Ironically, I was immediately offered some leading roles in major BBC productions but could not accept all of them, as by then I was happily working on a television comedy series with the wonderful Eric Barker, which kept me busy every other week until the end of the year.

My life did seem to be settling into the world of comedy. If that was true, I knew I had to tackle the next most challenging work after cabaret, that of the stand-up or solo comedian in the theatre. If I could do this, I thought, I would finally prove my versatility and be offered comedy roles in plays, which was where I felt my natural talent lay. As described in a later chapter, that is when I decided to seek a position, alongside the scantily clad girls, as resident comedian at the Windmill Theatre in London.

I enjoyed three stints at the Windmill, and then in January 1954 an engagement with tremendous possibilities came my way. I was asked to star in a late-night review show with Beryl Reid that was opening in March at the little Watergate Theatre, in Buckingham Street, off the Strand. The show was devised and directed by Ronnie Hill, an experienced producer who had been in the Light-Entertainment Department at BBC Radio until he left to concentrate on writing music. The show was staged by Ian Stuart, who went on to become a successful television director, and the material was drawn from a number of talented writers of the day, including Diana Morgan and her husband, Robert MacDermot, Peter Myers and a young Canadian actor called Donald Harron. My friend John Hurst wrote a witty number about a man who had changed his sex, which was brilliantly put over by Beryl. It was quite daring for its time, but you could get away with more in a club, as they were not subject to the rigorous censorship rules of the Lord Chamberlain's Office. This particular number received incredible press coverage, as a few days before the show opened one of the first sex-change operations on a woman was headline news. It was a happy coincidence, as John had written the number a year or more earlier for Hermione Baddeley to perform in cabaret. Beryl's superb delivery of the opening line brought the house down every night. As a hearty lady, dressed in tweeds, she strode on, came centre stage, said, 'Hello,' and went straight into the lyric:

I changed my sex a week ago today [huge laugh]
I don't know what my friend is going to say [huge laugh]
Though she can be cute She's naturally astute
And it is not easy to explain the thing away. [huge laugh]

Beryl Reid had become a star name through her work in variety. Perhaps her most successful stage character was the naughty schoolgirl Monica, which she also performed on the BBC and for a spell in the *Educating Archie* radio show. She later developed another popular stage character, Marlene, an empty-headed creature who hailed from Birmingham and who was very popular with the public. Beryl was a superb actress and comedienne but suffered from the same syndrome as I did: the dreaded British Labelling Disease. She always wanted to be accepted for her all-round talent and star in a revue in the West

End. She obviously hoped, as I did, that this revue at the Watergate, called *First Edition*, would be sufficiently successful to transfer to a major West End theatre. It is ironic that she became a national star only after the dramatic performance she gave sometime later in the play *The Killing of Sister George*.

I brought some of my own material to the revue, including my routine about the different ways people laugh. I was expecting to do my foreign-film act, but Ronnie Hill preferred a routine I had developed about foreign garages, which also incorporated gibberish. I included a send-up of animal programmes on television and a comedy number in which I said I had been put on the 'Windmill Blacklist' and ejected from that theatre for disobeying their house rules.

Before the rehearsals began, Ronnie had a meeting with me to discuss material and the show generally, in the course of which he asked if I had any suggestions for additional members of the cast. Robert Bishop, Ian Stuart and myself were the male contingent, and two girls were required to make up the female team to accompany Beryl. I suggested Denise Bryer, from the BBC Drama Rep, who could not only play comedy well but was also good at dialects and had a natural singing voice.

Denise turned down the invitation to appear in *First Edition*. She did, however, accept my invitation to take her out one evening. Within three months, I had proposed marriage and we were engaged. By August, we were married. The wedding took place at the lovely Queen's Chapel of the Savoy, off the Strand, and was a very happy occasion. The day was made even more memorable by the fact that I was working in cabaret at Quaglino's at the time and nearly all of the wedding party joined us there in the evening. I had the most fantastic audience ever. At the end of my show, I announced to the whole room, 'I got married today.' The British are delightfully sentimental. The audience rose to their feet and called for the bride. Denise joined me, and it was a lovely moment for us both.

The two girls who did make up the team for *First Edition* were a pretty blonde called Valerie Carton and an attractive, dark-haired Welsh girl, Petra Davis, who had a lovely singing voice. The show was well received, and we had excellent reviews and played to packed houses, but no transfer to a major West End theatre followed. The Watergate management then decided to capitalise on their success and followed with *Second Edition*. Valerie was not available, so Barbara Leigh joined the cast, and Ian Stuart left to be replaced by James Gilbert, who later joined BBC Television as a producer and eventually became head of comedy programmes. A young dancer with a most ebullient personality was brought in to stage the show: Lionel Blair. He was full of boundless energy and thrived on the work. He still does today – he is a true survivor in our business.

Second Edition was a success, and the management were still hoping for a West End transfer, perhaps with the best of the two *Editions*. It was not to be, in spite of continued capacity business. A third show followed, and Beryl and I were dropped, which was difficult to fathom, as we were the only ones at the time with any name or reputation. Perhaps it was thought that we created an imbalance and that an unknown, talented team would make a greater impact. If that was the reasoning, it did not pay off, for while the young cast did well the business was not so good.

I was disappointed in the outcome, but I had enjoyed working in revue and knew it could only be good for my career once again to broaden my repertoire. Surely now I would not be categorised as just a 'voice man', a 'cabaret artist', a 'comic actor' or a 'variety performer'. In fact, it did seem my versatility was being recognised at this point in my career, because, soon after leaving *Second Edition*, I was approached by Leslie Bridgmont, one of the senior producers in BBC Radio Light Entertainment, who invited me to come and meet Richard Murdoch and Kenneth Horne, the stars of the radio comedy series *Much-Binding-in-the-Marsh*. Whether it was my brief period at the Drama Rep, my growing reputation as a cabaret artist, my work on television with Eric Barker or my stints as a stand-up comedian or in revue that had brought me to Leslie's attention, I did not know. I was just delighted to be given the opportunity to undertake another new and exciting challenge.

RADIO AND
THEATRE WORK

Radio comedy has had a major impact on my life and career. I also believe it has played a role in shaping today's society. During the Second World War, the edges of the British class system began to crumble as people from every walk of life were called up, trained and fought together. This was in contrast to the First World War, where the officer classes were still very much in existence.

When the Second World War broke out, it was realised that comedy on the radio was a great morale booster for the troops and for the country as a whole. Comedy shows were encouraged, and more and more were commissioned. These also contributed to the blurring of the class distinctions, because comedy is classless. Arthur Askey was the first to develop this brand of humour in his pre-war radio show *Band Waggon*, in which 'Big-hearted' Arthur worked alongside Richard 'Stinker' Murdoch. They were from two completely different classes but came together to create comedy. The listeners loved them both, and they loved each other.

The theme was built upon in 1939 with shows such as *It's That Man Again*, the title of which referred to the increasing frequency of references to Hitler in the British press prior to the war. *ITMA* was packed with wonderful characters from every corner of society, from Colonel Chinstrap to Mrs Mopp. Again, we laughed at them all and we loved them all. In the '50s, programmes such as *The Goon Show* poked anarchic fun at the Establishment, and Tony Hancock portrayed a character from East Cheam who had ideas above his station. The humour was egalitarian, and I believe this seeped into the British psyche and slowly helped to break down class attitudes.

Much-Binding-in-the-Marsh was another broadcast that contributed to this shift in society, and I was thrilled when, in 1954, I was offered the opportunity to join the cast. The programme launched in 1944 and was set in an RAF base. After the war, the characters decamped to civvy street and the show continued to star both Richard Murdoch and Kenneth Horne, as well as Sam Costa. Maurice Denham was brought in to supply all the character voices, and in 1952 Dora Bryan was engaged to play the scatty telephone operator in the office occupied by Murdoch and Horne.

Towards the end of 1953, Maurice was offered a film engagement that took him to the Far East, which meant he could not appear in the new series early the following year. This was the reason Leslie Bridgmont made contact and invited me to meet Richard and Kenneth. They had as much charm in private as they displayed on the stage. What impressed me, in particular, was the ease with which they wrote the scripts, including the humorous lyrics for the song that finished each week's show. Kenneth, in fact, was a successful businessman, a director of Triplex, the glass manufacturer. To him, show business was a hobby that he fitted in between company commitments. He was the least theatrical man I have ever met, always immaculately dressed, usually sporting a buttonhole and very modest and naturally courteous. Even when he retired from the world of business and worked solely as a performer, he never changed. He was the epitome of the conventional straight man and had a natural instinct for comedy, something he exploited magnificently in the classic comedy shows *Round the Horne* and *Beyond Our Ken*.

He and Richard put together the weekly script for *Much-Binding* in about a day and a half. They would meet in Kenneth's office, and by the end of the day most of it would be done. They had been doing it for years, so the style was quite easy, but to keep up the standard for weeks on end – radio comedy shows ran much longer then – was a real challenge. They met the next day to tie up any loose ends and compose the rhyming stanzas for the finishing song. They could not work longer, as Kenneth had to return to his business. They were both quite shrewd, however, for they encouraged Sam Costa to bring a little bit of script for himself each week. He enjoyed this, as it guaranteed his exposure in each programme – it also meant they had less to write.

When I first met Richard and Kenneth, they asked if I had any particular voices or characters that I thought would fit particularly well into *Much-Binding*. 'Yes, there is one,' I replied. 'A Bristol voice, because my mother's family comes from Bristol. There is a Bristol accent that is subtly different from that of the West Country and is very interesting and attractive.' We created a character, Mr Greenslade, who was an excitable fellow. When asked by Kenneth what had particularly troubled him during the week, he would go into a long description of some situation in which he had been involved and how he had extricated himself or resolved the matter. He would speak faster and faster as he became more excited and always finished with the same phrase: 'Oh, I never let the grass grow under my feet,' which became so popular with the audience that it soon aroused spontaneous applause.

Actors acquire voices and gestures through observation and often subconsciously absorb them and later reproduce them without realising where they came from. As children, my brother, sister and I would often visit my mother's family and stay with my grandfather in Westbury-on-Trym. I used to enjoy those visits and particularly looked forward to going to his big department store, B. Maggs and Co., and being taken round by my mother's cousins. The younger of the two, Bertram, of whom I was very fond, had a slight Bristol accent, and it is quite possible that Mr Greenslade was an exaggeration of him. My mother certainly thought so.

After the second broadcast featuring Mr Greenslade, my mother telephoned me: 'I've been listening to your show. That Bristol character, that's my cousin Bertram.' I suddenly realised she was correct. Bertram's engaging manner and lovely personality had made an impression on me, and I had inadvertently reproduced his educated Bristol accent. My mother was not happy. 'It has got to go,' she continued. 'I will never be able to hold my head up in Bristol again.'

I tried to reassure her, as there was no possibility the character was going to be dropped: 'Look, Mother, don't worry. People do not recognise themselves. Anyway, it is not actually Bertram's voice, and even if it was I do not think he would assume I had based the character on him.'

About a week later, my telephone rang again: 'Nicholas, this is your cousin Bertram. I've been listening to that *Much-Binding*. I've got to tell you, that Bristol character you do, it is absolutely marvellous. I know people in Bristol who speak exactly like that. I don't know how you do it. I couldn't, and I come from Bristol!'

I'd been proved correct, but it did lead to a rather embarrassing experience some time later. I was staying down in Bristol with Bertram's family, and he took me on my usual visit to Maggs. On arrival, he asked me to do a quick impersonation of Mr Greenslade for some of his staff. With Bertram standing next to me, it was all a bit awkward when I was asked about the inspiration for the character. I had to think fast and explained he was based on a friend of my grandfather's, now dead.

Mr Greenslade proved popular with the audience, and Kenneth asked me one day, 'Why don't you write a little piece for that Bristol character and bring it along each week?' I was delighted that I was to have my own moment in the show, but that was typical of Richard and Kenneth. They were not comedians who worried if their supporting players got laughs, because it all helped the show. The further easing of the writing burden was, I am sure, merely a bonus.

In the early '60s, I was also enjoying the political satire that was appearing on television following the success of *That Was the Week That Was*. I realised, however, that there was nothing comparable on radio. In late 1964, I contacted the writer Alistair Foot, whom I had met through his work for the comedian Arthur Haynes. Alistair had written some wonderfully constructed and stylish sketches for us in the Arthur Haynes radio series. He also wrote material for Ronnie Barker on the radio. Together, Alistair and I developed a concept for a political satire show for radio, which I called *Listen to this Space*. I took our synopsis to the head of Radio Light Entertainment, Roy Rich, whom I had known as a theatre director, and explained the idea in more detail.

BBC Radio at the time was still influenced by its great Reithian past and in many ways was still very prim about the kind of programmes that could be transmitted and particularly what could be said or referred to in those programmes. Roy Rich, however, had faith in the idea, confidence in us and, as a recently appointed head of his department, was keen to explore new ground. He commissioned a pilot programme and passed it to the most experienced producer in Light Entertainment, Bill Worsley. I knew Bill from the many shows in which we had worked together and also knew how good he was. It was an auspicious start.

Alistair asked if we were going to write the show together. I said no. I thought my strength was in ideas rather than scriptwriting, and I preferred that he should find another experienced writer with whom he would be happy to work. If the series went ahead, I would always be on hand with suggestions. Alistair told me that there was a fellow writer in the office where he worked, Anthony Marriott, who was experienced and politically orientated. He knew that Tony would be interested in the show, and he thought that they could write well together. I liked Tony and trusted Alistair's instinct, and so the team was formed. None of us realised at the time that the two would become one of the most successful writing duos of the '60s and '70s. Their partnership blossomed when *Listen to this Space* became a success, and later they went on to write comedies and farces for the theatre, the most successful of which was the record-breaking *No Sex Please, We're British*.

As far as politics was concerned, our opinions differed, but that was a help rather than a hindrance. Professionally, we got on extremely well and made a good team. For the pilot, my wife, Denise, played all the female roles in the sketches, Roger Delgado and myself, the male parts. Libby Morris sang, and the music was supplied by a great trio under Tony Osborne. There was a special item in which we put a high-profile personality on the spot. Our 'subject' in the pilot was Robin Day, whom I interrogated about his own aggressive interview technique. As so often happens, he turned out to be very different from the personality

NICHOLAS PARSONS: MY LIFE IN COMEDY

he projected on television, and he was urbane and charming.

In 1965, programme producers were responsible for deleting from a script anything remotely sexually suggestive or even mildly vulgar. Swearing was strictly forbidden, and unsolicited advertising was not allowed – even the names of newspapers could not be mentioned. Lastly, the royal family was out of bounds unless the reference was respectful. The pilot show that we had devised was going to break nearly all of these edicts.

Before we began, we had to obtain permission to mention the names of newspapers, since we were going to quote from them and, specifically, take passages where misprints and sloppy journalism had created humorous inferences or ridiculous meanings. This is something that is done as a matter of course now, but it started on *Listen to this Space*. We obtained the permission we needed, which was the first breakthrough; the others we decided to leave until after the pilot to negotiate.

The recording went well, and we were all optimistic. Our spirits were dampened by Bill Worsley, who, while saying that he thought the show was good, did not believe that we would be granted a series because the content broke too many BBC ground rules. He had overlooked, however, the tenacity of Roy Rich, who loved the pilot and was determined to see a successful series. As far as I know, Roy had no support from the rest of his department and was going out on a dangerous limb. While he might have been breaking the traditional mould in the BBC with something so different, he might also have damaged his career if the show failed. Gerald Mansell, then head of the Home Service, liked it, but no series was commissioned. Somehow, by what means I do not know, the pilot landed on the desk of Hugh Carleton Greene, the director-general who had already blown many cobwebs away from 'Auntie BBC'. He enjoyed what he heard and sent word that a series should go ahead.

Bill Worsley was due to retire, and Roy asked John Bridges to produce the shows. John had recently joined Light Entertainment from the disbanded Features Department and had a fine track record. There were, however, problems from the start. John had never handled an audience show before, where you treat the recording as live and edit the fluffs and mistakes later to bring the programme down to the required length. Also, when playing in front of a studio audience, it is often possible to capitalise on a mistake and create a laugh out of the situation. John was used to working with a script prepared and approximately timed in advance and a recording that would be interrupted, if necessary, to eliminate mistakes as they occurred. To add to John's pressures, some of our new show was written by Alistair and Tony on the morning of the recording, so that it would be as politically topical as possible. The show was to be broadcast on Friday at 7 p.m. on the Home Service. The first programme went out on 12 April 1965. In order to preserve the topicality, Alistair, Tony and I had asked that we record between 5.30 and 6.15 p.m. and then do an incredibly rapid edit in 45 minutes to have the programme on air by 7 p.m.

I think Alistair and Tony instinctively realised that John was lost and, without discussion, took over. Alistair marked on his script the sections that were getting laughs and made notes for cuts. We could not go for the luxury of single-line edits; it had to be sections and, on occasion, whole sketches. Tony kept the overall structure in his head, so as rapidly to endorse or reject proposed cuts from Alistair. John's production assistant, who had timed every page of script during the recording, then worked out very quickly how many minutes had been cut and kept the two writers abreast of the total time, while the recording engineer, a talented technician called Mel House, with great skill cut and spliced the tape as the edits were explained. The finished show was down to the required length sometimes with only moments to spare. On one famous occasion, they were still editing the second half of the show while the first was being transmitted.

John Bridges was much happier in the pre-production and planning stage of the show. When Roger Delgado was unavailable, it was John who suggested someone to replace him. This replacement was a farmer, approaching middle age, who had little professional experience as a performer but was a naturally funny man with a gift for dialects. His name was Bob Todd, and *Listen to this Space* marked the beginning of his career as a full-time entertainer. He, of course, went on to achieve great success with Benny Hill. The thing about Bob, however, was that while he knew he could make people laugh he never understood technically how he did it, so if you asked him to repeat something he could not be guaranteed to reproduce the same intonation or inflections, which often meant he was at his funniest the first time he read a script or delivered a line. He was a rare and exceptional performer and a valuable asset to the small cast, as was Denise, who continued to play the many female roles. Libby Morris did not contribute to the sketches and, since she did not sing in every show, left at the end of her contract, when another performer was brought in. In the second series, it was the impressionist Peter Goodwright, then in the following series, at Tony's suggestion, we engaged Barry Cryer, who was then known principally as a scriptwriter and talented warm-up comedian.

Barry could do a brilliant impersonation of Harold Wilson, who, as prime minister, was obviously going to appear quite frequently throughout the run of the show. I could do a good impersonation of Edward Heath, the leader of the opposition, and the two often appeared in sketches together. Barry's impersonation was the finest I have ever heard, and he became a key member of the team. He also became a good friend.

Listen to this Space, after the struggles to get on air, made an immediate impact, and contrary to the expectations of seasoned broadcasters and producers we soon had a success on our hands. We even received a personal message of congratulations from the director of Sound Broadcasting. Alistair and Tony had the courage to be outspoken and critical in their sketches, yet they were always entertaining. They mocked the struggles of the Liberal Party through two elderly liberals, played by Bob and Denise, who were living completely in the past, recalling the great days of their party. They also made significant political comment on the social conditions in urban areas through a lovable family of Indian immigrants who were trying to come to terms with the vagaries of our health service, unemployment system and the general structure of society. Poor, likeable George Brown, then foreign secretary, never appeared quite sober in the show, and if any politician said anything remotely foolish he was fair game for satirical comment. We had most fun at the expense of Wilson and

Heath but always kept a balance. If one week there was a sketch knocking the Labour Party, the following week we would have a go at the Conservatives. We were also outspoken about the royal family, although we were never rude or cruel.

I initially thought that, by fronting a show that was having fun at the expense of those in power, I would soon be made a political outcast and certainly *persona non grata* with those in the Establishment. I had overlooked how the British respond to positive criticism and to those who are successfully promoting anti-Establishment ideas. They do not attack or deride; they accept you into their inner circle in the hope of seducing you away from your more radical opinions. In effect, they try to take you over, and it usually works. As our success spread, I received invitations to visit the House of Commons from MPs who were followers of the show. They clearly enjoyed the publicity, which was meat and drink to those in the public eye. I was introduced to Edward Heath when he was a guest in a show at Television Centre. I was initially quite nervous, but he was courteous and charming. Of course, it would have been foolish for anyone to state that they hated being 'taken off' and demonstrate that they had no sense of humour, but I did feel that his smile was rather being forced through clenched teeth.

The show's popularity grew, and it even had a repeat for a time on the Light Programme – now Radio 2 – on the Sunday following its Friday transmission. In 1967, the Variety Club honoured me at their annual awards ceremony by naming me Radio Personality of the Year. I was very flattered, and, while not wishing to sound like every show-business-award winner, it is true that it could not have happened without the talented writers and marvellous team.

One day, while *Listen to this Space* was at the height of its success, the phone rang at home. I picked up the receiver, and a voice said, 'This is Buckingham Palace.'

I thought immediately it was a friend playing a joke, so I replied, 'Really? This is Battersea Dogs Home. We don't have any stray corgis here at the moment.'

The voice became more pompous: 'Is Mr Parsons there?'

I suspected by now it was probably Tony Marriott winding me up, so I said, 'Come off it, Tony. What are you doing at the Palace? Getting copy for next week's script?'

The voice on the other end was now even more formal but very patient: 'This is the Controller of the Household at Buckingham Palace. Is Mr Parsons there?'

I then worried that perhaps it was real – but, if so, why were they phoning me? I spluttered a little, then said, 'Did you say Buckingham Palace?'

'Yes,' came the reply.

'I'm so sorry. This is Nicholas Parsons.'

There was no reaction to my embarrassment. He simply continued, 'Oh, good. I've been asked by Her Majesty to invite you to have lunch with her and Prince Philip. It would be a week on Thursday, and if you are free to join them we will put an invitation in the post.' It was genuine. What a fool I felt. I thanked him very much and said I would look forward to it immensely.

The next day, the beautiful embossed invitation arrived. The Queen and Prince Philip occasionally host informal lunches to which they invite six or seven people from different walks of life – there is usually a representative from the world of politics, the Church, the law, medicine, industry, sport and the arts. On this occasion, I was the guest representing the arts.

The lunch was magnificent. The Queen sat at the head of a rectangular table, Prince Philip in the middle and a young Princess Anne, who was on leave from school to keep a dentist's appointment, at the other end. I was placed opposite the F1 driver John Surtees, representing sport, and beside Princess Anne. It was a memorable occasion, and, as the Queen and Prince Philip talked to us easily and informally, it made me realise what a difficult task the members of the royal family have in maintaining a regal presence while trying not to appear too distant in our informal society.

I will always be grateful to Alistair and Tony, not only for their writing but also for the way they worked on the scripts and saw each show through to transmission. Their work on the editing was more than could be asked of any writer and well beyond the call of duty. It also, I think, left John Bridges feeling undermined and professionally impotent, which are the only reasons I can give for his subsequent behaviour. Instead of accepting that he was working with experienced performers and writers who all knew what they were doing, and then walking the corridors of the Corporation taking the plaudits that would be given to the producer of a successful show, he first became frustrated and then exploded. It was about the sixth show in the first series, and we were assembled for a read-through of the script. John called us into the auditorium and then went up onto the stage. The programme had by this time been acclaimed, and I thought he was going to congratulate everyone. Instead, he berated us for our unprofessional attitude. He finished by saying that, as someone who had led troops over the top in the war, he could certainly lead a rabble like us in the right direction, and then swept off to the studio control room, instructing us to get on with it. There was a stunned silence, and it was a while before we could put our minds wholeheartedly to the task in hand.

The next day, John went to Roy Rich and asked to be released from the programme. Roy immediately asked me to lunch to discuss the matter. I explained that John was not used to a show where everyone was very experienced, knew their jobs and was trying to make something work against time. We all made suggestions, and without Alistair and Tony working on the editing the show would never get on air. Roy was shrewd as always and said, 'I think I understand. Your programme doesn't need a general to lead. It requires a quartermaster sergeant to organise supplies.'

I replied, 'Exactly.' Roy then asked if I would like a different producer from his department. I did not dislike John and certainly did not want to harm his career. I said I would be happy to work with him, provided Roy could explain what we had just discussed. John returned, clearly embarrassed about his outburst. We got along fine after that, and the show went from strength to strength. In retrospect, however, I should have trusted my professional instinct and let John go. I believe that, deep down, he was still frustrated that he did not feel in control.

After a few years, when *Listen to this Space* was well and truly established, Alistair and Tony quite rightly asked for a salary in keeping with their contribution, pointing out that each show took the best part of a week to prepare, unlike most radio scripts, which could be put together more rapidly. Also, as it had to be topical, they could not finalise any of it more than a day or two in advance. They were spending the same amount of time as they would spend on a television script, for which the money was infinitely greater.

Their request for an increase in salary was refused; John Bridges did nothing to promote their cause, and they left the series. They suggested that Barry Cryer, who was already in the show, and Dick Vosburgh, a successful writer of satirical material, should take over the writing, which was an excellent idea. John would have none of it. He saw his opportunity to take control at last. He let Alistair and Tony go, ignored their suggestions and brought in two writers, Peter Myers and Ronnie Cass, who were talented but totally wrong for the programme, in my opinion. They had been very successful in the '50s with their clever, saucy intimate revues, which was a different kind of writing.

I agreed to continue in the show, which was now called *Hear this Space*. We struggled on for three further series, more on the reputation of our previous success than anything else, and then I really lost heart and it all petered out. I should have left with Alistair and Tony and started a new programme. It is never a good idea to stay with a show when it has lost its quality and style. You become associated with its decline, however good your performances may have been. A year or two later, a similar programme, without a studio audience, was begun called *Week Ending . . .*, which was excellent and always entertaining. It ran until 1998 and was the offspring of *Listen to this Space*.

The most frustrating thing of all when Alistair and Tony left and John insisted on all the changes was that he never consulted me. To some extent, there was no reason why he should have done, except out of professional courtesy, as he was the producer. From my point of view, the whole concept of the show had been my idea. I had made a fatal mistake, however, that excluded me from any say in, or control over, the format. I had failed to secure credit for the original idea at the outset. Some years later, I was to repeat the error.

In the mid '70s, I had the idea of producing a radio quiz based on the news. I sent the synopsis to David Hatch, who was then head of the BBC Network Production Centre in Manchester. His reply was not encouraging: 'Nicholas, we have got so much news on radio and television that I don't think anyone wants to hear another programme based on current events.' I was surprised by this response, as I had a huge amount of respect for David and his ability to recognise potential. I was not to be put off, however. If the BBC were not interested in a pilot at this stage, I decided to put one together myself with the help of two friends, David Lund, a schoolmaster at University College School in Frognal, Hampstead, and his brother Peter. We decided to produce the show in the little theatre attached to David's school, which he created and is now called the 'Lund Theatre' in his honour, to raise money for charity and also to demonstrate to the BBC how it could work. We invited a young John Lloyd, who was a BBC Radio producer at the time – John has since gone on to have a wonderful career, including being involved in the creation and production of classic series such as *Not the Nine O'Clock News*, *Blackadder* and *QI* – to come and watch it. We called it *Keep Taking the Tabloids*.

The show went well. John was impressed and was keen to push for a radio pilot to be recorded at the BBC. He succeeded, and we kept much the same team as had appeared at University College School, with John producing the show. From what I heard, the pilot received a favourable reception from much of the BBC but, unfortunately, not from the person who mattered most, the new controller of Radio 4, Clare Lawson Dick. I knew Clare well; she is a lovely woman, but she didn't have a great feel for satirical humour and she turned it down.

John Lloyd, however, was a very enterprising producer and realised there was something in the idea. Clare was Radio 4 controller for only a relatively short period of time before she retired, and at that point John put together a new version of the show for the BBC, with exactly the same rules, and called it *The News Quiz*. The programme was first broadcast in 1977, and at the time a number of people who had been at the recording of our pilot for the BBC congratulated me on the fact that my show was now being aired. I had to inform them that *The News Quiz* was not my programme. Once again, I had not taken the simple precaution of copyrighting the format to retain my intellectual property, leaving the BBC perfectly entitled to produce their own version. I love being creative and coming up with ideas, but I clearly do not have a natural business brain. If I had, as Roy Plomley, Ian Messiter and my good friend Derek Batey all exhibited when they created and protected *Desert Island Discs*, *Just a Minute* and *Mr & Mrs* respectively, I could be receiving royalties to this day every time *The News Quiz* is broadcast. Derek refers to his creation for Border TV as his little pension. I could have had one of my own. From my point of view, *The News Quiz* is the one that got away in my radio career.

From the mid '50s through to the mid '60s, many of my television and radio appearances were happily dominated by *The Arthur Haynes Show*, but that still allowed time for me to continue with my theatre work.

In 1961, I was touring with Peter Jones in *Doctor at Sea*, adapted by Ted Willis from the Richard Gordon novel. We launched on 8 May at the New Theatre, Bromley. The play was directed by the then resident producer, David Poulson, who had his own sparse style of directing, presumably because he was used to mounting productions on a weekly basis. He kept his instructions and advice to a minimum. The theatrical maxim 'Try to make sure you don't bump into the furniture' was about the extent of the direction we received. By the time we reached the second week of rehearsals, he seemed to be offering even less detail.

Peter and I were not only developing comedy business ourselves but were also devising moves for the rest of the cast, and we both felt that some of the scenes needed more work. After one run-through, we reached the end of the scene and waited for comments. The lone figure sitting in the stalls shouted out, 'Right, we're on to the next scene.'

'But aren't we going to get any notes? We can't all be perfect,' I called back.

He merely replied, 'On to the next scene.'

Peter Jones, who was normally very gentle, suddenly couldn't take any more and shouted back, 'Listen, before we start, we'd love you to say something. Even if it is only "Goodbye!"' It was so out of character that I have never forgotten it.

The tour that followed was reasonably successful but memorable for the final week at the Theatre Royal, Nottingham. Peter had developed mumps, and the glands in his neck were swollen to such a size that he was almost unrecognisable. There being no understudies, he was persuaded to soldier on to the end of the week. As if this was not bad enough, I then caught gastric flu and could not keep anything down. The flu reached its peak on the Friday night. A bucket was placed beside each exit on the set, and more than once I had to rush off in the middle of a scene, throw up while the other actors ad-libbed and then stagger back to carry on with the performance. I will always remember the forbearance of Patricia Garwood, who played my character's girlfriend and had to act with two performers who looked nothing like their normal selves, one of whom must have also smelled most unpleasant from his frequent trips offstage to the waiting buckets. Such is the glamour of show business.

Despite the ups and downs of the tour, I enjoyed being with Peter. He was a good friend and a truly talented actor. We worked together often on the stage, on the radio and on television. In 1965, we starred together in a television series for the BBC called *Night Train to Surbiton*, which was not as successful as it should have been. Peter had been touring with the play *Boeing-Boeing* in Australia previously, and within months I too was appearing in the same successful and popular play, in London's West End.

The year 1965 had marked the end of my ten-year partnership with Arthur Haynes. The break-up had made me sad, as I felt that we could have gone on to greater heights together, but I had little time to dwell on the situation. I was offered the lead in *Boeing-Boeing*, taking over from Leslie Phillips when the production moved from the Lyric Theatre, in Shaftesbury Avenue, to the Duchess Theatre, off the Strand, it was a wonderful opportunity, and I was determined to focus all my attentions on the role.

Leslie Phillips is a lovely man, and our paths have crossed on many occasions. I first met Leslie in 1949 when I went to see him play the juvenile lead in *On Monday Next*, Philip King's farce about a repertory company, at the Comedy Theatre, on Panton Street. After the performance, I was invited backstage and introduced to Leslie. He was very kind and said to me, 'This would be a wonderful part for you to play.' Actors do not usually say things like that. He continued, 'If I leave, I'll let you know so you can apply.' I have never forgotten Leslie's generous gesture that day.

When I joined the cast of *Boeing-Boeing*, I did not know that John Gale, who was presenting the show, had decided that the play had probably all but finished its run in London. After all, it had been on for three years. Apparently, one of the reasons he was pleased to cast me in the lead was that he had estimated that the stay at the Duchess would probably be very short, after which the play could go on a national tour, helped by the fact that the star name would be someone who was well known to television audiences. As I would be appearing in the play in London, albeit for a short while, it meant that he could advertise the show in each town not only as 'a record-breaking success from the West End' but also with the West End cast. Had I known all this, I might have been a little unsettled. The move to the Duchess Theatre, however, was far from disappointing. The play eventually ran for another 18 months in the West End, though I stayed with it for only 15. Peter Byrne, who took over from me, went on the provincial tour.

Boeing-Boeing had a chequered history. A clever farce, it was originally written in French by Marc Camoletti and was only an hour long. It had run for a long time in a small theatre in Paris and had subsequently been translated and extended into a two-hour play by Beverley Cross for performance in this country. John Gale had bought the rights, cast David Tomlinson in the lead and invited Jack Minster to direct. There is a certain symmetry that can arise in show business, and here was one such example. David Tomlinson created the role in *Boeing-Boeing* that, within three years, would establish me as a West End performer; David's career in films was kick-started when he played the part originally offered to me in my first film, *Master of Bankdam*, in 1947.

The play opened to very poor reviews in its try-out week in Oxford, and Jack Minster, who had invested in the production, had grave doubts about bringing it to London – it is even rumoured that he tried to sell his shares. It needed great courage on the part of John Gale to continue with the play. On Thursday, 20 February 1962 it opened in London and received good reviews from *The Times* and the *Telegraph*, but the popular press said it was dreadful. Bernard Levin, writing in the *Daily Mail*, even went so far as to say that the only things missing were sick bags on the backs of the seats for the audience.

Word of mouth is what creates success, but you need audiences to start the ball rolling. The two good reviews brought some custom to the box office, and this was helped by J.W. Lambert on the Home Service on the Saturday following the opening. He stated that the play was, 'a true, blue French farce'. The final boost that put the seal on its success, and confirmed John Gale's faith in the play, was an unexpected piece of good luck that occurred during the second week.

Around this time, the BBC were presenting excerpts from West End shows live from the theatre. It was not great television but wonderful for the box office of the show from which the excerpt was taken. The BBC always chose comedies and, naturally, always picked the most entertaining sections. They chose the second scene of the first act from *Boeing-Boeing*, which probably contained some of the funniest moments in the play. It was the last transmission of an extract from a London play that the BBC ever presented. The next day, the box office was inundated with calls for tickets; the play was soon established.

The character I played, Robert, is up from the country visiting an old friend, who has organised his private life in a most ingenious way. He has an 'arrangement' with three air hostesses, timed so that as soon as Air France flies out Lufthansa flies in, and as soon as Lufthansa departs TWA arrives. Something is bound to go wrong eventually, which is, of course, the basis of the play, and this begins to happen when Robert is in the flat alone.

When you have a farcical comedy, and you have a director who encourages the leading players to search out areas for extra laughs, any inventive performer will always try to improve the comic potential of the part he is playing. This was certainly true for David Tomlinson, and I am sure there were more laughs in the play when he left, a year after the opening, than when he began. It was also true of Leslie Phillips, who played the part for two years. Leslie had subtly altered the interpretation of the role from David Tomlinson's original portrayal, and when I took on the part I adopted my own approach, maintaining some of the elements of David's and Leslie's comedy business and introducing touches of my own.

When comic actors talk about 'comedy business', they are referring to what they do with their hands, feet and body, not how they deliver the lines. Working with a talented director, there is much that can be built in to a role using comedy business, and in *Boeing-Boeing* I embraced this approach wholeheartedly. The show had been running for a few weeks, and I had introduced and developed a number of new elements, which were getting laughs. One in particular involved a telephone. One of the girls arrives unexpectedly at the flat, and as she walks in I am seated and talking on the telephone with another of the air hostesses. The audience know I am in trouble. The moment she appears, I react. I keep the receiver in one hand, whip open a drawer with the other, put the receiver in and shut the drawer, all the time looking and smiling at the new arrival. All very rapid and neat, and the audience has a laugh. The girl then makes a quick exit to freshen up, and I go back to the drawer, open it, pick up the receiver and say, 'Oh, I am terribly sorry. I shut you in a drawer.' Another laugh. This does not sound funny when described, but like all comedy business it is the personal interpretation and the slickness you bring to its execution that brings a laugh.

I was keen to find out what our director, Jack Minster, thought of my performance and how it had developed and asked John Gale if he would invite Jack to come and watch the show and give any feedback, or 'notes' as we say in show business, that he felt appropriate.

When John approached Jack with my request, apparently his response was, 'He's a comic actor. They don't want directors coming back and telling them what to do. They just want to do it their own way.'

John tried to reassure him: 'Nicholas is different. He actually asked if you would be very kind and go and look at his performance and comment on what he is doing.'

Jack did come to see the show and came backstage afterwards. He was a quiet, unassuming man but a real character and lovely to work with. He looked at me and said, 'You've put some nice bits of business in there.' Then he said to me, and this is wonderful direction, 'That bit of business you did with the telephone: excellent. But why did you go for the second laugh afterwards?'

'Well, it got a laugh,' I explained.

'Yes, it did, but it is much better to get your big laugh and move on with the plot.' He was absolutely correct, a variation of the old show-business maxim, 'Leave them wanting more.'

It was a joy working with Jack, as he was one of the most creative comedy directors in the business. He also had a natural talent for acting but never had any ambition to be on the stage. I said to him once, when he was illustrating a bit of business we should do, 'Jack, that was brilliant. You really are a good actor.'

He shook his head: 'No, no, that's not me. I am too self-conscious. You actors want to show off all the time, and I am not a show-off.' He understood the profession very well.

While I was in *Boeing-Boeing*, I came close to experiencing what must be the actor's greatest nightmare: failing to get to the theatre on time. I have dreamed this many times, and the panic you feel is indescribable.

In the side street off the Aldwych, where the Duchess Theatre is situated, there were two parking bays in front of the theatre. The commissionaire kindly kept one of these for me every night, so I had the luxury of parking on the doorstep and just walking in. It is a rule of theatre that every artist reports in at what is called 'the half', 35 minutes before the curtain rises. On this occasion, I left my home in Hampstead, allowing the usual time to reach the Aldwych by 7.25 p.m. The curtain rose at 8 p.m., and I was on stage about ten minutes after that. I reached the end of Gower Street, and there was a solid block of cars, which was unusual. The queue began to crawl. I was not particularly worried, as it took me only ten minutes to get ready. The queue edged slowly forward, but the time was ticking away. It was now nearly 7.45 p.m., and I was about 200 yards from the theatre, just north of the Royal Opera House, where, I discovered subsequently, the Queen Mother was attending a special gala performance. This was the cause of the traffic jam. Another five minutes passed, and I had moved about fifty yards. At this rate, I was not going to be at the theatre until after 8 p.m. I was now desperate. I could not abandon the car in the middle of the road. I was going hot and cold. I was due on stage in 15 minutes.

In a crisis, you pump more adrenalin than usual, which fires you up and you do things you would never normally contemplate. In the car directly in front of me, there was a man sitting in the passenger seat. I jumped out of my car, ran up to his door and pulled it open. 'Can you drive?' I asked sternly. The man nodded. 'Can you drive an Alvis?' He nodded again. 'Then please get out of the car,' to which he meekly responded without a murmur. 'The key's in the ignition. I'm due on stage at the Duchess Theatre in ten minutes. Leave the car with the commissionaire. He'll look after it. The curtain's about to go up. I'm running.'

I arrived at the theatre at 7.55 p.m. No one seemed in a particular panic about my whereabouts. They were obviously under the impression that I was already there, as I had never been late before. The curtain was shortly to be raised, and so I sprinted to my dressing-room, slapped on my make-up, got dressed and ran to the stage just in time to hear my cue line. I made my entrance, and the nightmare was over.

The sense of relief lasted until the interval, when a different panic gripped me. What about my beautiful Alvis? I rushed outside, and there was the car, sitting happily in its normal place. The sense of gratitude I felt to this unknown man, who had saved me from disaster, was tremendous. Then another awful thought struck me: in my panic I had forgotten to ask him to leave his name and address with the commissionaire. I would not be able to thank him for his kindness or offer him tickets to the show. I live in hope that he might still contact me, and I will at last be able to thank him for his noble deed that day in 1965.

My work on television with Arthur Haynes had brought me a degree of public recognition, and my role in *Boeing-Boeing* had brought to life one of my theatrical dreams: to star in the West End. I saw no difference between the achievements. Television and stage were merely two different media that allowed me to demonstrate the same thing: my acting ability. The public do not always see things the same way, however. Back then, to some the two worlds were mutually exclusive – there was a television audience, and there was a theatre-going audience. Rarely did they overlap, and the perception was that you either worked in one area or the other. This was brought home to me during our run at the Duchess Theatre.

Covent Garden is situated near the Duchess Theatre, and in 1965 it was not a place full of boutique shops, cafés and bars, as it is today; it was a fruit, flower and vegetable market. A month or two into our run at the Duchess, I was standing outside the theatre talking to the commissionaire when one of the Covent Garden market traders wandered past. He stopped when he noticed me and said, 'Here, it's Nicholas Parsons, isn't it?'

'It is, yes,' I replied and shook his hand.

'I thought I recognised you. Now, Nicholas, we don't see you on the old box these days. What's happened? Have you retired?'

'Not at all. Look up there.' I pointed to the poster above the theatre, which proclaimed, 'Nicholas Parsons in *Boeing-Boeing*.'

He looked up and read, 'Nicholas Parsons in *Booing-Booing*. Oh, right, that's a play isn't it, Nicholas? Where they all get up on stage and . . . here, Nicholas, do you realise something? That geezer has got the same name as you.'

Many years later, I was once again reminded of the gulf that can occur between theatre and television audiences. It was 1982, and I was touring in Simon Gray's thriller *Stage Struck*, in which Alan Bates had starred at the Vaudeville Theatre in 1979. I was playing the lead, alongside Dermot Walsh, who produced and organised the tour.

There was a blank week in the tour, and Dermot said that the only date he could obtain was at the Rosehill Theatre, on the outskirts of Whitehaven, in Cumbria. Dermot explained that the theatre was run by some lovely people, almost as an arts theatre, and it was tiny.

'Nicholas,' he said, 'I know you are on a percentage, but this is such a little theatre that we won't make any money. But you get a glorious audience up there; in fact, some of them put on evening dress for the occasion. If you don't mind doing it, I think it will be a memorable week.'

'Of course, Dermot,' I told him. 'That's fine. Better than a week out with no income.'

We arrived only to discover that the people Dermot remembered as owning the theatre had retired and it was now being run on a commercial basis, not very successfully. The smartly dressed, sophisticated theatre-lovers whom Dermot had described had clearly abandoned the place. Poor Dermot was embarrassed. 'It wasn't like this the last time I was here, I promise,' he explained.

Business was slow, so the management decided to bus in an audience from the local old-people's home for the midweek matinee. It seems they had never been to a theatre before, but it soon became clear they must have enjoyed watching television in their communal living room and chatting about the programmes. The front row of the stalls was almost adjacent to the stage, so we heard nearly every word: 'Oh, I like him, don't you? Have you seen him before? What else has he done?' As the drama developed, they seemed to get more involved: 'Oh, what a thing to say'; 'Oh, I don't like the sound of him'; 'Oh, look, she's a saucy one'; 'He's nice, isn't he?'; 'I like his pinny'; 'What's he up to now?'

The play allowed me the opportunity to perform my first-ever death scene on stage. My character has arranged for his wife to shoot him in an elaborate plot he has set up to have her blamed for the murder. She produces a gun, aims it at me and pulls the trigger. I fall to the ground and die. Then there is silence on the stage before the next actor speaks. That afternoon, during this dramatic moment, a voice from the audience piped up, 'He doesn't have much luck, does he?' The cast immediately got the giggles, and the corpse 'corpsed'. It is not very realistic to see a dead body suppressing laughter.

Stage Struck gave me the chance to play a serious role again after many years being somewhat typecast as a quiz-show host on *Sale of the*

Century. Four years later, I was offered the opportunity to take on something entirely new to me, a major West End musical. The show was Harold Fielding's 1986 revival of *Charlie Girl*, starring Paul Nicholas, Cyd Charisse, Dora Bryan, Mark Wynter and Lisa Hull. I took the role that my good friend Derek Nimmo had played in the original 1965 production with Anna Neagle and Joe Brown. When Derek used to appear on *Just a Minute*, he often teased me about my age, as I was seven years older than him. So, when I landed the part of Nicholas Wainwright, I was pleased to be able to get my own back to some extent. I called Derek and told him I was playing the character with which he had become synonymous over 20 years previously. Derek was a good friend, a talented actor and a kind and thoughtful man. He died in 1999, and I still miss him.

Although I had never appeared in a big-production musical, I was not entirely unfamiliar with this form of theatre, thanks to my appearances in the '50s in revue, which included a lot of musical numbers. That gave me a good grounding for the work, although in my wildest dreams I do not think I ever imagined I would be singing in a West End production featuring a genuine Hollywood musical legend.

Cyd Charisse was a lovely, talented lady and a pleasure with whom to work, a true professional who was dedicated to her dancing and practised assiduously to keep fit. Even into her 60s she was more than able to perform a wonderful modern ballet routine with an outstanding dancer called John Paul Henry, set to a jazz tune, every night in the second half of the show. Cyd's fabulous career had been built on appearing in films, where the individual scenes are short and there are microphones everywhere to pick up the dialogue. Performing in the theatre is a different discipline, and Cyd sometimes struggled to project her voice or sustain a long scene, but that took nothing away from her natural charisma.

Charlie Girl opened to rather indifferent reviews, but Harold Fielding was not worried. His shows had survived poor press before. He believed that if you gave the public what they wanted they would come to the theatre, and he certainly tried to do that in this production with an attractive cast, a stunning set and a simple, romantic story with a lot of humour. Times had changed, however, over the previous two decades. The London public were more cynical and demanding and less willing to accept a show that relied a great deal on charm. At first, business was good, and those who saw the production enjoyed it. After the Christmas period, however, bookings dropped. Cyd Charisse had to return to America, and the show was too expensive to maintain when not playing to capacity, so our stay at the Victoria Palace finished in January 1987.

My time in *Charlie Girl* was memorable to me for many things, but principally for an idea that I instigated, based on a gimmick I had once previously introduced when playing dame in pantomime. In the play, I arrive at a large stately home where Paul Nicholas's character is working, to tell him that he has won the pools. Paul has fallen in love with 'Charlie Girl', and I also become enamoured of one of the girls in the house and decide to stay on as a temporary butler, quite an eccentric one.

During rehearsals, I approached the producer: 'You know in the ballroom scene when everyone is waltzing and I serve champagne? Would it be an amusing twist if I came on in roller skates?'

'Fantastic,' he said, 'but how is it going to work?'

He had a point. I was not entirely sure about all the logistics, but I had a feeling that it would be worth it. I already had the skates, so that was no problem. The real issue was that skating on stage is not straightforward, because every stage has what is called a 'rake', which means it slopes. You have to find a balance between skating up stage and freewheeling down. Having successfully done it once before, however, I felt I could pull it off.

As so often happens in musicals, we were getting behind in our rehearsal schedule, and as we approached opening night we had still not tried out the skating. 'We'll come to it, we'll come to it,' the producer assured me. By the time we got to the final tech run, we had still not rehearsed this difficult technical maneouvre. 'Don't worry, we can put it in the show once we open,' he said. I had been in the business long enough to know that never happens. Material comes out; sections are not added in. So I decided to give it a try regardless. We started the tech run, and as the waltz number grew nearer I called the musical director to one side.

'By the way,' I said to him, 'on this one I am going to do the skating.'

'Has it been cleared?'

'I don't know. I think so. But it will be OK. I am going to do it. Any problems, it is my fault.'

He was a good friend and said, 'Nick, I wouldn't do it for anyone else, but I will do it for you.'

'Thanks. If you can keep the music going, the others will continue dancing. I'll come on, but remember it will all take a little longer than in previous rehearsals, as I will be on skates.'

My heart was beating. 'This is absolutely outrageous,' I thought. 'What am I doing?' I sailed on, and the waltz continued. The couples kept dancing, but they were absolutely mystified. Out of the blue, there I was with a tray in my hand, to which I had stuck the glasses, skating between them and calling out, 'Champagne, champagne, who wants champagne?' Thank God I managed to avoid them all. They continued with the dance, and I shot offstage again.

When the scene ended, Harold Fielding walked up to the stage. I thought I was in for a telling-off at the very least. I might even lose my job. 'I haven't seen that before,' he said.

'I know,' I replied. 'We have been very busy and haven't had time to rehearse it before.'

Much to my relief, he continued, 'It is brilliant. Keep it in.'

That was that. The skating remained and was popular with the audiences. I was a bit miffed, however, that it had all been so last-minute and that our producer had not had the vision to see the potential and give us more time to rehearse.

Working with Dora Bryan was another memorable aspect of *Charlie Girl*. Dora had begun her career in repertory at the Coliseum Theatre in Oldham, and she and I had known each other since the late '40s, when we were both looking for work in the West End. Over the years, our careers have crossed, notably in *Much-Binding* and in a show called

The Lyric Revue in the West End. I have always been very fond of Dora, and it was a great joy to work with her again. She is a natural comedian. Similarly to Tommy Cooper, she has the ability make you laugh simply by talking. Dora has a way of delivering a line that is naturally funny.

We had one scene in which I was supposed to be a yoga expert demonstrating positions to Dora and Cyd Charisse. Dora was incredibly supple even then. She could perform the splits and bend over backwards, which the audience loved. In fact, we were rather naughty in a professional sense and built in some additional comedy business to the scene. We rather indulged ourselves, and Paul Nicholas, as the star of the show, said to me at one point, 'You know, it is good to have the extra laughs, but cut down all the business and move on. Don't overdo it.' He was quite correct.

Unfortunately, Dora and I did get a bit carried away on occasions. When we travelled to Manchester with the production, we introduced even more business. By the time we arrived in Birmingham, the scene had been cut. I think we probably deserved that.

My final memory of *Charlie Girl* is of performing a duet with Paul Nicholas in the song 'I 'ates Money'. Paul is a talented singer. I am not. I have always struggled with musical numbers and have adopted a speak/sing approach, which just about gets me through. Paul was very generous in his support of me and helped me enormously, but I would never have thought my performance merited an appearance in another West End musical. Certainly not a Stephen Sondheim production.

In November 1988, I was elected Rector of St Andrews University. The position of Rector in the four ancient Scottish universities – Glasgow, Edinburgh, Aberdeen and St Andrews – is decided by student vote and is not an appointment. That summer I received a letter out of the blue from a St Andrews student, Andrew Burnett, asking whether I would consider standing. I was delighted and flattered, and Andrew and his team led a brilliant campaign against formidable opposition from Glenda Jackson, Auberon Waugh, an Edinburgh art-gallery owner, Richard Demarco, a popular Radio Scotland presenter, Neville Garden, and Attila the Stockbroker. This last candidate, a rock poet, insulted everyone and created a lot of fun. He did not receive many votes, however.

On winning the election, I took my role as Rector very seriously. It was an important position. The Rector chairs the meetings of the Court, which is the governing body of the university. In my first year of rectorship, I visited St Andrews no fewer than 11 times, attending Court meetings, various formal celebrations and student graduations. When my three-year stint came to a close, I was proud that the university conferred on me an honorary degree of Doctor of Laws. I sometimes wonder what my parents might have thought if they knew. I know they would have been pleased and probably very surprised.

It was during my third year as Rector, while I was up in St Andrews to attend a Court meeting and appear at the graduation ceremonies, that my agent called: 'You are being considered for the part of the Narrator in Stephen Sondheim's *Into the Woods*. They'd like you to come down to London to meet Richard Jones, the director.' My immediate reaction was that I was not right for Sondheim. 'Well, it is going to be a big number, and I think you should go,' my agent responded. 'I am going to post you the script.'

In show business, there are jobs you particularly want and for which you think you are natural casting, and someone else lands the part. I never mind if that person is talented – that is the luck of the draw – but when that person does not have the ability you do feel a bit annoyed. There are also other jobs that make you nervous and for which you do not think you are suited, even if you believe you can do them. Having read the script, that was my feeling. There were other big names in the frame – Bob Monkhouse was certainly one – who I felt might be better suited. Then there was the timing issue. I would have to go down to London on the Tuesday, meet Richard at the Old Vic on the Wednesday morning, then get the train back up to Leuchars, the nearest station to St Andrews, that afternoon in order to be there for the graduation ceremonies on the Thursday. In this profession, however, you won't get anywhere if you are not willing to give it a go. 'What the hell,' I thought. 'I'll do it.'

Richard Jones is amazingly talented and has directed numerous operas across the world. He is one of those people who trust their instincts. When we met, we simply talked, about *Just a Minute*,

Kenneth Williams, Arthur Haynes and many other aspects of my career. He did not ask me to read a word of the script. I thought this was a very intelligent way of undertaking an audition. He wanted to obtain a feel for me as a person. He knew enough about my work to make a judgement on whether I was capable of performing the role. What he wanted to know was whether I was right for it. The following day my agent called me in St Andrews: 'You've got the job.'

The production was due to open in September. That was going to cause me a problem, as I was fixed to be in a pantomime over Christmas. It meant I had to buy myself out of that contract by paying for the advance publicity already produced. The producers of the pantomime were understanding, recognising what a wonderful opportunity this was for me. They would have to find someone else and prepare new publicity material, but, this being July, there was sufficient time for them to work something out.

It was an amazing show and a wonderful experience. I was flattered and thrilled to be part of it. Julia McKenzie was the star, and she was brilliant. Stephen Sondheim told me that he was a great admirer of Julia. He felt she interpreted his songs and music better than anybody. He was quite correct. Julia is at the peak of her considerable talent when she performs Sondheim.

In the role of the Narrator, I had difficulty with the musical element. The assistant musical director was extremely patient, giving me special private lessons as we tried hard to get my number, 'Ever After', to an acceptable level. 'I got away with it' is probably the best description. I only realised how true that was when, some months later, I read a review of the recording of the show, which had been released. The reviewer wrote that he had been impressed with my performance when he had seen me on stage, but listening to me now on the record he realised that I was 'not much of a singer'. I could not fault him for thinking that.

My character was involved in a dramatic moment in the show. The Narrator is drawn into the proceedings centre stage, offered to an unseen giant to placate her and then thrown to his death. Richard Jones had decided that my body should actually be seen being hurled back onto the stage. A dummy was to be created with exactly the same proportions, dressed in the same clothes and with a complete reproduction of my head and features. I was asked to visit the factory where the *Spitting Image* puppets were made. To create a complete likeness, they needed a mould of my head and face. My hair was held down with a stocking, and then plaster of Paris was spread all over my head down to the neck. I was told that it would be uncomfortable, that I would not be able to see or say anything and, once my ears were covered, that I would also hear nothing. To make sure I could breathe, they put straws up each of my nostrils, around which they then packed more plaster. I must have looked very strange.

If I wanted to communicate, I had to gesticulate, and if I felt I was suffocating I had to clap my hands and they would immediately break off the cast. I tried to relax but was suddenly seized by a mild panic. How long was I to stay like this? No one had told me. It might be half an hour. They might have gone off for coffee. I started to gesticulate and tried desperately to mime that I wanted to know how long I had to suffer this isolation. I got the message through eventually and was informed it would be about ten minutes. It was difficult to relax and it was not an experience I would like to go through again in a hurry. The dummy, with my facial reproduction, was apparently one of the most expensive items in the show, but Richard's brilliant idea was more than justified. When the body was thrown from a great height to hit centre stage with a thud, there was always an audible gasp from the audience, it was so realistic.

Into the Woods opened to universally good reviews, and some critics gave rave notices. We were packed until January 1991, when the first Gulf War broke out, and the whole of the West End was affected as audience numbers dwindled. David Mirvish Productions was presenting the show, and he himself had invested a significant amount of his own money. He needed capacity business over an extended period to recoup his outlay. How long could he carry a loss? Would the visitors return after the conflict ended? He waited as long as he could and then decided to close the show in March. We were all given three weeks' notice of the termination of our contracts. Almost the next day, the war ended, and the public slowly started to return to the theatre. Unfortunately, it was too late for David to change his mind, as the theatre had already been let for a new production.

My appearance in *Into the Woods* has not been my only exposure to the exceptional work of Stephen Sondheim. Two clever young directors, Richard Morris and Doug Pinchin, approached me in autumn 2005 with the idea of putting on a gala performance of Sondheim in aid of charity. They had the theatre arranged but wanted my involvement in terms of contacts and charities. I was delighted to accept and introduced them to ChildLine, for whom I am an ambassador. This amazing charity was launched in 1986 by Esther Rantzen and provides a confidential helpline where children and young people can seek comfort, support and advice from trained counsellors. It was with considerable courage that ChildLine decided to back the project, as there are no guarantees of success with fundraising events such as these. We adopted as the title of the show the wonderful number from *Into the Woods* 'Children Will Listen'.

The cast they assembled was spectacular, including John Barrowman, Eartha Kitt, Gemma Craven, Rosemary Ford, Bonnie Langford, Claire Sweeney, Brian Conley, Josie Lawrence, Millicent Martin and Marti Webb. They sang wonderful songs from a variety of different Sondheim musicals. The choreographer, Bill Deamer, had only two weeks to pull it together, and he performed miracles. Dress rehearsal was one day only on the Sunday, and we performed that evening, on 23 October. The performance was a huge success, raising a considerable amount of money for ChildLine. I did some compèring and was flattered with the audience reaction when I came on for one number and began with the words, 'Once upon a time . . .' which is the opening of *Into the Woods*. The Sondheim fans are passionate about his work and recognised it immediately, even though the show had not been seen in the West End since our production almost 15 years previously.

In 1994, I once again appeared on stage in the West End as a Narrator in a musical. This time it was in *The Rocky Horror Show*, and I remained involved with Richard O'Brien's show until 1996. After that, I appeared regularly in pantomimes at Christmas until about three years ago, when

I decided to stop. I had so much other stage work on then – and now, with my various one-man shows and the Edinburgh Festival, in addition to after-dinner speeches and the radio – that I just did not have the time to commit to an extended run. Being able to enjoy a civilised festive period with the family is a very welcome benefit of no longer appearing as Widow Twankey or other such characters.

My one-man show takes me to theatres up and down the country. For longer journeys I go by train, as I love rail travel. For shorter trips, my wife, Annie, often drives. Recently I have been to Brighton, Falkirk, Oxford, Darlington and Chipping Sodbury, to mention a few. A number of years ago, I was booked to perform at a small theatre in Wisbech, run by some friends. I asked Annie if she would drive, as the evening was likely to be quite demanding. 'Certainly, darling,' she replied, 'but on one condition: I don't have to see the show.' I quite understood. She had seen it many times and knew most of the stories and probably where every laugh came.

'Of course you don't need to see it again,' I told her. 'Why don't you bring a bottle of wine, a book or some magazines, and I'll make sure there is a comfortable chair in the dressing-room where you can relax while the show is on. We can then meet up with our friends afterwards for dinner, and you will enjoy a good evening.' We arrived at Wisbech, and, as I got ready, Annie settled into the armchair. As I was just about to go on, she suddenly realised she had forgotten a corkscrew. 'Don't worry,' I said. 'There is a small bar at reception. They are bound to have one.' She went down and asked.

'Of course, Mrs Parsons. Delighted,' said the barman. As the barman went to fetch the corkscrew, a man approached her.

'I'm sorry, but I couldn't help but overhear the name, Mrs Parsons. You're Nicholas Parsons's wife?' he asked.

'Yes, I am.'

'I suppose you have come to see the show, have you?'

'Oh, no, I've seen it far too often before. I couldn't sit through all that nonsense again.'

'That's very interesting. I'm the local critic. I've come to review it.'

Annie was a little worried that she might have put her foot in it. If the journalist had been from one of the tabloids, perhaps she would have. As it was, this local reviewer used the encounter positively. He told the story and went on to say, 'As I sat watching Nicholas Parsons on stage, my mind kept flitting back to what his wife had said to me. I had no problem at all sitting though the performance. The longer the show went on, the more entertaining it became.'

That Wisbech journalist was kind in his comments on the show. Not all reviews are so positive, of course, but in my opinion that does not mean you should ignore them. I have always felt it to be rather pompous when actors say, 'Oh, I never read my reviews.' I read every one, even the bad ones. There must be some reason for the criticism. Even if it is unfair, there might be some little grain that triggered the unkind remark. If you can find that, you may be able to improve your performance, to be more acceptable to a broader audience. Show business is a learning process that never ends.

When you are in a play, appearing night after night for perhaps a year or more, the challenge is to be able to go out there and perform as if it is for the first time. You have to find a way to keep your performance fresh while maintaining the integrity of the role. The key is to rethink each performance, introducing subtly different inflections. Only that way will you retain your sparkle and project what you want to convey across the footlights. If you merely go on and speak the words you know so well, you can sound dull and flat.

Some actors come offstage and blame the audience because the laughs weren't coming. 'Ghastly crowd tonight,' they will say. I always respond, 'No. No audience is "ghastly". They are all different. Some respond more rapidly and more easily. Some do not. If that is the situation, we have to step up our performance a notch to bring them on board. It is not the audience's fault. It is ours.' You must view it as a challenge. Audiences are fascinating. They are groups of strangers who come together, sit down together and suddenly react as a unit. That is an unpredictable dynamic. If you are lucky, there will be some catalysts who start laughing early, which quickly spreads. Ideally, these people will be near the front of the theatre, because laughter travels backwards not forwards. The same applies in a dramatic play.

The tension and emotion travel backwards. If you are not lucky enough to have these catalysts, then, as an actor, you just have to work harder. That is your job.

The acting profession has changed almost beyond recognition since I started. When I was young, many of my generation had the opportunity to gain invaluable experience in the wonderful repertory companies that existed. Students would come straight out of stage school and get taken on as assistant stage managers. Then they would play a few roles, all the time learning how a company works. That apprenticeship has all but gone now, and that makes life far harder for actors today.

In one sense, there is more work available, with the advent of multiple channels on television producing far more programmes – provided the cheaper option of 'reality shows' does not take over entirely. The trouble is, the increase in supposed opportunities means an increase in competition. It is a tough business. A young actor may get a role in a crime or medical series and think, 'Great, I have work. I am on my way.' That job then finishes, and they have not gained any depth of experience. If things do not go well for them immediately after that, with another part, they have no grounding to rely on. It is all too easy to fall by the wayside in such circumstances.

Through my years of acting, I learned that you must not give up. Keep trying. Do not sneer at the humble job; it might lead to something more significant. Gain experience. Keep plugging away. Do not become disillusioned. Something may happen. The comedian Jimmy Edwards once told me that he was asked what he thought the most important quality in show business is. His answer was quite simple: 'Stamina.' He was correct. You require physical stamina, because it is a demanding profession, you need creative stamina in order to generate new ideas when you are performing and you are lost without emotional stamina to cope with the inevitable setbacks. With stamina, you can survive; without it, you are lost.

Television talent shows project the image that one can become a star overnight. This gives a false impression. Those who do achieve success via this route have often had previous experience. There is always the exception, such as Susan Boyle, which is exciting, but for longevity nothing replaces experience. You have to learn from the hard knocks that this unpredictable business can hand out, and then bounce back. I have sometimes been asked to give advice to youngsters looking to enter the world of entertainment. My reply is always the same. First, you need talent, but that is not enough. You also require a certain dedication. Be under no illusions, this is a tough business. You are bound to face upsets, disappointments, frustrations, indignities and rejections. If you can cope with these and not become bitter, then carry on, as there are many rewards: wonderful characters, a lot of laughs and the unique joy of being received on stage by a warm, responsive audience. It is a privilege that has come to some of us, and it is worth fighting for.

THE STRAIGHT MAN AND
ARTHUR HAYNES

Nobody starts a career in show business by saying, 'I want to be a straight man.' That was certainly never my ambition. I fell into the role by chance, and it has proved to be both a successful and an enjoyable one for over 50 years. It came about because of my willingness to diversify and accept new challenges.

When I first became a professional actor, in the mid '40s, radio was the premier broadcast service. The BBC were producing television programmes, but the output was limited to a few hours in the evening. Some of the shows were good, but they did not have the slick presentation and timing you find today. It really was 'Auntie Beeb'. There was even a rather embarrassing but well-meaning short item offering thoughts on spiritual well-being at the end of every transmission, about 10.30 p.m., called *The Epilogue*. Television was ready for a shake-up, and it came in the form of a parliamentary Bill in the mid '50s that aimed to establish 'commercial television'. It did not have an easy legislative passage.

There was tremendous opposition in Parliament to the idea of the new broadcaster, particularly in the House of Lords. They thought the advent of this rival to the BBC would pollute and undermine the very fabric of our society. Happily, those sincere but short-sighted individuals, who seemed determined to keep their heads deeply embedded in the sand, proved to be unsuccessful in their arguments. Independent Television was launched on 22 September 1955.

The biggest impact of the introduction of commercial television was on the BBC. They suddenly had to increase the professionalism of their programme-making in order to compete with the new independent companies that were luring away trained production staff. To illustrate how deeply the BBC felt about the arrival of this new channel, they created a hugely dramatic storyline in their flagship radio programme, *The Archers*, to be transmitted on the opening night of ITV and in which one of the best-loved characters, Gracie Archer, was killed in a fire. The episode received huge listening figures and is still remembered, but commercial television was here to stay. It was one of the best things that happened for our profession. Not only did it create many more employment opportunities for actors and technicians, but it also forced the BBC to improve the quality of their shows immeasurably.

The independent network was divided into different areas, with separate companies supplying programmes for both local consumption and the network. The idea was to encourage a keen level of competition between the various programme-makers. Associated Television, ATV, was based in London and was one of the first to go on air. In some ways, ATV was the real power broker, with a team of people who understood show business. Lew Grade was the chairman, with successful impresarios Val Parnell and Prince Littler also on the board. They were all hugely experienced in providing high-quality family entertainment, and their aim was to maintain that standard on the small screen.

George and Alfred Black produced one of ATV's earliest variety shows. During the war, their father, George Black senior, had produced a famous show called *Strike a New Note* at the Prince of Wales Theatre in London. The aim was to discover new stars, and by that I mean professional entertainers who had already done good work but were not yet famous. It proved to be very popular with the public and made names of the great comedians Sid Field and Terry-Thomas and the singer Zoe Gail. When their father died, George and Alfred inherited his empire and decided to revive *Strike a New Note* as their first television production. ATV gave it more publicity than any show could possibly live up to. I remember the actual phrase they used: they were going to discover 'the new and unknown stars of Independent Television'. We were promised an exciting new shop window for all aspiring young artistes, and, naturally, I hoped I might be included. I had gained a broad range of experience by that time, but it did not happen. My telephone remained silent.

I made a point of watching the first transmission of *Strike a New Note* in January 1956, and I could not believe how bad it was. There was, however, one person in the show who I thought was rather talented, a comedian called Arthur Haynes. I remembered his name from his work with Charlie Chester in the radio show *Stand Easy*. Arthur's personality came over well on television, but he was working with terrible material. The following week, I happened to see the show again, and it was even worse. Nowadays, a show like that would be taken off immediately, but at that time they had nothing with which to replace it, so they had to keep it going. The following morning, my agent, Richard Stone, telephoned: 'Nicholas, have you seen a programme called *Strike a New Note*?'

'Yes, isn't it absolutely pathetic?'

'Well, they want you to join it.'

'Really? When do I start?'

'Today,' said Richard.

In show business, we do not question; we go where the work is. *Strike a New Note* was pretty poor, but it could only get better. I do not think George Black thought I could save the show; he merely wanted to strengthen the cast with some new faces. In one of his items, Arthur Haynes played a mischievous character called Oscar Pennyfeather, who never spoke. He mimed to an unseen voice. I was keen to meet Arthur, as it was the best thing in the show. In fact, it was the only good thing in the show, but the voice was not right. George felt I had the right style and asked me to take over. When Oscar mimed something, I would say, 'Oscar, that's a bit ridiculous, isn't it? Oh, look out, Oscar! Why did you do that? Oh, because . . . I understand . . . yes. Where are you going now, Oscar? The next counter? What do you want to do there? Oh, Oscar, are you sure about that?' It was excellent television, a creative idea that has not been done since.

I joined the show to work with Arthur and also to do some hosting and a little stand-up. I still remember the first joke I ever told on television. It was about a chap who was a racing enthusiast, a great betting man, and he had a system. He always backed horses with the colour yellow in their name. Then one day in the sweepstake he drew a horse called The Yellow, and it won him a lot of money. From that day on, he was obsessed with the colour yellow. He decided everything had to be yellow. He painted his house yellow, inside and out. He did the whole of the living room yellow: yellow carpets, yellow curtains, yellow walls, yellow ceiling, yellow furnishings, yellow fittings, everything yellow. Next he started on the bedroom: yellow walls, yellow carpet, yellow bedspread, yellow ceiling, yellow sheets, yellow pillowcases. Then he died. It was terribly sad. He got jaundice, and they couldn't find him!

I was enjoying myself on *Strike a New Note* and working with a very nice group of people, but despite the new additions the show was not reviving. George Black decided to change the name to *Get Happy* and bring in Kenny Morris and Joan Savage, who were a talented duo, and a singer called Maria Pavlou. George also said he would like Arthur and me to do some sketches together. That was really the start of our partnership. It is interesting the way things evolve in show business, rather than being the result of some grand plan. When Morecambe and Wise started working together, Ernie was the funnier of the two, but as their partnership grew Eric got most of the laughs and Ernie was happy to play the foil. Arthur and I came together by chance but found we had a natural rapport. We used to get together with George and Alfred Black's production manager, Roger Hancock, Tony's brother, and read all the sketches that had been sent in by aspiring young comedy writers. Together we chose the best, and, without realising it, we were becoming partners in a double act: the comic and the straight man.

I instinctively felt this was the way to go. If you are going to be a good foil to a comedian, you need to understand comedy. You need to know where the laugh comes and how it is phrased. I found myself using the experience I had gained as a comedy actor in a new and totally unexpected way. Arthur was a cockney comedian from the world of variety. I had the persona and delivery of the Establishment

116

figure and automatically fell into the role of the straight man. I was happy with that, because when the sketches worked I knew I had played my part. I was never envious of Arthur taking the gag lines. That is the unwritten law of the partnership: one is the comic, and the other is the foil. Nowadays, that relationship no longer exists, not in the traditional 'comic and straight man' sense, as developed by the great double act Murray and Mooney. The role of the comedy performer has evolved, with partnerships consisting of two comedians working together, both getting laughs, such as Armstrong and Miller, Mitchell and Web, Punt and Dennis. Having said that, Arthur was always very fair. If I got laughs from the characters I played, he was quite happy, but the gag lines were his, and that was something I respected, and we evolved into an extremely successful team.

There is a difference between being a good foil and simply being an old fashioned 'feed' who lines up the gag for the comic so that he can deliver the punchline. I used to resent it if anyone said to me, 'It's wonderful the way you feed Arthur.' I did not just stand there saying, 'I don't wish to know that; kindly leave the stage!' That was the music-hall approach. I like to think I took the role of the straight man into a slightly different realm, in the sense that I always played a character to whom Arthur could react. He played three different character roles: the likeable tramp, a rather conniving Mr Know-All and an aggressive East End cockney. All three represented different aspects of Arthur's professional persona.

As the Establishment figure, I played a doctor, MP, lawyer, policeman, employment official or vicar. I played lots of vicars. In fact, we broke ground with that, because up until then you could not have a vicar in a comedy sketch. It was considered bad taste, as if you were sending up the clergy or the Church. We proved that you could create a comedy situation as long as the vicar was portrayed as a genuine and sincere person. When one of Arthur's characters, played with great charm, tried to take advantage of this pleasant man, people could laugh at the situation. They were not laughing at the vicar. This meant my characterisations were important: they had to be convincing. *Get Happy* slowly became a successful show, and the partnership with

Arthur flourished. We got on well together. We came from different social backgrounds, we did not socialise often, but professionally we spoke the same language. That autumn, Arthur was offered a guest spot on a new ATV variety show called *Star Time*, and he asked if I would like to do a sketch with him.

'Do you remember that chap, Johnny Speight, who wrote some sketches for *Get Happy*?' he asked me.

'Of course,' I replied. 'Lovely fellow, I thought he was the best.'

'Well, I think we could ask him to write something new for us, and we'll do it in the *Star Time* bill.'

'Wonderful idea, Arthur. I will really enjoy that.'

Johnny Speight wrote a very funny sketch that proved popular, and ATV booked us for a second appearance. Our success was noted by Arthur's agents, Lew and Leslie Grade. As they were involved with ATV, they naturally wanted Arthur to have his own show, and I was asked to be part of it. In retrospect, friends have said my agent missed a trick. He should have pushed for naming the show *Haynes and Parsons* instead of *The Arthur Haynes Show* with Nicholas Parsons. I suppose they may have had a point, but we were a good team and I was happy with the terms of my contract. The billing was never a major issue with me.

Val Parnell wanted the new show to act as a platform for Aileen Cochrane, an attractive singer he was keen to promote. She had a warm and friendly personality and looked lovely on the screen. One evening, we were recording at the Hackney Empire and Val arrived to see the show. It was the first time he had come to a recording, and Aileen was tremendously nervous, which did not help her singing, and once or twice she missed a note and was devastated. Nowadays, they would stop the recording and go for a second take. Back then, it was all live. Videotape had arrived, but you could not edit it.

After the show, I went to Arthur's dressing-room and we sat there having a drink. Val had gone to reassure Aileen, who was very low. It was possible we were going to have to record the whole show again. Arthur and I knew perfectly well that our sketches would not work second time around, to the same audience. We were all feeling pretty low and held our breath as Dicky Leeman, our producer, came in to tell us the worst. 'It's all right,' he said. 'It's all fixed. I've seen Val, and he thought you were all lovely.' Then he smiled and added, 'He thought the whole show was great and Aileen was gorgeous. I'll let you into a secret, though . . . I think Val's a little tone-deaf!'

The Arthur Haynes Show began modestly. We went out at an off-peak time, 10.15 p.m., and it took some time to establish a following, but slowly people started to say, 'Have you seen that show? It's very funny.' That is the best way to build success. We started to receive some good reviews and gradually evolved from being a modest late-night comedy show to being moved forward to the 8 p.m. slot. That was when the top comedy shows were screened then, and by the early '60s we were established as one of ITV's most popular programmes. Aileen Cochrane had moved on by that time, and we settled into a mini variety show with top singing guests, like Anne Shelton.

Johnny Speight was soon writing all the shows on his own, and he made a huge contribution to the success we enjoyed together. His comedy mind was wonderful; he would think of these incredible situations and weave them beautifully into a hilarious script. He delivered material of the highest quality for many years. Johnny was friendly with a young and relatively unknown actor called Michael Caine, who had great charisma. Michael made an early television appearance in 1962 on *The Arthur Haynes Show*, playing the part of a young burglar trying to steal from houses on Arthur's patch. He was funny and worked well with Arthur. It was great to have these guest stars, because it added to the diversity of the show.

With the advent of The Beatles, the entertainment world was changing fast, and I thought it was an excellent move when we started booking pop groups for the musical spot in the show. We had The Searchers, Freddy and the Dreamers, Gerry and the Pacemakers, the Spencer Davis Group and The Dave Clark Five. In fact, the only new group that did not appear in our show was The Beatles. The group that generated the most excitement was the Rolling Stones. They looked a pretty dishevelled bunch, but the crude messages scrawled in lipstick on their old van by teenage fans left little to the imagination. They obviously had something special, although at the time I could not quite see what it was.

One performer whom Johnny Speight was responsible for turning into a household name was Dermot Kelly, a skilled and disciplined actor who had originally worked at the Abbey Theatre in Dublin. He appeared in Johnny's play *The Knacker's Yard* at the Arts Theatre and gave a fine performance. Johnny was struggling to think up new situations involving Arthur's tramp character and brought Dermot into the show as a second tramp, playing in the sketches with Arthur. He was introduced for one sketch only, but it was so successful that he then started to appear regularly – in fact, some of our most memorable sketches contained these two tramps.

Dermot was used to appearing in plays, where he had plenty of time to learn his lines thoroughly. The pace at which Arthur worked always put him under great pressure, and he never really knew exactly what he had to say by the time it came to transmission. 'Irish', the character he created, arose not out of deliberate planning but out of necessity. He would always appear to be searching for the word he wanted to use, which was exactly what he was doing. He did it with such style, however, that the viewers, and the critics, all believed it was a brilliantly thought out characterisation.

Of the supporting players who frequently came into different sketches, Patricia Hayes, an established actress in her own right, was undoubtedly the best. She played the cockney wife in some of the sketches with Arthur and, simply by her characterisation, contributed a tremendous amount. Arthur, not being a trained actor, never fully appreciated her value and often preferred to have Rita Webb play some of the character parts. Rita was marvellous at playing an outrageous cockney harridan but had none of the subtle comic timing at which Patricia Hayes was so adept.

The main partnership was between Arthur and myself, and that grew into something quite memorable. We worked intuitively together. It was almost as though each of us knew what the other was thinking. We could improvise when things went wrong and ad-lib our way out of the situation without ever stepping on each other's lines. Arthur liked to go out and greet the studio audience before every television show, and I would join him to help get them in the mood. We never rehearsed those warm-up routines, but they always flowed. Somehow we never spoke at the same time or ruined each other's lines.

Arthur did not enjoy rehearsing. When it came to performing the sketches, he always had a keen sense of what it was about but did not always remember every word. He would often dry. Luckily, I have a good memory and knew every line of Johnny's scripts, Arthur's and mine. When he dried, I was always able to read the message in his eyes. He would suddenly pause and look at me, and I knew he had gone, so I would feed him the line he had forgotten and Arthur would smile and say, 'Mr Nicholarse, that's very clever of you, because that's exactly what I wanted to say. How did you know that? You put the words right into my mouth.' Arthur usually called me 'Mr Nicholarse', with the emphasis on the last syllable. He said it once in an ad-lib, it got a laugh and the name stuck. Nowadays, situations like those when Arthur forgot his next line would be cut out and sent to programmes such as *It'll be Alright on the Night*, but our audience knew what was going on and enjoyed it. In fact, I think they looked forward to those moments.

It is amazing how someone can misread a situation. A journalist once wrote of Arthur, 'He has the most televisual face. When he looks at Nicholas Parsons with that humorous intensity he can display, you can read oceans of meaning into what he is trying to convey.' All he was trying to convey was 'What's my next ruddy line, mate?'

Johnny Speight sometimes became a little upset when it happened, because it spoiled the flow of his sketch, but Arthur enjoyed improvising and I was happy to go along with him. It was great fun, but in a professional sense we were living rather dangerously. You always feel tense when you are performing and the adrenalin is flowing, and when things went wrong I often had to suppress a laugh. Arthur would say, 'Mr Nicholarse, I'm just a poor, 'umble working man, and you're laughing at me!' Looking back, it is hard to believe we were able to improvise in that way, when we knew perfectly well that making a mess of the sketch could mean professional suicide, as the shows were live. To add to the pressure, we were constantly getting instructions from the stage manager, who was in touch through his headphones with the director and would be standing just behind the camera. It was his job to let us know whether to speed up a sketch or drag it out. Sometimes, he felt sure we were going to overrun and would give us a frantic signal to 'Cut! Cut! Cut!' but we always came out on time. It was exciting and thrilling and helped the quality of the show.

Arthur was never sentimental about our partnership. I had huge respect for his ability, and I believe he felt the same about me, but when it came to our work he was always blunt, and I liked it that way. We would read through Johnny's new scripts, and Arthur would adjust the words to his liking, saying, 'Nick, I think the gag's in that line.' We would then run through it a couple more times, and when Arthur was happy he had got the script just the way he wanted it he would turn to the director and say, 'Right, it's all yours now, Dicky. Where do you want us to move?' Sometimes, I would ask Johnny if I could rephrase my lines to suit the character I was playing. He did not mind as long as we improved on what he had written. That is how we worked together, and it was successful because we respected each other's talent.

There was only one break in my ten-year partnership with Arthur, and that occurred when the actors' union, Equity, went on strike against the Independent Television companies for better pay for all performers but particularly in television plays, where there were long rehearsals. Members were instructed not to work for any ITV company, and only those who had actually signed contracts should continue to fulfil them.

Equity called their strike in November 1961, and the other performers' union that existed at the time, the Variety Artists' Federation (VAF), came out for the same reason. The heads of the independent companies, some of whom had close links with variety performers, recognised that if they had a nucleus of artists who were available to work, particularly in the world of light entertainment, they could keep their channels open. They therefore made a deal with the VAF for better pay, and its members went back to work.

The strike was lost when the VAF struck their deal. When Equity could not persuade the VAF to present a united front, it should have settled for the best possible terms or insisted that all performers, whether under contract or not, refuse to work. The ITV screens would have gone blank, and the strike would have been over in a week. As it was, programmes continued to be broadcast. The independent companies already had a number of Equity performers under contract. Granada, for example, had contracted actors for *Coronation Street*, as well as Bill Fraser and Alfie Bass, who appeared in *Bootsie and Snudge*. With VAF members available for other shows, they could continue. On one famous occasion, Bruce Forsyth did the whole of *Sunday Night at the London Palladium* with only Norman Wisdom to help him.

The viewers' reaction was 'Three cheers for the Independent Television companies for keeping something on our screens when those greedy, inconsiderate Equity members are striking.' We got little, if any, sympathy from the public, because Equity showed no common sense in handling the dispute from the beginning. They should never have called the strike unless the VAF had agreed to stay out for as long as it took. Having called it, they should have insisted on every single member walking out, rather than make that exception for those who already had signed contracts.

The dispute dragged on. Arthur, who was a member of the VAF, quite understandably became fed up waiting for me and decided to do a new series with Tony Fayne, another member of the VAF. Though I had nothing whatsoever against Tony personally, nor against the other VAF members with small parts in the show, I was upset. Equity was incensed. It had already stated that it would not allow someone to do another person's work, and both the television companies and the VAF had agreed. Equity said it would fight the case on my behalf, but I told them they must not. I was not prepared to be the sacrificial lamb. I had no doubt that, if they fought my case, they would win, but I would never work for Independent Television again. I just suffered in silence while the strike lasted: five months and three days.

Tony Fayne did a good job, and I did not begrudge him his good luck; I was just utterly distraught at my own lack of it. I received a good deal of sympathy from people in the profession and, of course, from my own family, but sympathy does not bring in work. An irony about our industry is that if you become well known working with one person other employers do not rush to give you work if you suddenly become available. When Harry Worth suggested to his producer that I should join him in his BBC television series, the response was, 'But he's with Arthur Haynes.'

Harry said, 'He's not. Arthur's working with someone else.' The association, however, was too well established for them to want to use me with another comedian. The only broadcast work I had at the time was on radio, particularly in *Midday Music Hall* from the Midlands, which I presented fairly regularly thanks to a fine producer called Richard Maddox. You could not live on radio fees, however, even though working in that medium is invariably a real pleasure. My mind was turning to the problem of getting back to work with Arthur.

I came to the conclusion that my best course of action would be to try to do a summer season with him. Up until then, I had always resisted summer shows, whereas Arthur thoroughly enjoyed them because they allowed him to do broad, pantomime-type sketches. He was back in the realms of pure music hall and variety, which he loved. George Black was presenting Arthur in his summer season at Blackpool, and, in spite of the fact that Arthur was working with someone else in the television series, George preferred the idea of me doing a summer show with him. This gave my agent a little leverage, whereby he persuaded George to agree that, if I appeared in the show, at least one of the sketches would be written by Johnny Speight. I considered this to be a minimum requisite, since I was against the idea of performing in all of Arthur's music-hall sketches. George also agreed that I would do a solo spot.

While I was reassured by having a good contract, I still thought hard about the situation in which I now found myself. By going into the summer season, I was moving into a complete partnership with Arthur and stepping further away from the legitimate theatre that I dearly loved. Up to that point, I had been doing plays, film work, radio and cabaret while he went off to his summer shows and pantomimes. I regarded the step, however, as an investment, as a way of continuing to work with Arthur in the future, which, as I had a young family by then, seemed important.

The thought of spending 16 weeks in Blackpool did not fill me with excitement, not least because my children were very young and I did not want to be away from them. However, once I had found somewhere to live – in St Annes, a charming and attractive area outside Blackpool and utterly different from the commercial resort alongside it – my wife, Denise, and children, Suzy and Justin, joined me, and we had a lovely summer together. For my part, it was an exhilarating experience working to a Blackpool crowd, because they are the true British variety audience looking to have a good time.

There was one major problem with the show: it was too long. George Black had realised that there was too much material and was wondering what to cut. After the dress rehearsal, Arthur's response was typically blunt: 'Well, I think that sketch of Johnny's will be the one to go for sure.' I felt strongly about this and argued forcibly. To Arthur's credit, he listened. I said that, as an actor, I was sure the sketch would evolve and that by the end of the season it would perhaps be the hit of the show. Fortunately, George Black agreed with me.

We had performed Johnny's sketch on television but never on stage. The scene was a barber's shop that I entered as a customer. Arthur, the barber, thought I wanted a haircut. When he realised I wanted a shave and he would have to use his cut-throat razor, his hand started to shake. He regained control, but, as he began shaving, the shakes returned and got worse, until finally he went completely to pieces. It was a funny idea that, as I had hoped, did develop – even if not in a way I could have ever foreseen. As the season progressed, it raised an increasing number of laughs. We added business. We refined jokes. We worked on the comedy.

After every performance, Arthur enjoyed having an inquest over a drink to discuss that night's show with the object of improving it and, hopefully, finding even more laughs. One night, out of the blue, he suggested that we could actually mime the barber's sketch. He pointed out that we had cut a lot of the dialogue and that most of the laughs were coming from looks and reactions. We talked it through briefly and agreed that we needed the two opening lines of greeting. Then, once I had said, 'I've come in here for a shave,' we could possibly go to the end of the sketch without further dialogue, except for my final outburst. I said to Arthur that this needed some thought before we did anything so drastic, and that I would like to mull it over. He agreed to wait a day or two before we made any final decisions, and I put the matter out of my mind.

The next night, we reached the barber's sketch, did the opening dialogue and came to my line, 'I've come in here for a shave.' Arthur paused and looked at me but did not come back with his usual response or, indeed, any response at all. He looked at his assistant, played by Leslie Noyes, and then back at me. He was going into the mime version without rehearsal or further discussion. The professional rapport between us was about to be tested as it had never been before. We were now ad-libbing together not with words but with expressions alone. We did it. We achieved exactly what Arthur hoped we would without any rehearsal at all. The sketch became very successful, and an Italian film company that had made an international film called *The World at Night*, featuring cabaret and music that could be understood in any country, decided to include it in their next production, to be released under the same title. It was a great accolade for a comedy routine that had had such humble beginnings and, I suppose, a compliment for the two performers who had developed it into its finished form.

The 1962 summer season at the Winter Gardens turned out to be a tremendous success, breaking box-office records. We were back on track and riding on the crest of a wave. Arthur had been voted the Variety Club's ITV Personality of 1961, and he played the Royal Variety Performance that same year. In 1962, the BBC also commissioned a new radio series of *The Arthur Haynes Show*, scripted by Johnny Speight. Perhaps when things are on the up it is a sure sign that trouble is around the corner.

The Arthur Haynes Show continued to win praise and plaudits, but around this time the wonderfully talented Johnny Speight felt he was beginning to run out of fresh ideas for sketches. He thought we should move away from the variety format and do something completely new: a situation comedy. Johnny saw that as the way forward for us on television, and I supported him. We had a meeting with Arthur, and between us we began to map out a storyline.

In essence, it was based on some of our most successful sketches. Arthur was to play his Mr Know-All character, who lived next to an Establishment figure, played by myself. Arthur's wife was to be played by Patricia Hayes, and Wendy Richard was to take the role of Arthur's daughter. Wendy had already occasionally appeared in the show and once shared a classic sketch with Arthur and me, an excerpt from which has had almost 8,000 plays on YouTube. In that famous sketch, I had called to take her out. We were all sitting at a table eating shellfish, and Arthur said to me, 'You're not going to stick a pin in your winkle, are you?' Wendy started to giggle and could barely get out her next line. Then, surprisingly, Arthur 'corpsed' as Wendy and I tried to continue our conversation. In fact, the three of us got a terrible fit of the giggles. My character in the sketch was a pompous young professional who was mad about Wendy. I tried to keep the sketch going by pretending I was laughing at what they had said. It was one of those magic moments that audiences love because it was all spontaneous.

Following our meeting with Arthur, and after that current series was completed, we all went our separate ways with the possible new approach in our minds, but when I met up with Arthur again prior to rehearsals for the new show I was in for a shock. 'Have you spoken to your man?' he asked, referring to my agent.

'No, why?'

'We're not doing the storyline; we're doing the sketches,' he said.

'You're just marking time, Arthur,' I told him. 'The new idea is the future.'

Unfortunately, he disagreed, and that was that. Sustaining a character in a situation comedy would mean venturing into the unknown, and he did not feel comfortable with that. He preferred to stay within his safety zone. I still feel a great opportunity was lost. When Arthur backed out, Johnny Speight took the idea and transformed it into *Till Death Us Do Part*. In many ways, Warren Mitchell was Arthur Haynes's character without the gentleness and the compassion. The structure of the show was essentially what we had discussed. You had the ardent, rabid, prejudiced Tory, the long-suffering wife and their pretty daughter. In *Till Death*, the scruffy young boyfriend was a big Labour supporter. In our series, I was to play that role as a keen socialist who lived next door in a smart house, and the political arguments with Arthur, over the garden fence, were planned.

Johnny eventually took *Till Death* to an enterprising producer at the BBC called Dennis Main Wilson, who had worked with the Goons on the radio. Dennis was not afraid to take chances, and he made himself such a nuisance with the powers that be that they finally gave him the go-ahead to make a pilot. None of the executives had any confidence in the show, but, of course, it worked brilliantly and broke new ground by confronting prejudice in a most original and entertaining way. The writing was extraordinary: Johnny Speight at his best. This was after *The Arthur Haynes Show* had come to the end of its run. In the meantime, we continued with the usual variety-style format.

I enjoyed spending as much time as I could with my family, particularly when Suzy and Justin were growing up. It was very important to me, and I was reluctant to take on any work that meant I would be apart from them for long. A year or two previously, I had turned down appearing with Arthur at the Coventry Hippodrome in what was known as *The Birthday Show*. It was a well-known, traditional variety show of the time. For Arthur, however, work was always the priority. He was obsessed with it. In many ways, he did not have a lot else in his life. His wife, Queenie, was charming, and he was completely devoted to her, but she did not enjoy the show-business world and she rarely went out. She was shy and ill at ease travelling. In the years that Arthur and I worked together, I met her only once or twice and never got to know her well. Arthur sought the company of fellow professionals – one in particular, Leslie Noyes, became both a friend and right-hand man and would often accompany Arthur on trips because Queenie did not feel comfortable socialising. Leslie had come into the series from the world of variety to play small parts and, although he had a family of his own, was extremely loyal to Arthur.

Arthur had never been interested in holidays, and since Queenie was quite happy to stay at home he simply worked continuously. The more successful he became, the greater became his thirst for work – not simply for its own sake, or for the money, but because of the insecurity that I believe builds up in all comics as their careers progress. If they are not in constant demand, they feel lost and rejected.

Family holidays meant a great deal to me, however, and it was this subject that gave rise to the only occasion Arthur and I had strong words. It occurred in 1963. The television series was still going very well, and Arthur and I had been asked to appear at the Palladium in a musical variety show called *Swing Along* in May. Arthur was top of the bill, and then came the Australian singer Frank Ifield, who had topped the charts with 'I Remember You'. I had a good billing – along with Susan Maughan and Joan Savage – and would be doing my solo spot in addition to appearing in sketches with Arthur, which included the now-famous barber's sketch. To make it all the more pleasurable, there would be a two-week gap between the end of the television series and the start of rehearsals at the Palladium. I had made plans to take Denise, Suzy and Justin to an isolated little five-couple *pensione* situated near a beautiful, completely unspoilt sandy beach in the north of Ibiza, at Portinatx. I had discovered the location the previous year when making a travel film for Skytours and was looking forward to it enormously. At that time, Ibiza was a quiet paradise, and it was going to be a dream holiday.

Then, one day, Arthur came to rehearsal and said, 'Have you heard from your man? We're opening at the Palladium a week earlier.'

I said, 'You're mad. What d'you mean?'

He replied, 'They've been let down by one of the American artists, and they've asked us to step in. It's a great compliment.'

I could not restrain myself and exploded back at him, 'You really are an absolute fool, Arthur. We don't need that extra week. What we both need is a holiday. A break. A rest.' I cannot be sure I actually said this next line, but I know I thought it: 'If you go on working like this, you'll have a heart attack.' It proved to be prophetic.

At the time, Arthur's response was typical: 'If you don't want to do it, don't bother. We'll get somebody else.'

I replied, 'Arthur, of course I'll do it, but I still think you're a fool.' I was deeply disappointed. All I had now was a break of five days, which Denise, Suzy, Justin and I spent in Dorset. We had a lovely time, but it did not compare to that distant haven in Ibiza.

Everything was going well at the Palladium. We were playing to packed audiences, and there was such a huge demand for tickets that our run was extended into the autumn. Then, during the August bank-holiday weekend, which back then fell at the beginning of the month, I received a disturbing telephone call from the theatre: 'Arthur has had a heart attack. They've taken him to hospital. You'd better get down here as quickly as possible.'

When I arrived at the theatre, there was a real panic on. Everyone was desperately worried about Arthur, of course, but they were also trying their best to comply with the age-old show-business maxim 'The show must go on.' All the major theatrical agencies were closed for the holiday, and that made the search to find a replacement for Arthur all the more frantic. Finally, they contacted the comedian Derek Roy, who was free that night. He did a solo turn, and Arthur's understudy did one or two of the sketches with me. To have performed the barber's sketch, however, would have been out of the question, for that was a completely personal performance between Arthur and me. I extended my solo spot, and nobody asked for their money back. When the news came through that Arthur would make a full recovery, we all felt a tremendous sense of relief.

On the Tuesday, I was called to rehearsal again and discovered I was to be working with Tony Hancock. It was an exciting prospect, as I had always admired him. Tony deputised for Arthur until he returned at the end of September, looking somewhat thinner and more rested than I had ever seen him. The heart attack had not been a serious one, and he was now sufficiently recovered to work, although he had been instructed not to overdo things. He stayed out of the opening sketch, in which his understudy was by now fairly proficient, and we rested the barber's sketch for a while. Arthur concentrated on his opening, one other sketch and his closing routine. His illness, however, had not really changed his attitude to work one iota, and it seemed that he had no intention of curtailing any of his former activities in show business.

I again thought he was foolish, but this time I thought it wiser not to stress the point.

Swing Along became the longest-running variety show ever staged at the Palladium. Afterwards, we went without a break into rehearsals for yet another television series. I was sure that Arthur was still overdoing things, and I was struck by how tired and drawn he had begun to look. I did not remark on his appearance but did tactfully ask whether he was perhaps taking on too much. He said he had agreed to one or two 'dinners', which meant performing his act as a cabaret spot, generally at company functions. I know from personal experience that after-dinner speeches can be particularly hard work, and this must have been especially so for Arthur. Most speakers write their own material or adapt their routine to suit the occasion or audience. Arthur relied purely on his variety act regardless of whether it was wholly appropriate or not, which can only have induced more stress.

We made the new television series together in 1964 and were then booked to appear at the Futurist Theatre in Scarborough for the summer season. One evening, Arthur asked me to join him after the show for a drink in his dressing-room, which was not uncommon, but as my family had just arrived at the resort I asked if we could talk some other time. Arthur was insistent, which I thought a little strange. I was totally unprepared for what was to come. He started talking about the individual work I had been taking on, then added, 'I was wondering whether you would consider us separating? No disrespect. I think we have a wonderful relationship, but I know you are doing well with all the other work you keep doing.'

'Arthur,' I replied, 'if the show was called *Haynes and Parsons*, I would make a 100 per cent commitment to it. While it's *The Arthur Haynes Show* and you go off and do your bits and pieces in films and elsewhere, I have to do the same with my theatre and film work and stand-up and after-dinners.'

'I can see that,' he told me, 'but I've given this a lot of thought and I think it might be better for both of us if we went our separate ways.' There was no aggression in his voice, but it was clear his mind was made up.

'All right, Arthur,' I said. 'You're the senior partner; it's your decision.'

I was surprised but not too upset. Ultimately, he was the one who called the shots. He had already agreed to go to the US the following spring, and he said he would like me to appear in his next television series then go to New York with him for *The Ed Sullivan Show*. I do not think he was confident of going to the States without the support with which he was used to working.

The trip to New York helped to take my mind off our impending split. It was my first visit to the US, and our six appearances on *The Ed Sullivan Show* were to be my first on television there. Denise had managed to persuade her sister, Peggy, and brother-in-law, Greville, to move into our house to look after Suzy and Justin, which meant she was able to join me. We were looking forward to discovering New York in the two-and-a-half-week period over which the shows were to be recorded. I had been told by my agent that, for the sake of convenience, Arthur's agent was arranging the whole contract, which would also simplify the process of getting the necessary work permits. I thought nothing more of it. Arthur helpfully said I would need what the Americans call a 'tax lawyer', who would work out my tax on the spot before I left the States, otherwise I would have to pay tax twice – American and British.

When I visited the lawyer in New York, I explained my working relationship with Arthur in Britain and said that I was an artist in my own right. He found this confusing, because it did not tie up with the way I had been booked. He advised me to speak to American Equity, who had sanctioned my work permit. I duly phoned and was asked some searching questions, which I found unsettling. The union representative then perturbed me further by saying, 'Mr Parsons, I don't like the sound of what you're telling me. Where are you placed? The Blackstone Hotel? OK. Stay right where you are. We're coming straight over.'

I was alarmed and wondered what on earth I had done. It did not help that just before leaving England I had seen that magnificent film *On the Waterfront*, with Marlon Brando and Rod Steiger, about the corruption-riddled New York docks and the gangster union bosses who ruled them. I had visions of a couple of heavies in big black coats bursting into the hotel room and snarling, 'We don't like it. Get the hell out of here right back on that plane to England. Some other guy should be doing the job you're doing.'

The two representatives arrived. They certainly were not happy with the situation. After I had answered their questions, it dawned on me what Arthur had done and in what an awkward position he had placed me. I back-pedalled rapidly, not only to save further embarrassment but also to safeguard my job in New York.

Unsurprisingly, Arthur's wife, Queenie, had not wished to travel, and he was keen to have his friend Leslie Noyes make the trip to keep him company. In order to be able to bring both Leslie and me over for the fees on offer, Arthur had asked his agent to book us as 'Arthur Haynes and Company'. I was not even named on the booking form and contract. This was the reason – I now learned – I was on such a modest salary. If I had been listed by name and given the status of a performer in my own right, I would have needed a different permit and would automatically have commanded a higher fee. I had no option but to play Arthur's game. I was there, I wanted to appear on *The Ed Sullivan Show* and, for the sake of harmony, I did not even bother to raise the matter with Arthur. It was the only time that I became upset with him. Perhaps he thought that, as our partnership was coming to an end, the credits did not matter, but it was a very hurtful thing to do.

On the show, I was not introduced by name. Things, however, worked out in my favour in the end. As soon as the first show finished, Ed Sullivan came straight over to me and, in front of Arthur, said, 'You're one of the finest straight men I've ever seen. I just had to congratulate you.' Arthur's face was a study, but there was nothing he could say.

When we came back from the US, I fell on my feet. It was then that I was asked if I wanted to take over the lead in the hit stage comedy *Boeing-Boeing*. That had been the height of my ambition as a young actor, to star in a comedy hit in London's West End. I could not have been happier.

Unfortunately, Arthur did not fare so well. Once again, he took on Tony Fayne as his sidekick. Tony was a skilled performer who went on to work as Norman Wisdom's straight man. He appeared to be an ideal choice, but in show business you never can tell. The public liked Haynes and Parsons, but suddenly they were being given Haynes and Fayne, and somehow the magic was missing. The viewing figures for Arthur's next television series with Tony were disappointing. Following that, in 1966, they went to Blackpool for a summer season at the Winter Gardens, and the business was poor.

Tony Fayne told me later of the extreme pressure Arthur was under. He would go off to play golf in Blackpool and come back saying he had terrible pains in his chest. Naturally, Tony was concerned, but Arthur refused to see a doctor. He said it was indigestion, but the pain was clearly a warning sign that another heart attack was imminent. That autumn, Arthur's agent advised him to give his next series a storyline. Arthur agreed to go ahead with a situation comedy, working alongside the wonderful comedy actress Joan Sims, but it was not written by Johnny Speight, who understood Arthur's style better than anyone. It was to be directed by Dicky Leeman, in whom Arthur had confidence. On paper it looked a strong team, but as soon as rehearsals began in November Dicky knew it was not going to work. When we spoke afterwards, Dicky said it was clear Arthur was ill at ease with the new format and, to his professional eye, it was also obvious Arthur would prefer to be working with a man. All of this must have put him under even greater stress, because within three days of starting rehearsals Arthur was dead. He came downstairs one morning, opened the fridge to get some milk, collapsed and died.

It was tragic. I went to the funeral and remember it clearly. Charlie Chester, Johnny Speight, Arthur's loyal and gentle wife, Queenie, and I were beside the grave, and it seemed to me the end of an era. Arthur was symbolic of the new phase of comedy that had come in with Independent Television, and now he was gone. Our partnership had broken up, but there was never any antagonism between us. The time we spent working together was magical. For many years, ours was a true collaboration; we had a great professional relationship and also a friendship offstage. I still have framed photographs from our television series on the walls of my office in London, and a watercolour of Arthur is given pride of place. It is a beautiful painting of him in his tramp costume. In his eyes you can see that particular blend of good humour and uncertainty that was so much a part of his personality.

When Arthur moved on to work with Tony Fayne, he probably felt my career would fade slightly, while he would go on to bigger and better things. I think the success I achieved on my own surprised him. When we were together, he did not like it if I was praised for the part I played in our sketches. When he went to Lodge meetings with the Water Rats, his fellow Rats would tell him, 'That Nicholas Parsons is good. Hold on to him, mate.'

Arthur would say to me at rehearsals the next day, 'They were singing your bloody praises again last night!' He said it as a compliment, but I could tell that deep down he resented it. He probably wanted to hear them say he was a great comic and that I was lucky to be working with him. When I started to get more attention, it niggled him and he thought the way to handle it was to take on somebody else.

George Black, the producer who gave me my first big break in television, once told me I should concentrate on my solo work. He was a shrewd man and a highly experienced impresario, and I gave what he said considerable thought, but I was enjoying working with Arthur at the time and decided to stay with the straight-man role. I never regretted that decision.

With Arthur's passing and my run in *Boeing-Boeing* coming to its natural end, it was time once again to look for new challenges. Before long I was to embark on a phase of my career that has continued to this day.

JUST A MINUTE

Just a Minute was first broadcast on 22 December 1967 and has been running 'without hesitation, repetition or deviation' ever since. I have appeared in every programme to date and have thoroughly enjoyed my involvement with what is now one of the world's longest-running radio series. We continue to attract an audience of over two million listeners on Radio 4 and the Internet. All of which is rather ironic when you consider I was very reluctant to take my place in the chair I have now occupied for over 40 years.

The show was the brainchild of a friend called Ian Messiter. When Ian was a boy at school, a master noticed he was not paying attention and said, 'Repeat everything I have said in the last minute, without hesitation or repetition!' Ian used that classroom memory to create a radio show called *One Minute Please*, which, with the addition of 'no deviation' to the rules originally suggested by his schoolmaster, proved to be reasonably successful.

In the late '60s, I was, as ever, looking for a new challenge and decided it might be fun to be a regular on the panel of a game show. I approached Ian and suggested reviving his programme, which I had always enjoyed. Ian was happy to go along with my idea, and he gave the show a new name, *Just a Minute*. I then took it to the BBC, who commissioned a pilot for their brand-new station, Radio 4. I was to be a panellist alongside Beryl Reid and Clement Freud, with Jimmy Edwards as chairman. In show business, things rarely go exactly to plan, and this was to be no exception.

We needed one more female panellist, and, as Jimmy was busy elsewhere, I agreed to play the chairman for the auditions. Our producer was a young and talented BBC employee called David Hatch, who previously had been a member of the Cambridge University Footlights, along with Tim Brooke-Taylor and John Cleese, and one of the stars of the radio show *I'm Sorry, I'll Read that Again*. After the auditions, David said he felt I had done rather well 'in the chair'. I had enjoyed it but was not interested in assuming the role full-time. I was keen to break away from the straight-man persona I had developed through ten years' work with Arthur Haynes. As a panellist, I felt I would have the freedom to improvise, which is what appealed to me, but it was not to be. Jimmy Edwards was having difficulty freeing himself from his regular Sunday polo commitments – in the end, the BBC got tired of waiting for him – and I reluctantly agreed to be chairman for the pilot programme. Beryl and Clement were joined on the panel by Derek Nimmo and a witty American, Wilma Ewart.

We recorded the first ever *Just a Minute* at the Playhouse Theatre in Northumberland Avenue on Sunday evening, 16 July 1967, and it was a moderate success. In the original pilot, there were some specialist rounds. In one, the panellists were not allowed to use plurals, in another they could not use pronouns, and in a third the word 'the' was barred. We discovered, however, that this was very inhibiting, and when the series was eventually commissioned it was decided that the basic format was more than enough on which to build a show. It was a mark of Ian Messiter's genius that he could think of something so simple but also so effective.

After the pilot, we all felt that, while it had not been great, with some adjustments there was every chance that it could become an entertaining and popular show. David Hatch had confidence in the programme and was therefore dismayed when he was told, some weeks later, that a series would not be commissioned. It was only when he threatened to resign that the BBC granted him his series.

It was now accepted that I would be chairman when the series began recording in November. This may not have been what I originally intended, but, like everything in show business, you have to find a way to make something work for you and for the show, and I think I have evolved into the kind of chairman who is effective for the programme.

The arrival of Kenneth Williams proved to be another inspired choice by David, and the series proved popular with listeners right from the start. Peter Jones joined us for the second series, and the classic panel of Freud, Williams, Nimmo and Jones provided the show with a wonderful blend of intellect and humour. I settled into my role and soon realised I needed to adopt a slightly different approach for each panellist, and that still holds true.

Someone who came into the show much later was Paul Merton, and we have become very good friends and share a natural rapport when we are working together. I played a part in his joining *Just a Minute*. We first met on a television show Simon Mayo was presenting called *Scruples*. The format gave me the chance to improvise and show a different side to the personality I displayed in some of my other work. Paul got the biggest laugh of the night when he said, with his immaculate timing, 'You were never like this on *Sale of the Century*!'

I did not know it then, but Paul not only has an encyclopaedic knowledge of comics of the silent screen, as seen in his stage show *Paul Merton's Silent Clowns*, but he is also a great radio fan. He used to live in a bedsit in Streatham and spent hours listening to classic shows like *Hancock's Half Hour*. He told me how much he had enjoyed *Just a Minute*: 'I used to record it in my bedsit. I love it.'

As Paul was speaking to me, I thought how good he would be in the show. Kenneth Williams had recently died, and various special guests had been invited to fill the fourth chair alongside Derek, Clement and Peter. I had not suggested anybody before, but I was so impressed by Paul that I put the idea to our producer, Ted Taylor. 'If you are looking for someone new,' I told him, 'I met a young comedian recently who would be wonderful. He has the comic flair we need.'

What I did not realise was that Paul had also been writing to Ted asking to be considered for the show. Paul says it was the only job he ever applied for in writing. I'm not sure if it was my endorsement or Paul's persistence that paid dividends. Perhaps it was a combination of the two. All I know is that Ted Taylor called me to say he had decided to give Paul a try. 'I don't know anything about him,' he said. 'I assume he's one of these "alternative comedians", and I get very nervous about them. I will book him, but if it doesn't work it's your fault!' I was fond of Ted, but he was old-school and the image he had of new, young comedians worried him.

'What clothes will you wear?' Ted asked Paul when he called to discuss the show.

'I don't know,' said Paul. 'I'll just come dressed normally, if that's all right.'

'You do know we don't swear on the show?'

'Yes, I have heard it before.'

Paul says he had the impression Ted thought he was booking Sid Vicious. What was clear to Paul was that he had to make an instant impression and that there would be no second chance. Coming into a show like ours for the first time is far from easy, because you are working with people who have been doing it for years. Naturally, that can feel quite intimidating, and when it comes to playing the game newcomers can struggle. Paul was the exception to the rule, and to me that emphasised his natural talent. He was very good on his first show, which was broadcast in April 1989. He was so good, in fact, that Ted immediately booked him for two more. Paul had arrived in *Just a Minute*.

Now, he has become one of our regulars, and I think what he does in the show is amazing. He has such a feeling and understanding of what is required, and I like the way he improvises. He does not adopt the regular stand-up comedian's approach of using the subject as a platform to deliver a gag. Instead, Paul has the ability to launch into an original world born of his own imagination while keeping totally focused on the rules of the game. Paul's mind is incredibly agile when it comes to finding alternative words with the same meaning. I listen carefully to every word the panellists say, to make sure there is no repetition, and on many occasions Paul appears to have talked himself into a corner and seems certain to repeat a word in the next sentence. Then, at the last moment, he will think of a comparable word to replace the obvious choice.

The wonderful thing from my, and the show's, point of view is Paul's great love of *Just a Minute*. He has an intuitive understanding of what makes the game work. If things go a little bit quiet and he acquires the subject, he will inject a burst of energy and go into a surreal monologue. The other players could challenge for deviation at any time, because what Paul is saying often has little to do with the subject, but they show their generosity by letting him go on. They realise how entertaining he is and that the success of the show is more important than the final score. The experienced players understand that, and nobody epitomises this more than Paul Merton.

Everyone respects Paul for the flair and skill he shows when playing the game, but Wendy Richard did not like him, and this caused problems. When Wendy first came into *Just a Minute*, she was always great value. I met her in the early '60s when she appeared in some sketches in *The Arthur Haynes Show*. She was feisty even then, but she also had a real sense of fun. I could tell she was going to achieve great things, and I was delighted to see the success she enjoyed in *Are You Being Served?*, which ran for 13 years.

Sadly, I think Wendy changed when she joined *EastEnders*. She played Pauline Fowler, a fairly aggressive character, and in later life I felt Wendy in some way morphed into Pauline. She always seemed to get narky with people, and that affected her performance in *Just a Minute*. The listeners liked her because she was good at the game and sounded like a real character, but she was not popular with the audience in the studio because she looked miserable and appeared irritable. In one particular show, her feelings towards Paul Merton boiled over. Paul challenged her, as he was perfectly entitled to do, and Wendy snapped, 'You're having a go at me again! You're always like that. What have I done to you?' Wendy was not joking; this was said in deadly earnest. I did my best to cover, but I felt embarrassed – everyone did, including the studio audience. What makes *Just a Minute* so enjoyable is the fun we have together. Paul, who is very tolerant, could not understand the way she behaved. In fact, it reached the point that if Wendy was booked for the show Paul said he did not want to be cast.

Another awkward situation arose when we were recording at the Theatre Royal, Bury St Edmunds. Paul was on the panel, as was Tony Slattery, in one of his early appearances. The two of them were sparking off each other, and the show was going very well. One of the subjects was 'freeloaders', and Tony somehow began talking about 'levitating a bull'. Paul challenged for deviation, and the two of them, with interjections from me, proceeded to engage in some bizarre and extremely funny cross-patter, which had the audience in stitches. It was saucy but certainly not vulgar. When it was over, Wendy pressed her buzzer and in an unhappy voice said, 'I think you have lowered the tone of the whole show. I thought that was disgusting.' An immediate pall descended over the audience. The wonderful atmosphere that had been created disappeared in an instant, and we had to fight to get it back. That was Wendy. I do not think she realised what she was doing. She spoke from the heart. It was genuine, but often it was out of place.

Clement Freud was another of Wendy's bêtes noires. He had the ability to compile lists as a way of filling time when he was speaking. This sounds easy but is actually very difficult. Try making a list of vegetables: carrots, radishes, turnips, parsnips, potatoes, and then . . . you hesitate. Clement had the ability to go on at some length, and I appreciated the skill he had developed. Wendy, however, was less than impressed: 'He's listing again. He's listing again. Nicholas, stop him. We shouldn't have listing in the show.' I used to try and calm her down and remind her it was not against the rules. As Clement got older, his delivery became more deliberate. He was a shrewd man and knew that if he spoke at a measured pace, without actually hesitating, he was far less likely to be challenged. It was a clever tactic, but it infuriated Wendy.

In the end, the producer decided to stop casting her. Her contributions on the subjects were always good, but if an unwanted edge is introduced to the show the listeners and studio audience are sure to feel it and become uncomfortable. Whenever I met Wendy afterwards, she always asked why she had not been invited back: 'Why is that, Nicholas? You know I love the show.'

'Yes, and you're very good in it.'

'It's that producer, isn't it? She doesn't like me, does she? She doesn't like me!'

It was all very difficult. You cannot tell someone, 'No, it's not that. It's because you're not enough fun. You don't relax. You become critical and nark about people.'

It was terribly sad in a way, as I was very fond of Wendy. I have no idea why she disliked Paul. I regard him as the most generous comedian I have ever worked with. He often makes jokes at my expense, but I enjoy the banter as much as he does. He says outrageous things, but I can be cheeky back to him. His jokes are never spiteful, and I never take offence. Recently, the subject 'the Crimean War' came up, and Paul said, 'It's all right for you, Nicholas, because you were there, weren't you?' The audience laughed, and I laughed with them. That is Paul's great gift, and you know there is no hidden agenda behind what he says.

Things were rather different with Clement Freud. I had to have my wits about me when dealing with him. He loved to try to put me down by making facetious comments designed to get a laugh at my expense. That was part of Clement's natural, instinctive, bullying attitude, which could be funny, within the terms of the game, but I had to be very strong and, if necessary, come back at him.

Clement was an intellectual. He had the most incredible brain and achieved so much during his life as a writer, politician, restaurateur and broadcaster. He enjoyed huge success in everything he set out to do. I remember him taking part in a challenge to get from the Post Office Tower in London to the top of the Empire State Building in New York in the shortest possible time. He planned it all meticulously and pipped the other competitors to the post to win the prize. He researched every aspect of the journey and discovered there were two lifts to the top of the Empire State Building. One stopped on the way up; the other went straight to the top. He arranged for someone in a uniform to be at the bottom of the lifts and tell anyone who arrived there before him to take the stopping lift. He arrived, took the non-stop lift and beat his opponents with seconds to spare. That was Clement: he had to win.

The players in *Just a Minute* feel the whole occasion very deeply. They do not play the game frivolously and are keen to succeed and demonstrate their talent, which is natural, as they are professional performers. This is why they may argue or dispute a decision I give, but most players are sporting and look to create an overall atmosphere of fun rather than push their individual contributions. One player to whom this did not entirely apply was Clement Freud. He did not enjoy the way I ran the show, as he wrote in his autobiography. He would have liked the show to return to the casual, laid-back style in which it began, when it was more of a parlour game with clever individuals talking at length on a subject, with haphazard challenges and rulings by me, the intellectual content of what was said being more important than the fun we generated. If the show had continued down that route, I think it would have run its course by now and not achieved the longevity that it has established.

Over the years, the game has developed as we have become more precise. It is important not to damage the basic concept of the show, but you can embroider on it. I have instituted new elements, such as awarding bonus points when someone interjects with a funny line. Spontaneous humour is important and should be rewarded as such. Malcolm Messiter, who now runs his father's show, appreciates all this. It is not a matter of adulterating the original concept; it is just embellishing and polishing it. Nothing can stand still. It is very pleasing when people say *Just a Minute* is funnier now than when we started. It is a wonderful compliment and probably underlines how we have evolved.

There was one incident that demonstrates Clement's frustration with how the style of the game changed. We record two episodes each year at the Edinburgh Festival Fringe, and afterwards, as is normal, the BBC supply hospitality, with wine, coffee and sandwiches. On this occasion, while everyone was winding down and relaxing, Clement was even more silent and moody than normal, brooding over a decision I had made against him during one of the games. Any other player would have let it go, but he let his feelings fester until he was in the taxi back to the Balmoral Hotel with Peter Jones and myself and then exploded, 'Why did you take the subject away from me when I was challenged for deviation? It was totally ridiculous!' I calmly tried to explain my reasons, as I had done at the time, but he was having none of it. I could not believe such an intelligent man was making a fuss about something so unimportant. Did all this stem from the fact that he did not enjoy the way I ran the show?

He continued to argue until we reached the hotel and then stormed off, calling me a crude name. I was naturally upset, which is probably what Clement wanted. I do not like confrontation. Peter Jones, one of my closest friends, was most concerned and over a drink reassured me that what I had done in the show was very professional. He felt deeply about the unjustified attack and later came to my room and said, 'I've been thinking. You have to realise that Clement has achieved so much in his life that there is now only one thing left to him, and that is to win points in *Just a Minute.*' What a lovely man, and what a witty way to try and put my mind at rest.

I was at school with Clement, I worked in his restaurant many times performing my cabaret act and we were good friends and often had dinner together, but all that suddenly stopped nearly ten years ago. Something a journalist wrote about the show did not please him, and he blamed me for it. I never really fathomed his reasoning, but from then on there was definitely a distance between us. In any event, we were very different people. He once wrote an article justifying his usual demeanour by saying it was natural to be grumpy and that people who were not like that were just putting on a front. He also said, 'If I don't like somebody very much, I forget why but continue to dislike them.' My attitude is, if I dislike someone, I will tolerate them, work with them, even be pleasant, but I never forget what they did to upset me in the first place. It is a much easier and more comfortable way to live.

Happily, Clement's attitude mellowed during the last two years of his life, which was rather lovely, because basically he was a nice man, an interesting and complex person with a deep intelligence and an unusual personality. I had huge admiration and respect for Clement. Working with him was far from easy, but that should not detract from the fact that he had great talent and his contributions to the programme were excellent.

Derek Nimmo was another highly competitive player, but he did not have the same edge as Clement. He simply had his own way of playing the game, which drew upon the fact that he was a great traveller. Derek had his own theatrical production company and took shows to places such as Dubai, Abu Dhabi, Kuala Lumpur, Singapore and, I believe, China. I was the director for one of the plays, *The Mating Game*, which Derek sent on one of his Far East tours. It was a wonderful experience. Derek was extremely entrepreneurial and created his own little empire. He was always on an aeroplane going somewhere and built up an extensive knowledge of different countries all over the world. He enjoyed using that information in *Just a Minute* whenever the opportunity arose. He would launch into a flowing speech about some obscure fact concerning one of the countries he had visited. It was difficult sometimes for his opponents to challenge, because he was so fluent on his pet subject of travel.

I enjoyed Derek's contributions; they were always entertaining. We developed a close rapport, and I was fond of all his family. We knew each other well, and he delighted in making jokes about my age. On one occasion, he illustrated how old I was by explaining that it had been many years since I had been intimate with a woman, so much so that the last one had been a suffragette. Peter Jones was there at the time, and quick as a flash he added, 'Yes, and that was only because she was tied to the railings at the time.' It was all in good fun, and I accepted it in the spirit it was delivered. I believe that is part of the success of the show.

A lot of people used to say Peter Jones was their favourite player. He was very witty and a great comedian whose comic timing was brilliant. I always credit him with producing some of the show's funniest one-liners. If you listen to early recordings of *Just a Minute*, many of the wittiest comments come from Peter. His lovely, gentle, warm personality came over in the show. We often worked together in the theatre, and he became a good friend. It saddened me that he never quite achieved the position his ability deserved.

Peter is probably best remembered for his work in *The Rag Trade*, but he started on radio just after the war, with Peter Ustinov, one of the greatest-ever comic performers. They did the first improvised comedy radio show, *In All Directions*, which was terrific and groundbreaking. Ustinov came to be seen as the star of the show, but Peter Jones's contribution was just as strong.

When I look at all the talented people I have worked with on *Just a Minute*, past and present, I realise how lucky I have been. Many have had a significant impact, but none more so than Kenneth Williams. His contribution was utterly individual. He did sometimes allow himself to shine at the expense of the show, but he loved *Just a Minute*. When he first came on, he was awfully nervous. He did not want to do it, and for about three shows he was struggling, but once he found his way of playing the game he took off. Towards the end of his life, it was his favourite job. Kenneth was a neat man who liked things to be organised and orderly. He always sat in the same chair, stage right. That was where he felt most comfortable, and heaven help anyone who asked him to move. When the programme began, he focused his mind and always played to the best of his ability. When he got the subject, he would brace himself and then run with it. Kenneth came from a humble background. He was self-educated, and his knowledge of history was amazing. *Just a Minute* gave him an opportunity to show off his intellectual ability. That is one of the reasons he loved it so much.

Ian Messiter realised this and used to introduce topics in which he knew Kenneth was well versed. When I announced one of these specially chosen subjects – for instance, 'Aphrodite' – and it was Kenneth's turn to begin, Kenneth would preen himself in the knowledge that it had been planted for him. He hated interruptions and wanted free rein to demonstrate his erudition and knowledge, which would be funny and factual. Off he would go, and if somebody challenged him before he had the opportunity to show off Kenneth would go into a sulk. 'Oh, you've missed a very good story there,' he would say. 'You are being fools to yourselves. Fools to yourselves.' The audience would laugh; they did not realise this was real frustration. He would then just sit there, as if to say 'Sod the lot of you,' and it was my job to try and find a way to draw him back into the game.

I would sometimes even twist challenges around and make sure he got the subject back. The others knew what I was doing: 'Now, Kenneth, the subject is back with you. This audience are dying to hear from you again. I know you have a lot to tell us about Aphrodite. So brace yourself. There's your public, Kenneth. Give them Aphrodite!' Off he would go, instantly jumping back into action, playing to the audience and having a wonderful time.

I first got to know Kenneth when we were in rep together at Bromley. He was a very good, serious actor whose originality stood out even then. I warmed to him greatly. The public have always adored Kenneth, but he could be ridiculous. He took big likes and dislikes. In his diaries, he wrote the most terrible things about me, and people would say, 'Oh, it was awful what he wrote.'

I always replied, 'He said far worse things to my face when we were on the stage recording *Just a Minute*.' That was just how he was. Everyone laughed at his comments as I adopted the role of his straight man. Equally, he was the only player in *Just a Minute* who ever paid me compliments. He would often say on air, 'Oh, he's a wonderful chairman. Wonderful.' People seem to love put-downs, while compliments are ignored. They remember the way Kenneth insulted me but never the times he sang my praises.

I believe the reason that Kenneth wrote some of those things in his diaries is that it took him longer than most to come down from the high that every performer feels when they are doing their job. After a show is over, it can be a little while before the surge of adrenalin subsides and you return to normal. Kenneth's high may well have been on such a scale that the resultant slump was probably deeper than most people experience. After a performance, he would go back to his sparse little flat and start writing, and the depressed side of his character would emerge, which seemed to find expression in his diaries. He would say the most awful things about people he knew and liked.

Kenneth was responsible for one of my most embarrassing moments on *Just a Minute*. He decided to take great exception when I accepted a challenge from Clement as Kenneth was expounding on the subject of 'Snapshots'. I tried to move on, but Kenneth went into a strop and would not let the matter rest. Derek Nimmo joined in the fun, and I started to feel a little flustered. 'I'm sorry, Kenneth,' I said. 'I cannot agree. The subject is "Snapshots". You have deviated from that . . . [Interruption from Kenneth] . . . No, no, Kenneth, it was "Snapshots" . . . [Another interruption from Kenneth] . . . You were well away from the subject. Clement has it. There are 20 seconds, Clement, snopshops, er . . . snipshots, er . . . snopshits . . . snop . . . snap . . . snip . . .' The audience were now roaring with laughter, and I finally recovered enough to say, 'I am not going to repeat the subject. I think you know what it is . . . and I think I've just finished my career in radio!'

Kenneth used to have us in fits of laughter when we gathered in the Green Room prior to recording. He would tell the most vulgar stories, but the way he told them you never took offence. I remember one that involved Kenneth staying overnight at a friend's house. He said the chap came into his bedroom wearing a loosely fitting dressing gown and smoking a pipe, supposedly to try to woo him. Kenneth was not interested in the fellow's attentions, but he delighted in telling the story, building it up and stoking himself into a high pitch of indignation: 'So there I was, sitting quite innocently, and he's trying to seduce me . . . with a bleedin' pipe in his mouth!' He painted an hilarious picture.

It is impossible to overstate the impact Kenneth had on *Just a Minute*, and when he died there was talk in the upper echelons of Radio 4 that the show might never recover and that perhaps it had reached the end of the line. Then the World Service stepped in. They knew we had a loyal following worldwide and offered to take over. There is obviously such intense rivalry between the different departments of the BBC that Radio 4 refused to countenance this possibility, and we went back to recording. While Kenneth was a great loss, I always felt that the show was bigger and greater than any one participant, and so it proved. We still miss Kenneth, but the show goes on, and some people think it is funnier than ever.

Others have come in, and although they have not taken Kenneth's place they have brought their own style and comic flair, which is essential in keeping *Just a Minute* entertaining and amusing. If all the players were the same, the show would soon become far too predictable.

They are all individuals, and that also makes my job more demanding and exciting. The producer has a nucleus of regular performers who play the game well, and she casts from that group where possible, although newcomers are introduced from time to time. The rapport between the players is always important, as is an appreciation of the sporting spirit we favour, and these are key elements when selecting the panellists.

Sue Perkins is one of our best players. She has a brilliant, agile, academic brain and can keep going on a subject for longer than most people, sometimes until the final whistle. It is amazing to see her speak at the pace she does and not fall foul of the rules. Sheila Hancock is another excellent player. She originally joined us because she was very fond of Kenneth Williams. In those early days, she was often the only woman on the panel, and she knew she could give the boys a run for their money. She still does. Sheila used to send up the lads when they got niggled and argued with each other. 'They're off again, like naughty schoolboys!' she would say. Sheila came on the show again recently and was as funny as ever, a very intelligent and humorous woman.

Gyles Brandreth is another exceptional performer. He is a brilliant writer with a great gift for language. Gyles has the most tremendous encyclopaedic knowledge, and he uses it to the full in the show. He is competitive and loves to keep going once he has the subject. When he is challenged, he will invariably argue and justify what he has said. He makes a joke of it, but I know he is desperate to retain the topic and continue. I have to be firm with him. He brings all his considerable gifts to the table when he plays *Just a Minute* and gives it absolutely everything.

Liza Tarbuck is a very popular player. She has such a warm, effusive personality that the audience love her. She is not aggressive or pushy, and, while she may not be as good at the game as some, she plays it with such fun that it does not matter if she slips up. She is a skilled and successful performer and contributes greatly to the entertainment value of the show.

I felt a little sorry for Pam Ayres when she first joined us, because it took her a while to get the feel of the show. Having acquired it, however, she has become a highly accomplished player. She is a wordsmith and poet, and I always enjoy hearing the lovely Oxfordshire lilt in her voice. Pam spoke on the subject of 'Spring' recently, describing the buttercups and aconites bursting into life. It was delightful and all delivered in her own unique style.

Kit Hesketh-Harvey is another fine wordsmith. He works with Richard Sisson in a wonderful double act called Kit and the Widow. Kit is a superb writer, and his command of language shines through when he plays the game. He is a lovely fellow, intelligent, amusing and warm, and it is a pleasure to have him on the programme. We feel the same about Tim Rice, our country's top lyricist. Tim is not very strong on the comedy side, but he is clever with words, so his contributions are always entertaining.

Tony Hawks has been a stalwart for many years. He may not be as well known as some of the others, but he is always reliable. He contributes incredibly well and comes out with some of the most delightfully witty comments. The same can be said of Ross Noble, who is one of the most amazing and original comedians we have. He has a way with words and is always funny. Ross lived for a long time in Australia, but he made a point of joining us whenever he was back in the UK.

Jenny Eclair is another clever player of the game who is always very welcome. She has an individual style of play that is highly amusing. She takes a different direction and approach to the subjects on which she is talking, which adds greatly to the comedy elements and is valuable in keeping the show fresh and vibrant.

Stephen Fry is an occasional panellist. We would love to have him more often, but he is always so busy. He is an intimidating opponent when he does take part. He has such a fine intellect, and with his amazing command of language he does not often make mistakes. There was a memorable occasion when he had the subject of 'Shostakovich'. He talked lucidly for some time, then said that Sir Thomas Beecham, when asked if he had ever conducted any Shostakovich, replied, 'No, but I have trodden in some,' which received a big laugh. At that point, Paul Merton challenged for deviation, saying Beecham had actually made that remark about Stockhausen. I was not sure whether Paul was correct, but Stephen sportingly confirmed he was. Paul now had the subject and with supreme confidence talked of Shostakovich's life and career. He was most convincing and carried all before him until the final whistle. Later, he admitted he knew nothing about the man. Perhaps the other players felt the same way and did not like to challenge. It is far from easy to bluff the knowledgeable Stephen Fry, but this was superb one-upmanship by Paul. It is moments like these that make *Just a Minute* enthralling and entertaining.

Graham Norton first came to us when we did a series of stage shows at the Edinburgh Festival a few years ago. He was not a big name at the time and was happy to act as stand-by in the event any of our guests failed to turn up. Graham is the most delightful person you could possibly meet, and he loves the show. When I thanked him recently for finding time in his busy professional life to join the team, he said, 'It's so lovely. There is no preparation; we just come along and have fun. If I'm free, I love doing it.' It was good to know that we have become such an iconic show that well-known people are delighted to take part. I love Graham's enthusiasm. When he is performing and trying to get the words out, he concentrates so hard he makes some very funny faces. Many members of our studio audiences have said the show should be on television, because it is so enjoyable watching the expressions of the panellists as they endeavour to keep going. Graham, with his mobile features, is funnier than most in this respect.

Charles Collingwood, who plays Brian Aldridge in *The Archers*, is another popular player. His sense of humour fits in well, and he often comes up with very original thoughts. Charles was involved in one of the most extraordinary episodes of *Just a Minute*. We used to take the show on the road, which I always enjoyed. It was an opportunity to perform in front of audiences from different towns and cities, but unfortunately recent cutbacks have meant that we now record mainly in the Radio Theatre at Broadcasting House. I hope that in the future we can go back to the original policy. In January 2004, we were recording two shows at the City Varieties theatre in Leeds, a famous old music hall where the television show *The Good Old Days* was filmed. There is a wonderful story involving Eartha Kitt, who arrived at the

City Varieties to appear on *The Good Old Days* in 1972. Barney Colehan, the producer, showed her backstage to her dressing-room, which was small, primitive and, frankly, grotty. She was horrified. As a big Hollywood star, she could not cope with such basic amenities, and she threatened to leave on the spot, until Barney launched into a wonderful speech: 'This is one of the most famous theatres in the country. All kinds of major stars have performed here. In this very dressing-room, Charlie Chaplin changed to appear on stage.' Eartha Kitt was so impressed with such heritage and history that she announced to Barney that she would be delighted to do the show after all. Afterwards, Barney apparently admitted that he had no idea whether Charlie Chaplin had ever appeared at the theatre.

When I arrived at the City Varieties, the producer at the time, Chris Neil, approached me and said, 'We have a mini crisis. Our fourth player can't make it. I've been phoning around, and no one can get here in time from London.' He then had a moment of inspiration. 'Charles Collingwood will be in Birmingham recording *The Archers*. If I catch him in time, he might just make it.' He telephoned Charles and said, 'Do you think you can get up here to Leeds for the beginning of the show at 7.30? Get the fastest car possible!'

Charles replied, 'If the traffic isn't too bad, I can make it.'

Paul Merton, Liza Tarbuck and Kit Hesketh-Harvey were the other panellists, and we all knew it was going to be touch and go as to whether Charles would arrive on time. By 7.40 p.m. there was no sign of him and it was clear we could not wait any longer. Paul came up with the solution: 'I know what to do. Let's start the show as if Charles is here.'

'Brilliant,' I said. 'We'll get going, and I'll make my usual introduction as if he is sitting right there. When he arrives, we'll just slot him in.' This was living dangerously in a show-business sense, but it also showed the inventiveness that the *Just a Minute* format allows if everyone understands the game properly.

Obviously, the theatre audience had to be in on the secret. I explained the situation to them and said I was going to introduce all the players, including Charles Collingwood, and I would like them to greet him as if he was there. I think the audience rather enjoyed this. We started the show, and at different times I would say such things as, 'Charles Collingwood has yet to score any points. In fact, we have yet to hear from him. I am sure, Charles, you will be speaking up very soon.' The audience laughter at such remarks meant I eventually had to explain what had happened. There was more fun when 'Charles' scored points. I gave him the topic of 'A Slippery Slope' and said, 'Charles, would you like to talk on that subject for 60 seconds, starting now.' There was a second's silence, and then Kit challenged. 'On what grounds?' I asked.

'Because he still hasn't said anything. Repetition of silence!'

I ruled that an unfair challenge and gave Charles another chance on the same subject: 'Charles, there are still 59 seconds available on "A Slippery Slope", starting now.' Liza challenged immediately for deviation, claiming Charles was not paying attention. Again, I ruled this as unfair on the grounds that it did not matter whether you were paying attention or not – you could still carry on playing the game. In his absence, Charles notched up two points before I gave a correct challenge to Liza based on 'Charles's' hesitation when taking up the subject again.

We continued in this vein for two rounds, until, in the middle of the third topic, 'My Favourite Pudding', there was a sudden commotion. The City Varieties' stage door had recently been removed, and this meant Charles and all the other performers had to enter from the back of the auditorium. The audience had seen him and immediately applauded. I explained to our listeners what had happened and that Charles was attempting a challenge from the back of the theatre. Straight from *The Archers*, Charles came up on stage with the words, 'Oh, I'm up to my knees in slurry!' He then took the vacant chair and off we went with the rest of the show.

Julian Clary has the ability to use what I have said as a springboard to bounce back with a funny line of his own. It is always a pleasure to work with Julian. I know him well, and he is a very clever comedian. He can bring a hint of suggestiveness to what he says, but he does not go too far and is never rude. He understands the ethos of the game. The only person ever to swear on the show was, surprisingly, Peter

Jones, who said 'bugger'. It was so inoffensive in the context, and, coming from him, the producer kept it in.

There have been two attempts to bring *Just a Minute* to television. In 1994, Mike Mansfield, an intelligent and experienced director, approached Ian Messiter and negotiated a deal to produce the show for ITV. Ian controlled all the rights in his creation, and the BBC were not happy with this turn of events. They made threatening noises about taking us off the radio – as they had done when the stage version was put on at the Edinburgh Fringe – but in the end the threat came to nothing.

As so often happens when a programme moves from radio to television, the producers decided they needed to adapt the format. One addition was a positive move: the inclusion of a huge clock, clearly displayed, which allowed the audience and television viewers to see the time ticking away. This helped build the tension and excitement as the panellist who was speaking approached the final whistle. A 'mystery object' round was also introduced, in which an unusual item was shown to the panellists and they had to talk with authority about it, whether they recognised what it was or not. This opened up the possibility of challenges for deviation if one of the other players thought the speaker was bluffing. I knew what the item was and could therefore adjudicate on whether the speaker had deviated or not. It was a fun idea, but the show is so sound in its basics that it does not need extra gimmicks.

A second series was commissioned, but here again the powers that be demonstrated they did not fully understand the concept. *Just a Minute* is a game played by individuals, each player playing against the others, but ITV decided to introduce two teams, captained by Tony Slattery and Dale Winton. The show floundered under this restrictive new structure, with the original format clashing with the new rules. There was no third series.

A few years later, the BBC decided they would commission a television series, but to my mind they made one fundamental mistake: they aired the show at noon. I think they thought we would fill the slot vacated by *Call My Bluff*, which had come to a natural end. *Call My Bluff* was a marvellous show, with gentle humour, and was appropriate for a midday broadcast. *Just a Minute* is naturally an evening programme, with incisive and clever humour that can be a bit outrageous, even saucy at times. It did not sit comfortably in the middle of the day.

There was also another problem that could not have been foreseen. On the radio we know it is essential that we have a group of panellists who naturally spark off each other. The producer will check my availability, then that of the key players, and schedule a recording when everyone can make it. Television does not work in the same way. It is necessary to set a block of time aside, in this situation two weeks, in order to construct the set and record all the programmes. This was fine for me, as I was under contract for the whole run, but the same did not apply for the individual panellists whose availability over the fortnight varied. I found myself chairing the game with people who were great names in the industry but were not necessarily comedy performers or familiar with the show. One person had never even heard of it. We had a few regulars, like Tony Hawks and Gyles Brandreth, but a lot of the time I was struggling to make it work. The result was that we produced one or two excellent shows and one or two that did not quite take off. The executive producer reassured me that there would be a second series for the autumn. 'Don't worry, Nicholas,' I was told. 'We have proved it can work, and I am sure they will commission another series.' The message then came through that the show was regarded as being less successful than had been hoped. There would be no recommission. To my mind, the reasons were clear and could have been addressed, but there was no going back on the decision.

I am happy to say *Just a Minute* seems to go from strength to strength on the radio. Clement Freud and Peter Jones both vocally slowed down a little during their years with the show, but I think I have been fortunate in that respect. A former producer once said to me, 'It's amazing. I have listened for many years, and your voice has hardly changed.' It was something I had never thought about. I do some voice exercises, which help, but the truth is I am probably just lucky. I also love being part of the show, and perhaps that is what comes across. I want to make each episode as entertaining as possible, and when the recording begins the adrenalin kicks in and my brain moves into a different gear. It keeps me sharp, and I may not sound the age I am.

We record two programmes back to back, without a break. The producer might ask me to re-record my introduction or make a briefer summary at the end, but when it comes to the game itself there are no retakes. We record it as live. I always have a word with the audience at the start of the evening and introduce the players. We then check the buzzers and have a little fun with that, which helps to set the mood. There is always a brief technical delay before the second recording, but we stay onstage, chatting with the audience to keep the atmosphere alive. When the game begins, it is my job not only to judge the challenges but also to move things forward to maintain the momentum we have built. It is a necessity for me to concentrate very hard through every programme. I sit in a privileged position as chairman, and I never take that lightly. People often think I have some kind of backup when judging challenges, such as an earpiece to the producer. That would not work; the delays would kill the show. So I have to listen carefully and make instant decisions. I am not so much enjoying the show as paying attention to every word the panellists say. As a result, when I listen to the broadcast of *Just a Minute*, it is as though I am hearing the show for the first time. I thoroughly enjoy the atmosphere we all generate, and I can assure everyone that the laughter is genuine.

My wife, Ann, is very supportive of all I do. She drives me on long journeys for my work, and, although she understandably does not wish to sit through every performance of my one-man shows, she never misses *Just a Minute*. She says it is always different. I think that is the key to our success in the UK and around the world. We now reach a loyal international audience via the Internet, but unfortunately, since November 2004, no longer via the World Service. This is ironic when you consider that, when Kenneth Williams died, it was the World Service that was instrumental in keeping *Just a Minute* on the air. The reason, I have been told, is that the World Service has moved to a more news- and current affairs-based output, as this is what draws most listeners to the station. In addition, as over 90 per cent of the audience has English as a second language, it has been suggested that comedy does not travel. I know this has disappointed a lot of people. Not everyone has access to a computer to listen online. I have received numerous letters from Australia, Canada and in particular the US, where the show has always been popular. One American wrote to me in an impassioned manner after he could no longer receive the show. I replied, giving the reasons that had been explained to me, adding that the BBC, in their wisdom, preferred to send out programmes on the World Service that reflect our society, its ethos and culture. He responded in a powerful letter, stating that to him nothing better reflected British culture than *Just a Minute*. According to him, the show was quintessentially British. He felt so strongly about this that he said he was going to write to the Prime Minister about the matter. He then added a PS: 'I have also decided I am going to send a copy of my letter to your Queen.' I wonder what she made of it. She has not watched a recording of the show, but perhaps the letter prompted her to listen on Radio 4.

For me, the World Service's decision was a great shame, especially considering incidents such as when Paul Merton was talking to a listener who casually mentioned that he had heard us while driving across the Gobi Desert. That is quite a thought and may not happen now. I had a similar experience when I went to Bangalore to record a radio documentary for Radio 4 called *The Quiz Exchange*. The producer and I spent a week discovering how quiz shows have become part of Indian culture and how they are used as an educational tool in schools. It was all very interesting, especially when we heard how popular *Just a Minute* is over there. People have taken the initials and formed their own *JAM* clubs. We found one of these clubs locally and went to a session to meet them, where they put on an improvised version of the show and invited me to be a guest, which was great fun.

My involvement with *Just a Minute* has been one of the great pleasures of my working life. Today, it is certainly my favourite job. I look forward to each and every broadcast and have now made nearly 800 appearances. The fact that we still attract such a huge audience is a thrill. I am genuinely moved by the comments I receive from listeners. If they enjoy my contribution, I am delighted, but I am just one of the team.

Keith Matthews is someone who is dedicated to *Just a Minute*. He runs a fan club and contributes to a *Just a Minute* website created by Dean Bedford, an editor on New Zealand Radio and an ardent devotee of the programme. Keith has an encyclopaedic knowledge of the show and keeps details of every recording, the panellists who appeared and how long each spoke on any given subject. He has transcribed classic moments that have occurred over the years, and below I have set out some of his favourites that he has sent me.

Derek Nimmo: Nicholas is living proof that there is life after death.
Paul Merton: Do you call that life?
Nicholas: Oh . . . oh . . . oh, really!
(The audience applaud.)
Nicholas: And this audience applauds!
Paul: It's only a 12-volt battery that keeps him going!

Describing the seating arrangement of the panel:
Nicholas: I've got two on my left side and two on my right side.
Graham Norton: You should see a doctor!

Nicholas: What are you writing, Paul?
Paul: It's a suicide note . . . All you've got to do is sign it at the bottom of the page!

Derek was once plugging one of my theatre appearances:
Nicholas: He was referring to *The Rocky Horror Show*, where I dressed in fishnet tights and a suspender belt.
Paul: And that was just for going to the theatre!

Paul: Oh, by the way, you left your mug of cocoa under the bed last night.
Nicholas: I'm sure you drank it, Paul.
Paul: No, I didn't. It had your teeth in it!

Nicholas: The subject . . . 'House Mats'. I don't know what Ian Messiter's mind is thinking of here, but . . . No, it isn't! I misread it . . .

Paul: It's actually 'Copenhagen'!

Nicholas: Stephen Fry, it's your turn to begin. The subject is 'Mouse Mats'!

Paul on the subject of 'Myths':

Paul: Nicholas Parsons is an extremely well-loved entertainer that the British public have taken to their hearts over the last 65 years. This, of course, is a myth!

Paul: You're very big in Norway, aren't you, Nicholas?

Nicholas: Absolutely. My record was number three in the hit parade over there!

Paul: You made a pop record?

Nicholas: Yes. It's called 'Fantasy'.

Paul: I'm sort of wandering into the middle of one right now!

(The audience laugh.)

Paul: So when was that?

Nicholas: It came out last year. And it's a sort of dance record. They tell me I should take it to Ibiza. I can clean up over there!

Ross Noble: You could clean up in Ibiza?

Nicholas: Oh, they didn't mean financially. They thought I could . . .

Ross: Just clean up!

Paul: How did this record go? The Norwegians grasped it to their bosom! How did it go?

Nicholas: Well, it sort of said . . . 'I-I-I want to be-e-e-e-e . . . your fan-n-n-tas-y-y-y-y'.

(The audience and panel are beside themselves with laughter.)

Nicholas: And then we went into the beat, you know, and she went . . . [I start to impersonate high-pitched diva] 'You are my fan-n-n-tas-y-y-y-y'. And I went, 'Yes, I'm gone! You're coming on strong!'

(The audience were now enjoying the fun and banter and applauded. We carried on with this for quite a while. I took Paul's cues as he superbly egged me on to increase the fun by looking foolish and sounding funny. The publicity for the record did not make very much difference. I do not think I sold any extra copies.)

On the evening before the formal presentation of my OBE, Paul appeared to be about to pay me a compliment:

Paul: Nicholas, are you going to the Palace tomorrow?

Nicholas: Yes, I am.

Paul: Are they still looking for cleaners?

We have had so much fun over the years, and we all owe a lot to David Hatch. I will always be grateful to him for persuading me to take on the chairman's role, a job I have performed with increasing pleasure every series for over 40 years. David gave me some very good advice early on. It was about the third series, and I said to him that the panellists appeared to be changing their tactics of scoring points at each other's expense and were turning on me to get their laughs. He said, 'Nicholas, I think that is the way the show is going to evolve, and I am confident your shoulders are strong enough to take the strain.' I realised what he meant, and I took his advice to heart. I used my experience as a straight man to forge a role for myself within the discipline of the show, and it has worked. David sent me an amusing note, along with a raunchy fan letter, shortly after giving me that valuable piece of advice. It read as follows:

> This one is really for you. She is not asking for a photograph of everybody, just of you. She's obviously desperately in love with you, and I think you're obliged to reply to her. I don't think you're going to have to marry her, but I don't want to be the gooseberry in the initial stages of what is obviously destined to be a very tempestuous affair!

David also sent me a most charming and flattering letter before he handed over the producer's reins and moved onward and upward through the BBC. He eventually became controller of Radio 2 and then Radio 4 before taking on the top job at BBC Radio. After leaving the corporation, he served as chairman of the National Consumer Council and the Parole Board of England and Wales. He was knighted in 2004 and very sadly died in 2007. The letter David wrote was to encourage me to keep pursuing the course I was following as I evolved my skills as chairman in the early days of *Just a Minute*:

The most crucial thing in the whole programme is your chairing of it, and the only reason this programme has run so long, and I hope will continue to run for as long again, is by the masterly adjudications which you give each week: sometimes playing by the rules, sometimes by showbiz rules, speeding up, slowing down, etc. etc. Even if it seems that Nimmo, Freud and Williams are against you, it is only for the programme that they do it.

Producers do not usually send such encouraging letters to artists. It certainly helped me to feel confident in the role I never wanted to assume. My approach to being chairman today is simple: the essence of the show is fun, and I want everyone to share in that – the players, the audience, everyone. When *Just a Minute* is flowing, it is a wonderful place to be.

MY FILM CAREER

There are not many actors who can say they landed a film role thanks to their barber. The year was 1957, the barber's name was Jock Johnson, the barber's shop was Trumper's in Curzon Street, Mayfair, and the film was *Brothers in Law*. In time, I was grateful to Jock for his help, but when he called to say he had set up a meeting for me with one of the country's top film producers I was rather sceptical.

Brothers in Law was not my first film. That was in 1947 and was called *Master of Bankdam*, starring Tom Walls, Anne Crawford, Dennis Price, Linden Travers, a young Jimmy Hanley, Stephen Murray and, eventually, David Tomlinson. If cinema, and not the theatre, had been the premier form of entertainment in 1947, I would perhaps have appeared in many more films in the ten years between *Master of Bankdam* and *Brothers in Law*. As it was, I was cast in a few small character roles before Jock intervened.

Master of Bankdam was based on a novel by Thomas Armstrong and chronicled the lives of three generations of the Crowthers, a Yorkshire mill-owning family in the nineteenth century. It was a classic 'trouble at t'mill' story with a superb cast who performed well. At the time, I was appearing in *The Hasty Heart* at the Aldwych Theatre, and the film's casting director came to see me. The production was a big success, and they were looking for someone to play one of the mill owner's grandsons alongside Jimmy Hanley.

It was a wonderful opportunity and could have been the start of a very different career for me. The casting director thought I would fit the part well and offered me the role. The character, Lancelot Handel Crowther, appears throughout most of the film, and the producers asked the theatre management to release me from my Wednesday matinee commitments if I was required for filming in a particular week. This would not have been every Wednesday, but the producer of *The Hasty Heart*, Firth Shepherd, refused, and I lost the part to David Tomlinson. David had recently been demobbed, and he took his opportunity with great flair. He made a deep impression in the role, and, although he had already made a number of films, *Master of Bankdam* proved to be the launch pad for a successful career during which he notably co-starred in *Mary Poppins* and *Bedknobs and Broomsticks*.

In a similar situation nowadays, the outcome would be quite the reverse. The exposure an actor brings from being cast in a film would be regarded as a positive thing for the theatre. Back then, theatre management were all-powerful. Even so, I thought their reaction was rather unfair, especially as the understudy who would have taken over from me on those Wednesday matinees was a talented, unknown young actor called Joss Ackland, who was appearing in his first West End show and would have been excellent in the role. Joss was so good, in fact, that when I contracted jaundice during the run at the Aldwych Theatre and was off for over a week, I was well aware that he might become established in my role and probably returned to the stage sooner than was wise.

I was obviously disappointed, but the film people were kind, and as a consolation they gave me the small part of Edgar Hoylehouse, who was up to no good with the character played by the wonderful radio, film and television actor Stephen Murray, who was perhaps best known as one of the stars of *The Navy Lark*. Despite the fact that I lost out on one of the major roles, I found the whole experience terribly exciting. Being on the set and meeting well-known and talented performers was tremendous experience for a young actor, and I enjoyed every moment of it.

My film career made another false start at the beginning of 1951. It was all tremendously exciting. A friend called Richard Waring had written a script for a feature film. It was a thriller called *Full Circle*. He had managed to obtain some money, which I think came mostly from his family, and he was going to break into the film business. Anthony Essex-Lopresti was the director and lighting cameraman, John Childs was the sound engineer and the other technicians, who were few in number, were obviously friends and colleagues. Anthony's younger brother, Francis Essex, was going to compose and arrange the music. Richard himself was playing the leading romantic role, an attractive young actress, fresh out of drama school, was cast as the love interest and I was invited to play the other leading role, the villain of the piece.

The film was going to make stars of us all. It was a good story, centred on two young men, one wicked and evil, who exercised a domineering influence over the weaker but nicer character, the hero, played by Richard. It was a relationship that had begun in their school days and continued into their adult life, until eventually the hero manages to assert himself and everything is turned full circle.

At least I think that was the plot. I am not sure, because the film was never completed and Richard was regularly rewriting scenes during the production. It is one thing to have talent and youthful enthusiasm, but in the difficult world of film-making you also need experience. We spent many days filming in a large room in a deserted property in Hyde Park Gardens, an elegant row of Georgian houses just off the Bayswater Road that had obviously suffered severe bomb damage during the war. My memories are that everything took an age. After every take, there seemed to be a problem. Sometimes it was the lighting, if not the camera, and on occasion the sound. I now realise that Anthony, whose experience had been with documentary films, had no idea how to direct actors or organise a film shoot.

We filmed one scene in a club, for which Extras were employed who stayed around for days, no doubt costing a fortune. Food was regularly produced and was always excellent. I suspect Anthony and his team knew how it was done on the big film sets and were trying to emulate that. In reality, they were simply behaving like amateurs. The publicity that was put out focused on the fact that their location-filming was groundbreaking. In that respect, they were innovators, since most feature films in this country are now made on that basis, instead of incurring the huge expense of building sets in large film studios.

The sad thing was that no one had the skills or experience to plan economically and film efficiently; they were acting the part of film-makers. It was a happy atmosphere, however, and we all became friendly. At times, I felt as though we were a bunch of undergraduates trying to put together our end-of-term production, in which time did not matter and the budget was of secondary importance. We were soon working long hours, with no extra pay, and often found ourselves standing around doing nothing while a discussion went on about the scripts or how a scene should be shot. Then more food would be produced.

During these periods of inactivity, we would stand by the window and look across to the Bayswater Road, where the prostitutes were plying their trade. We observed how they would pick up a man, bring him to the quiet street below us and, when they became aware they were being watched, descend down the basement steps to earn their money. I, too, was supposed to be making a living, playing an excellent role in an exciting new film, but it was all rather quickly becoming unreal.

The next location was a schoolhouse in Bromley. The production team seemed more taken with the loquacious caretaker, who talked in clichéd sentences that amused them immensely, than in making the film. To this day, I cannot remember what scenes were shot there. It was then decided we would move on to the dock area of London, where the final scenes were to be filmed, involving some dramatic chase sequences down dimly lit, eerie backstreets. These were night shots, and they found an excellent location in Wapping, not far from Tower Bridge. I had never visited this area before, and in 1951 it had a certain Dickensian atmosphere about it. We assembled in a small pub in Wapping Old Stairs, right on the edge of London Docks, which were very active in those days. The pub seemed to have only a few customers in the evening, and when I arrived Richard was seated at a table with his typewriter, yet again rewriting the script. He was looking worried, and he told me that they had run out of money. He asked if I would be kind enough to finish the film without pay and take a slice of the profits. By this time, I did not think there was going to be any return on the film, let alone profits. Out of friendship, I agreed to work for nothing, hoping they might salvage something to compensate for the long hours and high hopes. Richard was grateful and continued with his rewrite of the final sequence, which we were shortly to film.

It is quite usual to shoot scenes out of sequence, but there had been so many rewrites on this film that I was beginning to lose sight of the original story. I do not think I was alone. During these night sequences, I would be told to run down a dimly lit street then disappear up an alley, and I was often unsure if I was chasing the other man or if he was chasing me. We spent so many nights in the Wapping area that I grew to know it quite well and enjoyed visiting the famous pub The Prospect of Whitby in between the endless takes.

On one occasion, I had to run so far into the distance, looking over my shoulder as I was doing it, that I ran out of earshot and did not hear the instruction to 'Cut.' I continued running and acting in a suspicious manner, until the next thing I knew was a heavy hand on my shoulder belonging to a burly policeman.

'What the hell do you think you are doing?' he asked, eyeing me curiously.

'I am making a film, Officer. Acting out a scene,' I replied.

'A likely story. Where are the film people and camera?'

I protested my innocence, but to no avail, and was taken off to the local police station to make a statement. Whenever you film on the streets in our country, it is necessary to obtain police permission, and, providing it is of no inconvenience to the public or the traffic, it is usually granted. This inexperienced lot had failed to take that elementary precaution, so my remarks about being in a film, with no other people in sight, sounded most unlikely to the police. While I was being cross-examined at the station by an aggressive sergeant, I had visions of the team searching the dock area and wondering whether in the darkness I had accidentally fallen into the river. As it turned out, they thought I had returned to The Prospect of Whitby and were proceeding to shoot another scene.

My story sounded implausible to the police, since I did not know the names of any local streets and could not tell them where the crew were filming. I had visions of spending the night in the local jail and asked them if they would phone my parents, who would be able to vouch for me. I was not happy about waking them up at 3 a.m., but I was becoming fairly desperate. They dialled the number, and, as fate would have it, my parents were away for the weekend. I asked the sergeant for what crime I was being detained.

'For loitering with suspicious intent.'

'What intent?' I asked.

His answer surprised me. 'That is what we have to establish. Whether it was robbery, larceny or homosexuality.'

My sense of humour was beginning to return as I began to see the ridiculous side of this situation, and I said, 'What happens if you have me for all three?'

He came straight back, 'Then you will need a very good lawyer, sir.'

It does not pay to be facetious with the police at 3 a.m., when they have probably endured a stressful time with drunks, vagrants and genuine criminals, and I foolishly continued to reason with them in the same light-hearted vein. 'I can see the headlines tomorrow,' I said. 'Effeminate burglar picked up in Wapping. Obviously looking for a bit of rough.' I saw they were writing it all down and asked what they were doing.

'I warned you, sir,' replied the sergeant, 'that anything you said could be taken down and used in evidence against you.'

This was getting serious. Fortunately, I remembered seeing similar situations unfold in various films and knew what I had to say next: 'I would like to speak to my solicitor.'

'Certainly, sir. What is the number?'

Rather pathetically, all I could say was, 'I don't have a solicitor. I've never needed one.'

'Well, I think you are going to need one now,' he replied. With that he nodded to the other police officer who had brought me in, and I was taken firmly by the arm and propelled towards the door.

I was still trying to make light of the situation and said, 'What, no handcuffs?'

Perhaps not surprisingly, his response this time was rather curt: 'Watch your lip, young man.'

As we passed down the corridor, I saw through an open door the reception area of the station, where one of the film crew, John Childs, was talking to the duty officer. I shouted, 'It's Johnny!' and made towards him. The officer with me reacted immediately and put me in an arm lock that made me shout out in pain. I think he thought I was about to escape, and he was on the point of pushing me to the ground when Johnny, who had heard my cry, hurried forward.

'What the hell are you doing here?' he said. 'We thought you were in the pub.'

As the officer forced me to my knees, in considerable pain I managed to say, 'I've been enjoying tea and sympathy with the constabulary. Johnny, for God's sake, explain what is happening. They don't believe me.'

The policeman then said to Johnny, 'Do you know this villain?'

Johnny was so amused at my being referred to as a villain that he began to laugh and said, 'Nick, what on earth have you been doing?'

'Apparently, I'm under suspicion for committing a homosexual burglary. Whatever that means! Why the devil didn't you get police permission for your filming?' Johnny replied that they had. 'Well, according to the police you haven't, and I am on my way to the cells.' Johnny realised what had happened and tried to explain the situation to the officer. He was still sceptical, and I was still in an agonising arm lock.

Johnny then added, 'Oh, come on, Officer, I appeal to you.'

'I wouldn't try that tack, Johnny,' I told him. 'They are not very appealing people here.'

The sergeant had now joined us, and eventually an officer from the station was persuaded to come to where we were filming in order to clear things up. It was all very well to work for no money, but to spend the night in a police cell seemed to be stretching friendship too far.

Back at the location, the situation was explained to the police, and permission to continue filming was informally sought and granted. Richard and Anthony apologised to me, but I think they were too preoccupied with their professional problems to have much sympathy for my ordeal. Instead of asking whether I needed treatment for my strained shoulder, they proceeded to explain what the next shot would be and what I had to do. The following night, we were back again in Wapping, running down more side streets, but by now the strain of an ill-planned, under-budgeted, overwritten film was affecting everyone. Young Francis Essex collapsed and was taken to the London Hospital, where he was kept in overnight, suffering from stress. The incident damaged still further the sagging morale of the production team. The final scene was to be filmed the next evening, and it involved me leaping from a jetty onto some barges, making a run for it and in the process slipping between two of them apparently to drown in the river. Being fit, I was able to perform this stunt myself. When the director shouted, 'Cut!' I clambered back onto the barge to which I had been clinging, unaware in my youthful ignorance of the inherent dangers I had faced. Certainly no one had warned me that it was necessary to have various injections if you were planning to fall into the horribly polluted River Thames. Even in retrospect, however, I was not too worried. I was pleased to be able to show off my athletic prowess, and it certainly made a dramatic end to the film. I was also happy to get it all over with and return to earning a living.

The next day, we were told no more shooting would take place, as the company that they had formed to make the film had become bankrupt and was in the hands of the Official Receiver. The dream had come to an end. None of us was going to become a star from this project. Anthony Essex-Lopresti went on to make some fine documentary films but died relatively young. Richard Waring became a successful writer of revue material and situation comedy at the BBC. Francis Essex moved into television shortly afterwards and finished up as a top light-entertainment director with ATV. Nothing in our strange profession is ever lost, however. The experience of being close to the other side of the camera during the making of *Full Circle* was invaluable when I eventually formed my own production company.

There was an unexpected sequel to this sad story. A few years later, when I was becoming established in television, some friends mentioned they had seen me in a film in the cinema the previous week. I explained that I had done little film work, to which they replied that it was a second feature, which they thought was called *Full Circle*. I said, 'But that film was never finished.'

They agreed. 'That is exactly what it looked like; it was pretty ghastly. In fact, it was difficult to make head or tail of it.' I then discovered that they had featured me as the star of this dreadful film. Obviously, the receivers who were handling the winding-up of the original company had invested a little money to do a rough edit on the available material in return for making more money from a cinema showing. Instead of advancing my prospects in the cinema, that ill-fated film seemed to have pushed me the other way.

Full Circle was not my only unfinished film to later receive a cinematic release. In 1966, I was engaged to play the manager of a pop group in a film entitled *The Ghost Goes Gear*. My character had the improbable name of Algernon Rowthorpe Plumley, and the band was the Spencer Davis Group. The project was basically a vehicle for them, with the hope, perhaps, that it would have an impact similar to The Beatles' films. Sadly, this was not to be.

The plot revolved around my character's dilapidated, haunted mansion and a scheme to put on a concert to raise funds for a renovation. We had two weeks on location in the English countryside, working to an exceptionally tight budget. It poured with rain every single day and was an absolute nightmare. Everyone and everything was drenched. I think it was the young director's first film. His name was Hugh Gladwish, and he spent the entire time pulling his hair out. I think it nearly killed the poor man. It was sad, and I am not sure if he ever worked in films again. The atrocious weather meant we could film only sporadically, which left very little footage available at the end of the shoot. I could not see a way to patch together any narrative and soon forgot about it, thinking it would never see the light of day. I was wrong. The producers must have adapted the few sequences of action we had filmed and spliced those together with some musical numbers, presumably shot separately. A friend who saw the 'finished' article described it as having a few 'hiccoughs'. I suppose it was decided that on the strength of the name of the Spencer Davis Group it was worth putting out. I would not say it was exactly released. It escaped.

By 1957, it was time for Jock Johnson to make his intervention. Up to that point, my film career had consisted of my two false starts and a handful of small character parts, including *Eyewitness* with Donald Sinden, in which I was a young doctor who, memorably for me, shared some scenes with the gorgeous Belinda Lee and Susan Beaumont, and as a policeman on the beat in the Ealing production *The Long Arm*, with Jack Hawkins.

For a number of years I had been having my hair cut at Trumper's, and Jock was my regular barber. I stayed with him until he retired in the '60s. Jock was an engaging Scotsman, and I enjoyed his company. He lived near Penge, not far from Bromley, and while I was in rep there he used to come and see me. I often gave him my two free tickets for Monday night, and over the months he saw me in numerous different plays.

Another regular customer of Jock's was Roy Boulting. In the early '50s, the Boulting brothers, Roy and John, were reaching the peak of their film-making careers. They were identical twins and almost impossible to tell apart, which sometimes made working for them confusing. They shared the responsibilities equally; when Roy was directing, John would produce, and vice versa. They also undertook the screenwriting. They made a number of extremely successful comedies, including *Private's Progress* in 1956, which made a star of Ian Carmichael, *Lucky Jim* in 1957, again starring Ian Carmichael and with Terry-Thomas, and in 1959 *I'm All Right Jack*, in which Peter Sellers played the union firebrand and won a BAFTA for his performance. Initially, Peter Sellers had not wanted to take on this role.

Peter always liked to be a big character in whatever part he was playing, and Roy told me years later that when they had first sent him the script he had turned it down. In his private life, Peter was an eccentric, over the top, and sometimes he was completely off the wall. You never knew what he was going to say next, but the people who knew him loved him. I met Peter once or twice and worked with him and Terry-Thomas in the Boulting brothers' film *Carlton-Browne of the*

F.O., also in 1959. He was a delightful person and a brilliant character actor. His Inspector Clouseau creation was nothing short of genius.

Peter Sellers's personality reflected the way he played his characters. He was not interested in straightforward roles. He had to see something more in the part, something he could work with and turn into his own. He 'became' the roles he accepted. When Roy sent him the script to play the shop steward Fred Kite, he told Roy he could not see it at all. He thought the role was just a down-the-line union hothead. Where was the comic potential? Roy Boulting was not to be put off. He was a brilliant director, and he knew Peter was perfect for the part. He spoke to Peter about how he saw the role developing and managed to convince him that he could draw something unusual out of the character. Peter had not recognised that potential, but when he realised that Roy believed in him, and was happy for him to develop the part as he saw fit, he accepted. The performance he gave was outstanding. It was exaggerated but real. We laughed at him in spite of the fact that we did not like his character's behaviour. It was Roy's ability as a director that allowed one of the stand-out performances of British cinema to happen.

Whenever I visited Jock to have my hair cut, he would tell me in his wonderful Glasgow accent, 'I had Mr Boulting in the other day. And I was talking about you. I was telling him I had seen you in your plays. I told him straight, I did. I said, "You should have Nicholas in one of your films. He's a good actor. You should cast him. I saw him doing these plays down at Bromley, and he was marvellous, he really was."'

I used to say to Jock, 'I wish you wouldn't. Please, leave it to my agent.' I thought the last thing a top film producer would want to do is consider a relatively unknown actor for a part on the recommendation of his barber. Especially if that barber went on about it every time he saw him.

One day, my phone rang and a voice at the other end said, 'Hello, it is Jock.'

He had never phoned me before, and I had no idea who it was. 'Jock who?'

'Jock Johnson, your barber.'

'Oh, I see, Jock. Yes, right.'

He started to talk like an agent. 'It is all fixed. I had Mr Boulting in the other day. I spoke to him. He wants you to call him. Have you got a pen? Take a note of the number. Tell him Jock Johnson told you to phone. Go and see him, and tell me what happens.'

I did nothing for three days. I felt convinced that, if I phoned Roy Boulting and said that my barber had told me to contact him, Roy would tell me not to bother him again. Eventually, however, I decided I should give it a shot: 'Can I speak to Roy Boulting, please?'

'Hold on a moment. I'll see if he is available.'

Then Roy came on the line and said, 'Hello, Nicholas. I've been waiting to hear from you.'

I explained: 'Well, I thought, after my barber, Jock Johnson, had been plugging me to you for years, I'd be the last actor you'd want to meet.'

He said, 'Well, I thought about it, and I decided that if I wanted to get my hair cut in peace I had better see you.'

I went to his office, and we hit it off. I talked about what I had done, and I think he was quite impressed. He was casting for a new film called *Brothers in Law*, from a novel by Henry Cecil. It is a comedy about two young men, played by Ian Carmichael and Richard Attenborough, beginning careers in the legal profession. I was tested and offered a very nice part. I played Ian and Richard's friend who is not connected with the law, is mad about motor cars and, eventually, much to the lawyers' chagrin, drives off in an old jalopy with the girl they both fancy. It was an extremely attractive supporting role. Probably the best I have had in a film. Many other parts stemmed from it. The role of the girl was played by Jill Adams, who was most attractive, with a look of Marilyn Monroe. I always thought she had the potential to become the British equivalent, but for whatever reason no one in this country seemed interested. I am sure that in America someone would have groomed her for film stardom.

In those days, the film producers used to place people under contract, and the Boultings had established a sort of rep company. They were not unlike the producers of the *Carry On* films in the sense that they were loyal to their team and would always cast them first and then fill in with other people. Ian Carmichael and Richard Attenborough were under contract in this way. When I was offered my part in *Brothers in Law*, Roy and John also negotiated a contract for me. They had first call on my services for a film. In fact, I think mine was the last long-term contract they gave out, and when it expired the spirit of it continued. When Roy was directing, I would frequently be his first choice if there was a part I could play. I was one of many young actors around then, so this was an excellent situation for me. If my face fitted, I had a strong chance of landing the role.

I owe a lot to the Boultings, especially Roy, and I was delighted when they cast me in their next film, *Happy Is the Bride*, a remake of the 1941 film *Quiet Wedding*, which was adapted from the highly successful Esther McCracken play of the same name. I played the lead in the play in the early '50s at Windsor Rep. Opposite me then was a young and extraordinarily talented actress called Geraldine McKeown – she later changed the spelling of her name to 'McEwan'. She had been discovered by John Counsell, who ran the Theatre Royal, Windsor, and everyone could see she was destined for a distinguished future. She was charming, unassuming and had a distinctive voice. I took her out one evening after the short run of the play finished. We went to a West End show and for supper afterwards. She was the kind of girl about whom you would only get serious. She was too delightful to be treated frivolously, and I was not ready for commitment. I had a lot of struggling to do before I became established and reached a position of professional security. I also discovered she was being courted by the resident director at Windsor, Hugh Cruttwell, who had directed us in *Quiet Weekend*. This troubled me somewhat, and so our mini-romance lasted only one night, but I still remember it. Hugh went on to teach at RADA and married Geraldine, who became one of this country's most distinguished leading actresses.

The story of *Happy Is the Bride* revolves around the plans of a young couple for a quiet, English country wedding, which are soon disrupted by various family members. I played the brother of the bride, who returns home to be best man accompanied by his hip girlfriend, played by a young Elvi Hale.

We had great fun making the film. The cast featured many of the Boulting brothers' stalwarts, including Ian Carmichael, Cecil Parker, Edith Sharpe, Terry-Thomas, Eric Barker, Irene Handl, Athene Seyler, Miles Malleson, Thorley Walters and Joan Hickson. I also got to know John Le Mesurier for the first time during the filming. John played the bridegroom's father. Janette Scott was charming as the young bride. She was Thora Hird's daughter, and this was one of her first big roles. She had been a successful child actress, yet there was nothing precocious about her. I got to know her well in the years to come, because I was friendly with her mother.

Janette's aunt was played by Joyce Grenfell, who was absolutely lovely, one of the most atypical stars with whom I have ever worked and an inspired amateur who was brilliant at what she did. She was most charming, with none of the professional aura that a lot of actors acquire when they are aware of their status. She was thoroughly natural, with that rare ability to make even a straight line funny. She was so wonderfully 'ordinary' in the best sense of the word that she would do her knitting on the set. I am sure her absence of any front was one of the things that endeared Joyce to the British public.

Roy Boulting taught me an invaluable lesson during the making of *Happy Is the Bride*. It was my big scene, with a lot of dialogue. My character had just come back home and was excited about the wedding. I was determined to give it my best. I delivered my lines, playing my heart out in the scene. When the first take was over, Roy gently took me aside and said, 'Darling boy, that was fine. The feeling was good. You have done a lot of work in the theatre, and that was an excellent interpretation. You have to remember, however, that in the theatre you are playing to someone in the back of the dress circle. In films, your audience is just there, behind the lens of the camera. Now, I want you to do it exactly the same again; play it with the same energy but with 25 per cent of the effort. We'll have another rehearsal and bear that in mind.'

That piece of direction was a wonderful, technical touch that helped me enormously. Not many directors have the ability, or would have taken the time or trouble, to describe it so well. Roy was very influential in my life, and I was extremely fond of him. Years later, he fell on hard times financially. He lived near one of his sons in a little flat in Eynsham, in the Cotswolds, which was not far from my home, and I used to call on him from time to time. I do not know what happened to his money, but he was married three times, which may have had something to do with it. He was writing his autobiography, and I used to say to him, 'Roy, get on with it. You have such a wonderful story to tell.' His nearby son used to keep an eye on him, but it was sad to me that this brilliant, successful man was living so modestly. I do not think he ever finished the book.

Roy was always lovely. I remember bringing him to our house for a meal when he was about 80. I could not help but think how times had changed. When I first met Roy, he was in his prime, a big-time producer, an icon of British cinema, and I was a striving actor whom he helped enormously. Years later, there we were in very different circumstances, but he did not seem to mind. He was appreciative and warm. 'Dear boy, so kind of you. Thank you. I've had a lovely time. Just lovely,' he said. 'Please do thank your charming wife.' He always had a way with women, and his charm had not left him. He flattered Annie no end, and she enjoyed it thoroughly.

In addition to my work with the Boulting brothers, I was offered many attractive roles by other producers. In *Too Many Crooks*, a Mario Zampi film made for the Rank Organisation, I played a tax inspector, Tommy Weston, who is engaged to Terry-Thomas's daughter, played by Rosalie Ashley. My arrival on the scene is not welcomed by Terry-Thomas's character, who is a philandering businessman involved in a dispute with the Inland Revenue. Added to the mix is a gang of crooks attempting to extort ransom money for the kidnap of Terry-Thomas's wife, played by Brenda De Banzie, who in turn helps the gang steal all his money once she learns of his adulterous lifestyle. Mayhem ensues in this delightful comic thriller.

The cast included some of the greats of British comedy. In addition to Terry-Thomas, George Cole, Sid James, Bernard Bresslaw and Terry Scott all had roles. Rosalie Ashley was a lovely person who had great potential in the film business because she was pretty, but with limited acting ability her career never fully materialised, and she later married Raymond 'Mr Teasy-Weasy' Bessone, the celebrity hairdresser.

There was a wonderful scene in the film that sticks in my mind particularly. Rosalie is introducing me to her father for the first time, with the words, 'Daddy, I want you to meet my friend Tommy Weston. He's a tax inspector.' At that precise moment, Terry-Thomas is opening a suitcase, the contents of which he wants to keep secret, especially from the Revenue. When he hears what his daughter has just said, he slams down the lid. Unfortunately, on the first take he slammed it so hard he caught his fingers, and, overacting magnificently, he ran around the set, effing and blinding in some style. He had actually hurt himself, and we had to do a retake, for which the director had some words of advice: 'Terry, that was wonderful, but can you do it without the language this time.'

Terry was an interesting man, but you could never really make any rapport with him. He lived in his own little world and was not easy to get to know. He was certainly very talented, but he was conscious of his position and his ability. He was not a communicative person and kept people at a distance, although he was always perfectly affable and utterly professional and easy to work with. It was terribly sad when he developed Parkinson's disease and was eventually unable to work. His last film was in 1978. I remember seeing him in a role during the early stages of the disease, and because one of his hands was shaking so much he had to hold it steady with the other while he delivered his lines. He spent a lot of time in Ibiza, and having gone through his money on medical bills and various attempted cures he eventually ended up in such a bad way, in both health and financial terms, that the writer and broadcaster Richard Hope-Hawkins and the *Carry On* actor Jack Douglas organised a charity event in aid of Terry and the Parkinson's Disease Society. A considerable amount of money was raised at the spectacular gala evening, and although Terry died less than a year later at least he was able to live out that time with dignity and in some comfort.

I remember seeing Terry for the first time when he appeared in *Strike a New Note* at the Prince of Wales Theatre during the war. At that stage in his career, Terry was an impersonator. He had a super stage routine in which he played a disc jockey. With that wonderfully distinctive voice, he would say. 'And now the next record I am going to play for you is that of Vera Lynn.' At which point he would suddenly work himself into a panic trying to find the record, which he couldn't locate anywhere. 'We'll be putting that on in just a moment, yes. Ha, ha, just trying to find it.' This went on throughout the entire routine. He could never find the record he wanted and would end up having to impersonate each of the singers. It was very funny.

Muriel Box, one of the few female film directors in the '50s and '60s, had directed me in *Eyewitness* in 1956 and also a year previously in *Simon and Laura*, in which I played a television producer in a lovely comedy set around a television soap opera. Four years later, I was working with the Box family again, this time in a film produced by Muriel's sister-in-law, Betty Box, and directed by Betty's husband, Ralph Thomas. The film was *Upstairs and Downstairs,* a delightful domestic romp starring Michael Craig, Anne Heywood, James Robertson Justice and the stunning French actress Mylène Demongeot. As the film's poster eloquently put it, 'M-M-M-M-Mylène's M-M-M-M-Marvellous!' She certainly was. She played a French au pair who causes havoc in an English household. I was in one short scene with her in which Daniel Massey and I, along with several others, vie for her attention. She was incredibly sexy, and everyone fancied her like crazy. According to Betty, it was me who caught Mylène's eye: 'You know, she was mad about you. You could have feathered your nest there.' I was flattered, of course, but that was as far as it went. I was happily married with a young family, and the thought of taking it any further never crossed my mind.

My second film with Betty and Ralph was the fourth in the *Doctor* series, *Doctor in Love*. This was the first sequel not to star Dirk Bogarde, Leslie Phillips taking a lead role instead. Filmed down in Pinewood, the plot followed pretty conventional lines, but for me the most poignant memory is of the lovely girl who played the lead, Carole Lesley. I had a scene with her, and she was absolutely gorgeous, a sexy Diana Dors-style peroxide blonde. It looked at that stage as though her career was about to take off, but she did not really have the talent. She landed a few more roles, but she soon disappeared from public life, only to reappear tragically in 1974 when she was found dead following an overdose of pills, which some suggested may have been suicide. It was a sad end indeed, when I think back to the vivacious girl I briefly knew.

The *Doctor* series ran to seven films in total, but by far the most successful movie franchise in British comedy is the *Carry On* films. With my reputation for playing character roles in comedy, coupled with the fact that I knew and got on well with many of the regular cast, it might have been supposed that I would have featured in more than one of the *Carry Ons*. As it was, I only ever appeared in 1961's *Carry on Regardless*.

The *Carry On* producer Peter Rogers and the director Gerald Thomas – brother of Ralph, with whom I had worked so happily – had a specific approach to the making of the films. Each *Carry On* was made on a modest budget, and the production schedule was intense. The team, therefore, had to be made up of very talented performers who could be relied on to work quickly and, hopefully, get everything right first time. The ethos was that if it was OK, it was in the can. Some of the actors felt that they were not paid as much as they could have commanded in a major feature production, but their reward was the loyalty shown to them. Once you were part of the team, wherever possible a part was found, or even created, for you in subsequent films.

It was through my agent, Richard Stone, that I was offered a supporting role in *Carry on Regardless*. Unfortunately, I innocently blew my opportunity of ever working again with Gerald Thomas. I failed to grasp the professional ground rules by which these films were shot. I had been working with the Boulting brothers, and others, on higher-budget films, in which there was more time for retakes to ensure every scene was as polished as possible. This was not how Gerald worked, and I should have had the common sense and professional instinct to realise it.

After a take of a long and complicated scene that featured Joan Sims and myself, Gerald, in the gentle and courteous way he had of speaking, asked me how I felt. I replied quite truthfully that the run-through in rehearsal had been better. He agreed but said that he was satisfied. My reaction should have been, 'If you're happy, Gerald, that's great.' Gerald then asked if I should like to go again with the scene, to which I should have replied, 'No, not if you're satisfied.'

It was my big moment in the film, however, which ended with Joan pouring a bottle of wine over me, so I tactfully replied that I thought I could make the scene funnier. Gerald considerately said that he would do another take, which we did, and he admitted it was better. The following day, however, Richard Stone told me that I had been reported as being 'difficult'. This is a word much used in our profession. In this country, if a performer makes any kind of fuss or complains, and the director is not comfortable with the artist, this word is applied to them. Without any factual detail or context, the information spreads, and slowly that individual finds he is receiving less and less work. It has happened to many. If only Gerald had behaved like a conventional director and said quite firmly that he was satisfied with the scene or that time did not permit a retake. He did not, and I had put my head in a professional noose, and it tightened round me. The others may have carried on regardless in many more films in the series. I did not.

The situation came back to haunt me in 1967, but thankfully without the same result. I had an excellent part in a film called *Don't Raise the Bridge, Lower the River*, which starred the US comedian Jerry Lewis. It was being produced over here by the American Walter Shenson, who is probably most famous for producing The Beatles' *A Hard Day's Night* and *Help!* The director was Jerry Paris, who had directed most of the episodes of *The Dick Van Dyke Show*. He was a lovely man, a typical wisecracking American character who generated a warm, friendly atmosphere on the set. The only problem Jerry Paris had was that Jerry Lewis was almost the exact opposite to him – dour and difficult, impossible even – and he did not appreciate some of his star's antics. Fortunately, Jerry Paris and I hit it off magnificently. This proved important during the filming when a moment arose that led me to worry that I had once again blotted my copybook, just as I had in *Carry on Regardless*.

We were shooting a big scene. I was lying on a bed feeling unwell.

We rehearsed and went for a take. I put in some funny business, but there was a technical problem, so we had to go for another take. 'OK, we'll print that one,' Jerry announced.

I called him over to my bed. 'Jerry, I didn't quite get what you wanted that second time, did I?'

'No, no, don't worry,' he said. 'It doesn't matter. It was good enough. Why? Do you want to go again?'

'Well, I can do a better one for you if you want.'

'All right, let's do it.'

That's when it struck me. I suddenly remembered what had happened with Gerald Thomas. 'Jerry, Jerry, please come here,' I called, gesticulating madly from the bed. I was beginning to panic. 'Jerry,' I said, 'I'm sorry. I don't want to go again. If you are happy, we'll leave it.'

He looked at me, mystified by my change of heart. Then he came out with a wonderful, made-in-America line. 'Listen, pal,' he said, 'you are the one in front of the camera. If you think you can do a better take, you are the boss in this situation. We go for another take.'

'Well, if that's how you feel about it, Jerry.'

'Sure do. But mark my words,' he said with a wicked smile, 'it had better be better.' Then this delightful, engaging character started shouting in his usual jokey manner. 'Right, we're going for another take on that one. Nicholas is not happy. Nicholas thinks he can do a better one. Nicholas is happy to go on spending Mr Shenson's money. He says he's not bothered as long as . . .'

'Jerry, Jerry, come over here again. Really, do forget it this time. Please, please forget it.'

He looked at me with genuine concern and said, 'Nick, I was only kidding. We'll go for another take. I am happy to do so. I couldn't care less if it isn't better. We'll just see what happens.' Fortunately, it was an improvement, but Jerry said afterwards, 'Listen, Nick, I wouldn't have minded if it wasn't. We'd have kept the other one.' That is the Americans: they take great pleasure in working hard to get everything as right as possible.

I did not have much to do with Jerry Lewis. I had scenes with him but found that, while he was always polite and courteous, you could hardly talk to him. He was used to being a big star, and it appeared to me that he put on the big-time act to a great extent. In America, the stars have the power, and he seemed to act as though he knew that. Away from the camera lens, I did not see much evidence of charm, but Jerry Paris still managed to get a good performance out of him.

Tight budgets in films can have implications other than a concern about the number of retakes. In *Murder Ahoy!*, the fourth and last of the Margaret Rutherford Miss Marple films, made in 1964, I had a lovely little cameo role. I played a doctor who had four or five small scenes where he would breeze in and be efficient and down to earth. He would make a few comments and be gone.

In this fairly small-budget production, the director had worked out that, to save money, we could film all of my scenes in one day. One after the other. The set was not a problem, as I only ever appeared on the ship. I had one day's filming and was paid for one day's filming. If we had filmed in chronological sequence, I would have had well over a week's work. My friends Derek Nimmo and Lionel Jeffries were in the scenes, and they found the whole thing hilarious. 'What's the next one, Nicholas?' they'd say. 'We are all just your stooges in this film. You are a star for the day.'

Murder Ahoy! has since become popular on television and is often repeated, but the actors do not see any income from that. In the cinema, your contract is a buy-out. You receive a one-off payment. In fact, that is increasingly the situation today for everything. A consequence of all these repeats, however, is that the film has built up quite a following and I continue to receive fan letters requesting an autograph and any anecdotes regarding working with the great Margaret Rutherford. I have to reply, 'I don't know. I never met Margaret Rutherford.' She was not in any of the scenes in my one day's filming, and I was never back on set when she was around.

Most of my film roles have seemed to be typical Establishment figures, including various doctors, a tax inspector, vicars, MPs and policemen. Perhaps that is the sort of face I have, or the sort of face producers and directors think I have, but I do love to play baddies from time to time. I have done so a few times on the stage but only twice in films. My first villainous role was in the ill-fated *Full Circle*, and my second was in the 1976 adaptation of Len Deighton's *Spy Story*, which, despite such a pedigree, never really took off. I played a sinister, smooth, evil character, and I loved it. They are the easiest parts in the world to play. In one scene, I was being quizzed and I was being utterly smooth, calm and chilling. 'I don't think you realise what you are suggesting,' I insinuated. 'If you pursue that course, I think you will have a very unhappy result.' What fun!

In the same year that I appeared in *Murder Ahoy!*, I also played the part of a producer in a teen musical called *Every Day's a Holiday*, which illustrates rather well the diversity of working in show business: from Miss Marple to Freddie and the Dreamers. They were the top billing in this sunny, lightweight seaside film, and although it was being made on a shoestring budget we had quite a starry cast. Alongside Freddie and the Dreamers were the singers Mike Sarne and John Leyton, the brilliant character actress Liz Fraser, a young Richard O'Sullivan playing the mouth organ and the truly wonderful Ron Moody. I used to watch Ron in revues, and he always gave the most incredible performances. It was no surprise that after playing Fagin in the West End production of *Oliver!* he reprised the role in the film, even though he was not a big name at the time. He had so much talent.

We filmed on location in Clacton, and thank goodness the weather was far kinder to us than it had been on *The Ghost Goes Gear*. One of my scenes took place in a television producer's box, where I was supposedly directing a sequence. I asked the director, 'How do you want me to play it? Do you want me to be eccentric and over the top?'

He liked the approach. 'Yeah, yeah, go for that.' I did and was totally outrageous and neurotic. I overacted like mad. I think I was probably ghastly, but they did not mind. They thought it was all good copy. A number of the actors in *Every Day's a Holiday* went on to become well known, not because of the film but in spite of it.

Four years ago, I was cast to play myself, twenty years younger. I was surprised but took it as a great compliment. It was a lovely challenge.

The enquiry came from BBC Four, who were producing *Kenneth Williams: Fantabulosa!*, starring the brilliant Michael Sheen. He found Kenneth's voice and the way he moved perfectly. There was a scene in the film in which we are recording *Just a Minute* and Kenneth is being very flamboyant. We arrived at the set, and the moment I walked in I said, 'You've got it wrong.' Kenneth and Clement Freud, who was played by someone who looked like him but did not say anything, were in the wrong seats, and my positioning was totally incorrect. They had designed the scene from the television version, which had me sitting on my own with a big clock in front. I explained that this was not how it is on the radio show, where our producer's assistant sits next to me with a stopwatch and keeps a note of the points. I pointed out the errors and wondered if I was being 'difficult'. In fact, they were genuinely concerned at the inaccuracies and delighted with my input. Authenticity was vital to them, and they quickly redesigned the set and found a larger table and someone to sit in as our timekeeper.

It was a strange experience when we finally started filming and felt our way into the scene. It was as though I had stepped back in time to be with an old friend. I have similar feelings whenever I see one of my films on television. I find myself immediately transported back to the laughter and companionship of Ian Carmichael, Derek Nimmo, Lionel Jeffries and many others whom I have had the privilege of working beside on a British film set.

THE JOYS OF TELEVISION

My television career has spanned almost 60 years so far, and in addition to the characters I played in *The Arthur Haynes Show*, and presenting *Sale of the Century*, I have been seen and heard on the small screen in a wide variety of roles – from playing alongside Robin Hood to the voice of a magical Texan cowboy; from a Martian to a vicar who turns into a Haemovore creature in a *Doctor Who* series. Along the way, I have enjoyed myself thoroughly.

My first break in television came in the autumn of 1951, when Graeme Muir rang to ask me to play some character parts in a new series he was directing at Lime Grove. The show was to be called *The Eric Barker Half Hour*, written by and starring Eric Barker. This was not only a wonderful opportunity; it was also the beginning of a friendship with an exceptional comedian and his delightful, down-to-earth wife, Pearl Hackney, who also appeared in the show.

Graeme and I had first met when we performed together in a lovely little theatre in Stratford-atte-Bow rented by the actor David Horne. David played character parts in dozens of films from the early '30s through to the late '60s, but he never became a 'star'. I do not think that bothered him too much; he just loved acting. David had some private money, and he took on the theatre partly to give himself and his wife acting roles. He staged ridiculous productions, such as Charles Morgan's *The Flashing Stream*, an erudite play about a group of mathematicians developing a secret weapon. It ran for over two hundred performances at the Lyric Theatre in 1938 but was a flop on Broadway, closing after only eight nights. Margaret Rawlings was in both productions, and it is said that after the first night on Broadway, when the audience booed, she stood in front of the curtains and said, 'You can't throw pearls before swine.'

Spotlight, the theatrical casting contacts, sent me down to see David when he was casting for *The Flashing Stream*, and I landed a part in the play. Back then, *The Spotlight* engaged in more hands-on casting than it does today, and I had a good relationship with them. Quite why David thought the residents of Stratford-atte-Bow would want to see this play was never clear, and we would sometimes have an audience of only two or three. David did not mind: he enjoyed giving a performance and could afford to lose some money.

David and I got on well together, and I ended up doing two or three plays for him, one of which also featured Graeme Muir and his wife. Graeme did not quite make it as an actor, and he subsequently embarked on a career in television, where he became a successful producer, working on programmes such as *Comedy Playhouse* and *It Ain't Half Hot Mum*. Eric Barker's series was one of Graeme's first jobs, and when Eric asked, 'Who do you think we could get to play these supporting roles?' Graeme replied, 'I remember an actor when I was in a play at Stratford whom I thought was talented.' Graeme got in touch with me, and I secured a contract.

At the time, Eric had his own show on radio called *Just Fancy*, which ran for many years. Prior to that, he had written and starred with Jon Pertwee in the naval edition of the wartime programme *Merry-Go-Round*, which, week by week, went 'round the Services bringing music and fun to boys and girls in khaki and two shades of blue'. Eric's show was set on HMS *Waterlogged* at Sinking-in-the-Ooze. Richard Murdoch and Kenneth Horne wrote the RAF edition, which featured Laughter Command based at Much-Binding-in-the-Marsh, and Charlie Chester wrote *Studio Stand Easy* for the army, which featured Arthur Haynes. After the war, *Much-Binding-in-the-Marsh* and *Stand Easy* carried on into civvy street, but *Waterlogged Spa*, as it became known, came to a natural end and Eric branched out into television.

Eric, in appearance, was not an obvious comedian. Reserved by nature, he appeared more like an unassuming bank manager. He did not have that big, star personality, but he was an intelligent man and a shrewd observer of people with an uncanny ear for recreating them. He was a natural satirist with impeccable comic timing. I enjoyed both his humour and his wisdom and learned a great deal from him, about both comedy and acting. We were a very happy company, and Graeme Muir made work easy and fun, directing with great skill and always supporting Eric whatever the content of the sketch.

Together with Eric and Pearl, the cast for the first series was made up of Cameron Hall, who joined Eric in his famous sketch from *Just Fancy* in which two old men discuss life, Patricia Gilbert and Daphne Anderson. Ronnie Boyer and Jeanne Ravel performed an elegant dance routine in evening clothes, the Malcolm Mitchell Trio played a number, additional music was supplied by Eric Robinson and the BBC Orchestra, and there was a different music group and solo singer in each performance. We made six programmes in all, which were transmitted fortnightly. In subsequent series, the musical groups were dropped, Deryck Guyler replaced Cameron Hall, and we had the same singer for all six shows. In one series, it was Sara Gregory, wife of my future agent Richard Stone, in another Janet Brown, singing but not doing impersonations. Later, as Eric's writing became more satirical, the title of the series was changed to *Look At It This Way*. He was a pioneer, the first person to do 'topical satire' on television, but as the phrase had not yet been coined, and as the sketches were part of a conventional variety show, he never received the credit he deserved for his originality.

When Eric's fifth television series ended, the BBC did not renew his contract – his individualism did not endear him to an organisation, which at the time liked conformity and conventional thinking. Soon, however, he was being offered good supporting film roles, particularly by the Boulting brothers, and on radio *Just Fancy* continued to win a large and loyal following. Then, at the comparatively young age of 52, he suffered a stroke that more or less ended his professional career. He made a good recovery but was left with slight paralysis on one side, and while his mind was as sharp as ever he lost some of his sparkle. In later years, he worked a little in local radio, and he died in 1990 aged 78, which is a good age and probably exceptional for someone who had suffered a stroke so young. It says much for the love and care lavished on him by Pearl and his family.

I think the biggest impact Eric made in his first television series was with the send-up of the television coverage of the 1951 general election. It was the first time television had covered an election, and he created a marvellous skit on the whole proceedings. We were all anxious about how it would be received, and while it was quite gentle compared with what is seen today, and viewers enjoyed it, messages were sent to Eric from above advising him to be careful and not to satirise too many of his employer's serious programmes. Eric, however, continued to take off most of what was on television, which gave me an ideal opportunity to do my impersonations. Pearl, too, was clever at impressions, but it was her subtle characterisation in one short sketch that created the biggest furore imaginable and nearly lost Eric and all of us our jobs. Above all, it illustrates how dramatically respect for authority and the Establishment has changed and how far ahead of its time was Eric's thinking.

He wrote a short sketch in which a regal-looking lady wearing a coat with a fur collar, played by Pearl, is on a platform surrounded by a group of important-looking civic dignitaries. One of the group solemnly passes her a bottle of champagne on a rope – she is clearly about to launch a ship. She takes the champagne, names the ship and lets go of the bottle. The scene cuts to a film clip of a ship slowly sinking into the river, then back to the group, and Pearl, in a studied voice, but by no means an impersonation of the Queen Mother, says, 'Surely, she should have floated?' End of sketch, big laugh and, before the show was over, a major crisis. The telephone lines to Broadcasting House and the national press were jammed with callers. Someone had dared to impersonate Her Majesty. The royal family had been mocked. The fact that the person in the sketch could have been anyone in the public eye, and that it was also an amusing situation and a funny pay-off, did not matter. The inference was there, and the bounds of good taste had been breached. The next day, it was headline news in the papers. Eric and Pearl were besieged by reporters – they could not get out of their normally peaceful Kent cottage and had to take the phone off the hook. Eric was asked to present himself to the then head of

Light Entertainment, Ronnie Waldman, who gave him a severe lecture and a warning about overstepping the mark. If he transgressed in the future, he was told, the series would be cancelled and he would not work again for the BBC.

Television in those days was transmitted live, with huge cameras that were difficult to manoeuvre. The production had to be carefully planned in the large studio at Lime Grove so that it could house the sets of all the items on Eric's show in such a way that the cameras could move from one to another to keep continuity. Cameras 1, 2 and 3 might be moving to their next position while camera 4 was taking the final shots on the piece that was finishing. Also, a set that had been used for an opening sketch might be dismantled and another erected at one end of the studio while filming was proceeding at the opposite end. Such construction work had to be done in silence, as the sound system picked up every stray noise. On one occasion, Ronnie Boyer was bending his dance partner, Jeanne Ravel, backwards in an elaborate movement. As her back nearly touched the floor, a stagehand dropped a huge iron counterweight. His timing was perfect. It sounded as if something Jeanne was wearing had snapped. The funniest sight, however, was the stagehand, who had dropped the counterweight on his foot and was now hopping about in agony, trying not to make a sound and swearing the most ghastly oaths in mime.

The camera rehearsals on the day of transmission were not only to establish positions and angles but also to make sure that, in the time available, it was possible to move them between sets and give the artists the opportunity to change their clothes as the sketches required. These changes were made behind the 'flats', the backdrop scenery to any set, and there were inevitably some awkward moments that simply could not happen in today's pre-recorded world. Such incidents made television much more fun for the viewers, as well as more of a challenge for the performers. If a mistake was made, you recovered with a gag if you could and got on with it.

Eric was very short-sighted, and after one sketch, in which he was not wearing his spectacles, he was searching for his dresser, who usually led him to where he made his next quick change. They missed each other.

Eric failed to see that the cameras were filming on a set near him and, instead of walking behind the flats, rushed in front, dressed in football gear and carrying the kind of clicking rattle that fans took to matches. Janet Brown was singing a song about some man in her life. Eric passed behind her, looked puzzled and then realised his mistake. Janet had not seen him and kept going while Eric, smiling weakly at the camera, crept to the door in the middle of the centre flat, only to discover it was false. He then tried slinking along the back of the set, hoping the cameras would cut the other way, when his dresser rushed on and dragged him off. Viewers must have been puzzled by the sight of an odd-looking stranger in Janet's flat, a door that did not open and another man appearing from nowhere. Of course, no explanation could be given.

I had an even more embarrassing experience in one of the shows, for which Eric and Pearl pulled my leg mercilessly afterwards. I had found the area where I was due to make a change. My dresser was waiting. He took my jacket, and I released my trouser braces and then bent forward to pull a shirt over my head. As I did so, my dresser, standing behind, pulled down my trousers to speed things up. At that precise moment, a cameraman bumped his machine into a flat, which swung to one side, and in the middle of an elegant dance routine I was revealed, trousers down, with a man standing in a most provocative position behind me. Ad-lib your way out of that one! I then had to continue in the next sketch, playing a very sincere vicar. The joys of television in the '50s!

The budgets for television programmes were always extremely tight back then, which meant that if you were producing a drama series it was essential to complete a certain amount of filming every day. Such strict requirements did not always lend themselves to actors producing their best work. In 1956, I played a small part in the first series of *The Adventures of Robin Hood*, which was filmed at Elstree and produced by Douglas Fairbanks's company. My character was Sir Walter of the Glen in the episode entitled 'Trial by Battle'. For some reason, the filming had run late with only about ten minutes of the day remaining when we came to my scene, in which I was to lie wounded in the forest.

The instructions the director gave me were a study in controlled panic: 'Nicholas, lie down. Cover yourself with leaves. Get some blood on him. Have you read the script? Good. Wait, he hasn't got his hat on. Right, now, remember, you are suffering. You have just been wounded. Action!' That was it. One take. I do not think I understood what I was talking about, but it did not matter. 'Cut. Finish.' We were done for the day.

The year following my brief visit to Sherwood Forest, I teamed up with Arthur Haynes, and my television appearances for the next few years were almost exclusively with him. The public might not have seen me on many other programmes, but they could hear me. In 1960, I was the voice of Tex Tucker on the delightful Gerry Anderson puppet series *Four Feather Falls*.

My wife at the time, Denise Bryer, was well known as a brilliant voice artist. She was also a talented actress, but she was not keen on working in the theatre. This meant she was rarely off touring and was able to spend time at home with our young family, which was a great bonus for us. She enjoyed her work in radio with the BBC Drama Repertory Company, but it was her amazing ability to produce different voices that brought her deserved success. Throughout her career, she has been the voice of some famous characters, including Kiki the Frog in *Hector's House* and Noddy in *The Classic Adventures of Noddy*. One of the most amazing jobs she did was for the medication Alka-Seltzer. The company ran a number of successful advertising campaigns, including a series of animated commercials featuring a character with a distinct and quirky manner of speech. Apparently the actor who originally provided the voice began to ask for too much money, presumably thinking himself indispensable. This was going to cause continuity problems until someone suggested that Denise might be able to help. She could, and reproduced the voice perfectly, going on to record many Alka-Seltzer commercials.

Denise first worked with Gerry Anderson when she was the voice of the title character in his puppet show *The Adventures of Twizzle*, which ran from 1957 to 1960. During this period, Gerry was developing a new show based on a western, featuring magical happenings and talking animals. Gerry wanted Denise to be involved and came to our house to discuss with her some of the voices she would provide for the characters. He brought some scripts and asked me to help by reading the other parts, including the sheriff, Tex Tucker. When we had finished, Gerry said, 'Well, we've worked out Denise's characters, but I also think we've found our Tex Tucker.'

We recorded at his studios, AP Films, in Slough. The wonderful *Carry On* actor Kenneth Connor was also a member of the cast. It was similar to working on a radio series. We read the scripts, and they were recorded. The puppets were nowhere to be seen. Gerry synched the recording and the action later. We produced 39 episodes, but a second series was not commissioned, perhaps because the audience were limited by age. Gerry was also beginning to turn his thoughts to his next show, which became the hugely successful *Supercar*. *Four Feather Falls* is a beautiful series with real charm and was one of the most imaginative things, from a child's point of view, that Gerry ever created. It also featured Tex Tucker singing some delightful songs – Gerry wisely chose the singer Michael Holliday to perform those.

Professionally, Denise would be linked with puppets for many years to come, but it was to be another 50 before I worked with them again: as the narrator in a children's series involving two aliens, called SpottyWot and DottyWot, who have landed their spacecraft in a zoo. I interact with the two aliens and translate for the viewers. The show is called *The WotWots* and is delightful. It was created in New Zealand and has been broadcast in a number of different countries, each of which records its own narrator. I was intrigued as to why I was chosen for the UK version. 'How did you come to approach me?' I asked one of the senior executives.

'You must be big in New Zealand,' was his rather surprising answer. *Just a Minute* was popular there, but that was about it as far as I knew. He explained that when they decided to bring the series to the UK a number of names were put forward, and when I was mentioned the producer said, 'That is the one I want, Nicholas Parsons.' Apparently he had worked in Britain many years previously and remembered my performances with Arthur Haynes and others.

I am delighted to be involved in the series, but it has put my son and

Much-Binding-in-the-Marsh in 1954, my first major break on radio. Left to right: Kenneth Horne, Dora Bryan, Richard Murdoch, Sam Costa. (© BBC)

Radio's first satirical show, *Listen to this Space*, in October 1967. Left to right: Peter Reeves, Bob Todd, Denise Bryer, Barry Cryer. (© BBC)

The early days of *Just a Minute*. Clement Freud and Derek Nimmo, with Ian Messiter and Kenneth Williams at the front. (© BBC)

The 40th anniversary recording of *Just a Minute* with four of the classic players: Clement Freud and Sheila Hancock, with Paul Merton and Graham Norton at the front. (© BBC)

Arthur Haynes (right) and Dermot Kelly (left) as their famous tramp characters, giving me a mouthful.

Four Feather Falls. I was the voice of Sheriff Tex Tucker. Kenneth Connor, on the right, supplied many of the other voices.

I was thrilled to be in my
first film in 1947, *Master
of Bankdam.*

Interviewing Fred Scuttle on
The Benny Hill Show.
(© Freemantlemedia Ltd/Rex Features)

The Boulting brothers film *Happy Is the Bride*, in 1958. Front from left: John
Le Mesurier, Ian Carmichael, Janette Scott, Edith Sharpe, Cecil Parker. Back
from left: Richard Bennett, Elvi Hale, me, Eric Barker, Virginia Maskell,
Thorley Walters. The bridesmaid is Sarah Drury.

A very early performance at a fancy-dress party, aged three.

My wonderful Alvis in the early '60s. The first of three I owned.

Having fun with my children, Suzy and Justin, after lunching with the Queen. (© Getty Images)

Suzy and Justin grown up.

Honoured with an OBE in 2004, accompanied by Suzy, Annie and Justin.

Annie and me on our wedding day in Barbados. (© Steve Cumberbatch)

Rector of the University of St Andrews, 1988.

Charity cricket at Lord's with the Lord's Taverners, 1988. Left to right: Willie Rushton, Henry Kelly, Barry Norman.

With two of the warmest, funniest men I know, Ken Dodd and Norman Wisdom, at the Children's Royal Variety Performance.

As the Narrator in the stage production *The Rocky Horror Show*.

Celebrating Annie's birthday.

daughter-in-law in a tricky situation. Justin and Louise have two children, Lara, aged six, and Jack, aged three, and they sensibly try to enforce a no-television rule for weekday mornings. Unfortunately for them, *The WotWots* goes out at around 8 a.m., and when the children heard that I was in the show, that was it: 'We want to hear Papa.' Justin and Louise had no comeback and had to relent.

Recording *The WotWots* is similar in many ways to the days of *Four Feather Falls*, although, of course, the technology has vastly improved. I go to a studio, read the script and do not see any of the on-screen action. We record 13 episodes in a day, and at times I do lose track of what is going on and have to ask the director. He will check the storyline and explain which section of the zoo the aliens are visiting. 'Oh, I see,' I will say. 'It is an elephant they are looking at. Now it makes sense.'

When the series was first broadcast, we held a press launch, and a young journalist telephoned me to gather some information. 'Which is your favourite episode?' she asked.

'Well, I've only seen one,' I replied.

'But you've recorded dozens, haven't you?'

'Yes, I watched one episode so that I knew how the characters behave. I then went to the recording studio, read the scripts and used my imagination as to what these two cute little aliens were doing. It is called acting.' I do not think she understood.

Denise was reunited with Gerry in the '80s on the hugely popular *Terrahawks* series, but the three of us worked together on only one other occasion, not long after *Four Feather Falls*. In 1960, I formed my own production company. I had been wanting to do some independent productions for a while, and the opportunity arose when a travel firm called Blue Cars, who were principally concerned with coaching holidays in Europe and for whom I had written and appeared in three television commercials the previous year, asked if I would write and appear in three more, to be broadcast at Christmas. I agreed but asked that my own production company should make them. (I did not say at the time that the company had not yet been formed.)

The managing director of Blue Cars was a delightful man called Ken

Fox, uncle of the actors Edward and James Fox, and when I went to see him to discuss the format of the three commercials I discovered that he also wanted a documentary and a 15-minute film to fill the 'advertising magazine' slot that existed then on commercial television. I had three separate ideas for the commercials – two in fairly conventional settings and one off-the-wall. Instead of producing storyboards, I decided to perform them in front of Ken. When I had completed all three, I waited for his reaction. I was surprised. 'Well, for me there's only one there. That idea with the funny voices. Let's do all three commercials like that,' he said. We were going to be breaking new ground. Until then, comedy had not been used in commercials.

Ken was straightforward when we discussed the money: 'The entire budget available is £3,800.' While this was worth considerably more in 1960 than it is today, it was still a small amount from which to make three commercials, an advertising magazine programme and a travel film. I already had an income from *The Arthur Haynes Show*, and, as I wanted a contract to get my production company off the ground, I accepted. I then had to decide whose production facilities to use. Gerry Anderson was the obvious choice.

I went to Gerry and said, 'I've got a commission to make three commercials and an advertising film. I have no studio facilities, and I'd love to work with you again.'

He asked, 'What's the money?' I told him the total figure. 'I'll tell you what, Nicholas,' he said. 'I'll split it with you. I'll take half, you can use my studio, and we'll make the commercials.' It was a pittance for the service he provided, but at the time Granada had just said they were not going to renew *Four Feather Falls* and he was in limbo while he was negotiating with ATV to produce *Supercar*. He needed cash flow to help keep AP Films afloat during this fallow period. Gerry did a wonderful job directing the three one-minute commercials, and while we were filming he clinched the contract for *Supercar*, which was fantastic news.

For two of the commercials, I devised dramatic scenes involving characters who looked and sounded as though they were appearing in foreign films: French in one, German in the other. The dialogue was unintelligible yet authentic-sounding nonsense. This was something I had previously developed for one of my most successful cabaret routines. Denise made one of her rare appearances in front of the camera, playing the female character in each commercial. Being a voice expert, she was able to speak the gibberish with total conviction, which was just as well, as I could not afford to employ an actress outside the family. The scenes depicted in the commercials were accompanied by English subtitles that purported to be a translation of the 'dialogue', extolling the benefits of Blue Cars holidays.

The third commercial was set on Mars, with two Martians looking through a telescope, fascinated by a sudden flurry of activity on Earth. They discuss what they see and discover that the interest is all to do with something called Blue Cars holidays. Again, subtitles were used to convey this. When Ken Fox viewed the final versions, he liked them immensely.

I filmed the documentary abroad with the help of Gerry's cameraman, and as I did not know much about film-making it was a steep learning curve. We ended up having to make two trips, which ate into what little finance I had. Finally, we had to produce the film for the advertising magazine.

The broadcaster, Associated-Rediffusion, produced a 15-minute show that was known as an 'advertising magazine'. Companies could buy time in order to promote their products. They could purchase thirty seconds, one minute or five minutes. It was far cheaper than producing one's own commercials. The show was called *Jim's Inn* and featured a pub in which Jimmy Hanley was the landlord. Various people would come in and start talking to Jimmy about products in a conversational way. For instance, someone might approach the bar undecided as to what to drink, and Jimmy would say, 'I've got this new beer here. Do you want to try it? It only costs X,' and he would clearly show the label of the beer. This was all sanctioned by the Independent Television Authority, the regulators for commercial television.

For our piece, Blue Cars asked if they could buy the whole fifteen-minute slot and produce a one-off show. There was nothing in the ITA charter to indicate this was not permissible. I persuaded Arthur Haynes to appear in the film in return for a holiday. The 'plot' was that I am at home showing some friends my holiday cine films when the camera breaks down. Suddenly a fellow – Arthur Haynes – appears from the back, and I ask, 'Who are you?'

'Oh, I'm your plumber, mate. I broke off from fixing your pipes, and I've been watching your little films there. I thought they were lovely. But, you know, if I was to go abroad, I would . . .' and off he goes describing the wonders of Blue Cars holidays. Time and money were tight, but because Arthur and I were so used to working together we managed to do the whole 15-minute filming in one take.

This monopolisation of the advertising magazine was not what the ITA had envisaged. It might not have been against the letter of the charter, but they felt it was against the spirit, not least because Rediffusion owned Blue Cars. The ITA decided to reassess the concept and eventually cancelled it. In many respects, I am the man who killed the advertising magazine.

Our three commercials, transmitted over Christmas 1960 and into January 1961, made a big impact with their humour, and I decided to enter them into the Television Mail Commercials Awards, which were being presented for the first time that year. I did not think we had much chance of taking away a prize but hoped we might warrant a mention in one of the categories.

I was not intending to go to the ceremony, but as the day approached one of the directors of Television Mail – Derrick Baker, who later became a good friend – rang up and asked if I was planning to attend the banquet, which was being held at the Hyde Park Hotel in London. 'No, I don't think so, Derrick. I don't think I'll bother. It isn't really my world,' I said.

He replied, 'Well, I think you should. I think you'll enjoy it.' Derrick could not say anything else, but by the tone of his voice I thought that perhaps we had won something. I telephoned Gerry, and we decided we should be there. Denise, Ken Fox and his wife joined us.

We won two awards in the consumer category, one for the French version, which was my favourite, and the other for the Martian commercial. The announcements were well received even though we were regarded as interlopers, having not used an agency. That did not make us popular in a room full of advertising people on their gala night, celebrating the work of their profession. Then it came to the Grand Prix Award for the best overall commercial. The host drew out the tension for a long time. He started from the tenth best commercial and worked his way up. As the winners of each category were slowly being ticked off, I kept thinking, 'Well, what's left?' The third placed commercial was announced, and I thought, 'Oh, yes, that deserved to be there. I thought that might have won actually.' Then number two: 'I forgot about that one. I'm surprised that didn't win. What on earth has won the top prize? We've seen them all.'

The host continued, 'And now we come to the Grand Prix Award. This, I have to tell you right away, was a unanimous decision. In fact, the judges were asked to reconsider one final time to make sure they were perfectly happy with the decision. And they were. It was unanimous . . .'

I began to think, 'He's going on a bit,' when suddenly he said, 'And the winner is . . . the Blue Cars Martians.' I could not believe it. Gerry's jaw dropped open. Denise was mortified, because she worked with a lot of the people there doing voice-overs. She just slid under the table. I did not know which way to look. Only Ken Fox and his wife were applauding madly. Gerry and I sat rooted to our chairs, too embarrassed to move, until the host announced, 'Would the winners please come and join me to be presented with the award.' We walked up to the faintest of hand claps.

We were pariahs when we retook our seats. Only one person approached us for the rest of the evening, a lovely Canadian fellow whom Denise had worked with on various commercials. He had enjoyed a bit to drink and swayed as he said to Denise, 'You naughty, naughty girl. We spend a lifetime in the industry, and you come along and steal the big prize from under our nose. You are naughty.' This was his way of paying a nice compliment while letting us know it was not a popular result.

I later found out that Television Mail had not wanted us to win, which was why they had asked the judges to reconsider. The awards were run by a group of very fair-minded young men, and when the judges confirmed their decision they went with it. Not that winning the award did us any good, beyond the prestige. Neither Gerry nor I were ever commissioned to produce another commercial again. The industry did not forgive us.

The Martians may have put paid to further commercials for my production company, but I did continue to produce and direct other features and comedies, many of which were made commercially possible through the system of the Eady Levy. I made no real profit from these activities, but I found the work extremely satisfying. The levy, named after Sir Wilfred Eady, was basically a tax imposed on box-office takings, the money from which was used to support young or independent British film-makers to produce shorts that might not otherwise find a distributor. It was an excellent idea that encouraged creative thinking. The exhibitors were paid to show the films, and some of the money also went to the producers. The levy was abolished in 1985. At that time, Margaret Thatcher was instituting her policy of market forces, and as the levy was a subsidy, and therefore clashed with the concept of commercial independence, it was cancelled. It was a sad loss that has not helped our industry.

I produced and directed two films for the Lord's Taverners that benefited from the Eady Levy and which were distributed by the Rank Organisation. *Mad Dogs and Cricketers* was made in 1976 and followed the Taverners' cricket tour of Corfu, and a couple of years later I made *A Fair Way to Play*, chronicling the Taverners on a golf trip which I organised to Tobago. When I went to Rank with the idea for the second film, Fred Turner, the head of the company, paid me a lovely compliment.

I had called him up and said, 'I've got an idea for another film, Fred.'

He said, 'Good, come in and see me, and we will talk about it.' This I did, and he commissioned it on the spot. I was delighted but a little puzzled that it could all happen so smoothly. Rank did not put money in the film, but with their promise of distribution I could approach potential backers.

I said to Fred, 'You are very trusting. I put an idea to you, and based only on that you commission the film.'

He replied, 'The bottom line is that I know you, Nicholas. You are a conscientious so-and-so, and I know that if I like the idea, and you like the idea, you will make a success of it. I back talent.' This is far more of an American attitude than a British one, and I am afraid things do not work like that any more. It is incredibly difficult to have anything commissioned these days. There seems to be an endless stream of faceless bureaucrats who have to be convinced, and no one seems to want to make any decisions.

The Lord's Taverners was one of the first charities with which I became involved, and I continue to remain so. I was on the Council for many years, and in 1998 I was honoured to become President. The Taverners was set up in the '50s by a group of actors who, as cricket enthusiasts, wanted to put something back into the game that gave them so much pleasure. The money the Taverners raise goes to help underprivileged and disadvantaged children, to 'give them a sporting chance', to quote our slogan. I first turned out to play cricket for them in 1956, and it has never ceased to excite me, walking out to field in a team containing some of the great cricketers, now retired, whom I have admired for a long time. We now arrange many more activities and events besides cricket matches, and have branches throughout the country, as well as the Lady Taverners and the Young Lord's Taverners.

In 1975, I discovered that they played cricket in Corfu, a relic of the period when the island was under British rule, and decided to take a team of celebrities and cricketers there to promote the Taverners and film the whole event, including the arrival and reception. All the stars gave their services free, and I had a magnificent cast, which included John Cleese, Willie Rushton, John Alderton, Brian Rix, Ed Stewart, Bill Simpson, Roy Kinnear and Peter Gordeno, as well as the professional cricketers Ken Barrington, John Price and Jack Robertson. The feat of organisation was only possible because of help in the planning from a good friend, Brian Langford, who was then working in the travel business. The budget went on the film crew, led by a superb freelance cameraman, Ernest Vincze. In fact, I ran out of money and had to use some of my own capital. I was also helped by a donation of £2,000 from David Evans, a generous member of the Taverners' Council.

The Corfiots treated us royally. There was only one slight misunderstanding: they thought they were welcoming and playing against a top MCC team sent out from Lord's, the home of cricket. I had given all the non-cricketers fictitious teams for which they were supposed to have played, and these were printed in the programme for the match. Ken Barrington was correctly down as having played for England and Surrey, John Price and Jack Robertson for England and Middlesex. Alongside John Cleese I had put 'Python Irregulars' and 'The Towering Faulties'. Brian Rix turned out for the 'Whitehall Farcers', Willie Rushton for the 'Tele-Eccentrics' and I represented 'The Old Centurians' and 'The Ancient Order of Straight Men'. Every player had two teams against his name, and the local Corfu paper, in promoting the match, mentioned all of them as if they were clubs almost as famous as the MCC itself.

The day of the match arrived. All cars were cleared from the rock-hard boundary area, and a tannoy system was installed. During the planning stages, I had asked if it might be possible to have the local band playing at some point. I assumed they would perform during the tea break. Since the mayor of Corfu, who was looking after all the arrangements, was so fired by my enthusiasm, and since he thought I was bringing an England team with me, he had organised a complete parade to open the proceedings. We had not only the local band, colourfully dressed in their uniforms, but also the Boy Scouts and Girl Guides, followed by a contingent from every cricket team in the Corfu league, all in pristine whites. There were civic dignitaries present from Corfu and Athens, speeches and presentations and then the national anthems of both countries. It was a delightful and moving occasion, and an original way to begin a cricket match.

I had asked Ken Barrington to captain our side, which he did with great style and authority. He also understood our charity cricket. By tradition we go through the formality of tossing a coin, but, irrespective of which side wins, it is arranged that the Lord's Taverners bowl first so that all the celebrities can be seen on the field from the beginning. More important, this means we can stage-manage the game so that as many runs as possible are made in the allotted time, thereby making the match as entertaining as we can for the spectators. If, for instance, the opposition is weak and begin to lose wickets, our professionals are taken off and the less able bowlers amongst the celebrities come on. The opposition is asked to do the same if the situation is reversed.

This was explained to the captain of the Corfu side, Yannis Arvanitakis, who was bemused, especially by the request for his team to bat first regardless of who won the toss. We tried to explain that this was how our charity matches were played. 'I do not understand,' he responded. 'What has charity to do with cricket?' I realised the significance of this remark when his team later took the field and his players threw themselves about on the hard ground with an abandon that was in complete contrast to the relaxed attitude of the Lord's Taverners.

The game was extraordinarily close. With only two balls to go, we needed five runs to win. Ken Barrington was batting and he hit the penultimate ball magnificently for four. The crowd and the teams felt the tension as the last ball was bowled. Ken steered it somewhere between mid-wicket and mid-on, and he and John Price ran two for good measure. They came off the field exhausted and elated. The Taverners and the spectators swarmed onto the pitch, and as the batting heroes walked off – John Price had scored a century – the Corfu team applauded. They had not won, but they had played well and everyone felt they had witnessed one of the most exciting games ever to take place on the little ground in front of Corfu's famous Esplanade.

Cricket is my great sporting love, and it was instrumental in bringing my wife, Ann, and I together. I had been asked to host a benefit cricket quiz for Norman Gifford, a left-arm spin bowler who played for Worcestershire and England. The event was taking place at the Duke of Westminster's stately home Grosvenor Hall. The team captains were Bob Willis, ex-England captain, and the Duke himself. Annie, who lived in Worcester, was a keen follower of Worcestershire Cricket Club, and as she was friendly with a lot of people there she came along with a large party of them to support Norman and help raise money. The quiz was a big success and tremendous fun. I remember Norman got so drunk he fell off his seat at one point. When it was over, a number of us, including Annie, went for a nightcap at the Grosvenor Hotel in Chester, where I and others were spending the night. I was on my own at that stage, as my marriage to Denise was breaking up, and although it was perfectly amicable we were leading separate lives.

According to Annie, she saw me at the bar and said to one of her friends, 'He looks rather lonely. I think I'll go and chat him up.' Which is exactly what she did. I found her very attractive and warmed instantly to her personality. I took her telephone number, but as Denise and I had not yet formally separated it was at least three months before I called. Annie was very surprised to hear from me. I told her I was coming to Worcester for a show and asked whether it would it be possible to meet. She agreed, we had a lovely lunch at the Gifford Hotel and as we said our goodbyes we exchanged a kiss in the car park. With my marriage over, Annie and I began to see each other frequently, and after a time we moved in together, to a little cottage I had bought in the Cotswolds. Annie found a job in Cheltenham, and our relationship prospered. A few years later, Annie told me that she would like to get married. I said that I believed we were together because we loved each other, which was all that mattered, and as we had both been married before, and had children of the same age, I did not see the need to formalise our love. She persisted and pointed out, quite fairly, that when we went to functions together it was embarrassing for her to be introduced as my girlfriend or partner or even just friend. 'It would be so much nicer to be your wife,' she said. I saw her point of view, and, of course, she was absolutely right and we agreed to get married.

I did not want this to be an impersonal ceremony such as you have in a registry office. I then discovered that it was possible to marry in the Caribbean, and I decided to take Annie to my favourite island, Tobago. Through a travel agent, Warren Rumsey, the son of the cricketer Fred Rumsey, we booked the holiday. I was growing excited at the prospect of going back to Tobago and kept telling Annie how lovely it was. Warren then phoned with some bad news: 'By law you can get married on any Caribbean island, except Tobago.'

When I told Annie she just laughed and accused me of fixing things:

'It was deliberate, wasn't it? You will go to any lengths to get out of this wedding!'

I told her not to worry and said, 'Warren has been wonderful. He has rearranged our itinerary. We are still going to Tobago, and then after five days we take an internal flight to Barbados, where he has fixed a wedding package at the Colony Club. They are experienced in these things, and it will all work well.' Ours was to be one of the first celebrity marriages on a Caribbean island, and as a consequence *Hello!* magazine decided to cover the event. In our agreement, they stipulated that there were to be no photographs other than those taken by their official photographer and we were not to speak to any other press about the wedding. As the only people who knew we were getting married were our immediate family, who would keep the secret, this was not going to be a problem. Until we landed in Barbados.

On arrival, we discovered a theatre festival taking place, organised by my friend Christopher Biggins, for which half of the actors in Equity seemed to be in attendance, together with journalists from just about every British newspaper. Our plans of secrecy were well and truly scuppered. Fortunately, John Rendall, the social columnist at *Hello!*, was on the island, and he called the magazine and explained the situation. 'Right, it is all fixed,' he told Annie and me. 'They don't mind you talking to the newspapers, but absolutely no photographs.' This was a relief, as it would have proved almost impossible not to explain to the journalists why we were there.

Our original plan had been for a quiet, private ceremony, just the two of us, with witnesses arranged by the Colony Club. Christopher Biggins was having none of it. Many of our friends were at the festival, and we ended up having a large wedding party, which was tremendous fun and added to a very happy day. Christopher acted as my best man and Lesley Joseph as Annie's maid of honour and, having ended up with a full-blown celebration, we were only sorry that our families were not with us.

The Colony Club arranged everything wonderfully well, including the vicar. When I asked him whether he agreed to marry everyone who applied, he explained that he insisted on meeting the couples beforehand

and if he felt they were being frivolous or were not committed he refused. It also turned out that he was a big fan of *Just a Minute*, which he listened to on the World Service. I was delighted to send him a copy of the *Just a Classic Minute* CD by way of thanks when we got home. The Colony also arranged the paperwork. We were required to present the necessary documents at the Ministry of the Interior in order for them to be stamped. We did as instructed, and when we entered the office of the relevant official he had music playing in the background: Tom Jones singing 'Delilah'. As we put our hands on the Bible and swore that we were telling the truth, the whole truth and nothing but the truth, Tom was belting out his classic about a lover's betrayal and murder. It was one of the most incongruous situations I have ever experienced.

It was 1965 when my involvement with *The Arthur Haynes Show* ended, and in the same year my dear friend Peter Jones, who was a lovely man and a huge talent, returned from Australia, where he had been touring in the play *Boeing-Boeing*. Peter was a great comedian who did not gain the recognition he deserved. We worked together a great deal, not least on *Just a Minute*, where his witty interjections and sometimes caustic remarks frequently produced the biggest laughs on the show.

Peter had returned to star with me in a comedy-thriller series on BBC television called *Night Train to Surbiton*, in which two unsuspecting businessmen become innocently involved, while travelling on their commuter train, with murder, spies and all kinds of skulduggery. The series was written by John Chapman, and the pilot show had been directed by David Croft. Unfortunately, he was not available to direct the series, which I am sure he would have turned into a successful spoof spy story. The director who was put in charge was Bryan Sears, who appeared to have no sense of comedy and certainly no feel for this particular storyline. He seemed more concerned that the actors always arrived at rehearsal on time and knew their lines rather than working with us to develop the comedy inherent in John Chapman's scripts.

Peter had wisely given up trying to work with Bryan and make the show funnier. At one point he said to me, 'Stop struggling to make it funny, Nicholas. He's talking a different language, and in this medium producers can damage you professionally. Keep your nose clean, and just try to survive.' I wish I had listened to him.

In one scene, I was standing behind a door with a gun in my hand, ready to make my entrance. There was a camera on my side of the set, and as my character had no experience with firearms I was performing some comedy business with the gun, believing I was being filmed. This was the way we worked on *The Arthur Haynes Show*. Suddenly, over the studio tannoy, Bryan's voice was heard: 'Nicholas, this is your entrance. Where are you?'

I opened the door, walked on and said, 'Bryan, I was doing some business with the gun before my entrance.' There was silence, so I continued, 'I thought you were shooting on camera 2, but if you have already cut to camera 3 on this side of the door I'll drop the business and make my entrance.'

There was a further silence, which seemed ominously long. Then the voice came back over the tannoy, 'You get on with the lovely acting, and we'll make the pretty pictures.' From then on I took Peter's advice. I ceased trying to be inventive and just hoped I would survive to be asked to work for BBC Television again.

In fact, it was eight years before I returned to comedy at the BBC, and even then it was because Peter put in a request for me. He had written a play for the *Comedy Playhouse* series called *The Rescue*, which featured me as a successful businessman who rescues someone from committing suicide and takes him back to his house only to discover that he is an ex-employee. This character, played by Peter, turns the businessman's life upside down. I was playing the straight man to Peter's character, and the whole idea had great possibilities. The show was successful in the *Comedy Playhouse* slot but was never taken up for a full series, in spite of the excellent direction of John Howard-Davies. Once again, I think the powers that be had not recognised the great comic potential Peter displayed in all his work, which was often underplayed. While he had many major successes and would have been the last person to say he was unhappy, he was the type of comedian that for some reason the British do not turn into big stars.

Two years after *Night Train to Surbiton*, I landed a marvellous job in an American television comedy series, *The Ugliest Girl in Town*, being made by Screen Gems. The company, based in Hollywood, had produced a number of successful situation comedies and hoped that, on the strength of the pilot, this new one would be taken up by the NBC Network. They had decided to set the whole thing in Britain, as the technical costs were much cheaper over here. The story was rather strange. A young man, for a dare, dresses up as a girl and enters a beauty contest. He/she wins and is adopted as the modelling world's face of the '70s. I was cast as the head of the British public-relations agency that promotes the 'girl'. A young Canadian actor, Peter Kastner, was cast in the lead, and Patricia Brake was his English girlfriend.

The script for the pilot was well constructed, and, as always with American productions, a small fortune was invested in the show in the knowledge that, if it was successful, a lucrative network series could follow. We spent a whole two weeks filming at Shepperton, but the final result, while impressive, stretched credibility too far, because we were inhibited by rules laid down, presumably by NBC, to make the story acceptable to American audiences. The young man must never act effeminate, must appear in male attire for at least one-third of the time and must never kiss the girl when dressed in female clothes. The result was that Peter Kastner always looked what he was: a young man in drag and not a beautiful girl who fooled the press and public and fascinated the public-relations agent. If a British company had produced the show, they would have found someone as glamorous as a young Danny La Rue to play the part. You could have believed that he really was someone of the opposite sex whom everyone fancied. As it was, I was amazed when I was told, some months after the pilot, that a series had been commissioned and we were to start filming later in the year.

Screen Gems signed me to a five-year contract, which contained an option after thirteen shows, another after twenty-six and then one every year. I was paid what was then a good salary, £400 a show, with increases if the options were taken up. When the tabloid press reported the story of the contract, the headline read, 'Nicholas Parsons signs £50,000 film deal'. What they did not add was that to earn the full amount all the options would have to be taken up, and I would have to work on the series for five years. The headline made impressive reading, but it was difficult to live up to, as people wondered why I had not bought a more expensive car or started to throw lavish parties.

It was great fun working on *The Ugliest Girl in Town*. The filming, however, was not without its problems. The producer of the series, Gerry Davis, and his team had been told little about how the film industry was structured in Britain and were obviously ill-informed about crewing. They approached the technicians' union, the ACTT, asking them to recommend people. In Britain, however, the union exists only to look after the interests of their members and not to find them work. I know from taking on crews myself that you engage technicians who have worked with you before or invite a company that you are familiar with to crew the film in consultation with you. On this occasion, however, because they had been asked the union did help find technicians but their priority was not to select the most talented people for the job but merely to obtain work for any member who was unemployed at the time. The result was that the cameraman who was booked for the first episode was unable even to get the scene in the centre of the frame. He was dismissed, and presumably arguments with the union followed.

In America, because so much money is involved in a project, the producers will sign a binding agreement with the union for the length of the production or for an agreed period. This means that the film-makers can get on with the costly work without fear of industrial action while the agreement lasts. In Britain, where the technicians earn less, if problems arise they are negotiable on an ad hoc basis. The Americans were not used to this and became irritated when a request they considered normal was treated by some technicians as a matter for discussion. Screen Gems swore they would never make another series in Britain. Word would have got back to other production companies in Hollywood, and a great potential source of work for film technicians in this country dried up, which is a pity because the best British crews are some of the most talented in the world. As a member of the ACTT, I saw both sides of the argument and tried to explain the situation to Gerry, but it was too late.

It is difficult to judge whether these problems contributed to the early demise of the series. Perhaps the American public did not take to the basic idea, in spite of the excellent reaction to the original pilot. The series ran for 13 episodes. Three weeks before filming finished, we heard that no options were being taken up, which resulted in every possible economy being introduced. The writer, Gerry Kaufman, was told to keep his storylines, as far as possible, to the four main characters under contract for the series and not to introduce unnecessary scenes or expensive sets. This entailed some concise writing as well as much more dialogue for the principal characters to learn.

There is always a sad feeling on the set of a show that is coming to a premature end. It is better not to know until after the filming has finished. It becomes harder to give your best, but if you let your performance slip you could be blamed for contributing to the demise of the production. Also, there is a reluctance on the part of potential employers to rush and offer you more work. They have a psychological resistance to anyone connected with a 'failure' and may also think you contributed to it. This is particularly so in America, where the stakes and rewards are so much higher.

Young Peter Kastner was terribly distressed that the series was to end. He had already appeared in a couple of films, but this could have established him as a big name in Hollywood. He was a talented actor with a fine sense of comedy, but he realised that the failure of a show in which he starred might knock him so far back that it could prove impossible to recover. We lost touch after the series. He returned to America and, I understand, appeared in some minor supporting roles but led a troubled life and sadly died in 2008 at the age of 65.

Throughout the period I was presenting *Sale of the Century*, from 1971 to 1984, I did little other television work. Instead I concentrated on the theatre, appearing in a number of successful plays and pantomimes and making guest appearances in various shows. I was also busy on other activities, such as my production company and developing my one-man shows. When *Sale of the Century* eventually came to an end, the impression that the press, and to some extent the industry, had of me – that I was a quiz-show host and nothing else –

meant that this was a slow period in my television career. It was not until 1987 that things took an upward swing in this area. I was about to attract a cult following and a new, younger audience.

In the late summer of that year, I received a phone call from Dave Morley, a producer who had worked in radio and seen me presenting *Just a Minute* in the studio recordings. He was now at London Weekend Television, working as a producer of a new youth-orientated show to be called *Night Network*. Jill Sinclair was the executive producer. Transmitted in the small hours following Friday and Saturday night, between 1 a.m. and 4 a.m., and in the early hours following Sunday night, between 1 a.m. and 3 a.m., it was to include pop videos, interviews with singers and groups and revivals of the Gerry Anderson puppet series *Captain Scarlet*. There was also to be a quiz show, *The All New Alphabet Game*, which they needed someone with experience to front, since there was neither time nor money for retakes. The overall budget was very modest, all the other presenters were young and comparatively unknown, and the show itself was recorded in the smallest studio imaginable.

Dave and I met in the elegant tea room at the Waldorf Hotel, a strange setting for a discussion about an innovative, up-to-the-minute, pop-orientated television show. We immediately hit it off. His opening remark was, 'Nicholas, how would you like to do a television show for radio money?'

I said, 'I'd rather do a radio show for television money.' He then told me what the fee actually was, and I realised that he was not joking. He explained that it was an insult fee but that their budget was genuinely low and they had a large cast and eight hours of screen time to fill at a time of day when there was little revenue coming in from advertising. He outlined the format of the quiz, and we discussed the way in which we could make it different and zany. I saw the potential in the idea, and we decided to turn the whole thing into a pastiche of a conventional quiz, with two teams of celebrity guests. The money became secondary. If it worked, it would be fun. It is only in retrospect that I see it as the unexpected beginning of my climb back.

Night Network began in early September 1987 with a great deal of pre-publicity. I was photographed in my nightshirt and also with a number of young presenters, who included Craig Charles and Emma Freud, and much was made of the weekly item in which Emma was to interview someone while in bed with them. Rowland Rivron did an interview each week from his nuclear bunker, which, when you have a guest with as brilliant a sense of the absurd as Mel Brooks, produced an interview that was a classic of its kind.

The All New Alphabet Game was promoted in the advance publicity as a 'new, hip spoof quiz'. Dave Morley worked extraordinarily hard on it, and there is no doubt it required more of his time and energy than a lot of the remaining eight hours of programming. Once the show was running and we had discovered the kind of off-beat questions that were fun and made the quiz work best, he would telephone two days before the recording and sometimes spend up to three hours with me going through all the questions that the creators of the game had devised, to see where we could improve them or even substitute better ones. It was not our responsibility, but we were both anxious to make each recording as strong as possible. It paid off: the quiz developed a strong following, and we heard that viewers who went to bed at a civilised hour were taping it to watch at a more convenient time.

Dave Hillier was the director responsible for the look of *Night Network*. Such were the restrictions of the budget that he had only one full day to record six hours of programmes for the Friday and Saturday transmissions (Sunday was mostly film). With a schedule that did not permit retakes or even breaks in the recording, I was under instructions that if there were mistakes of any kind – technical, verbal or otherwise – I had to ad-lib my way out and keep going. That was not particularly difficult for someone reared in live television, but I did not expect to have to contend with practical jokes from some of the production team. I would introduce the quiz as if we were in a huge studio, playing to a vast and excited audience, at which point the director cued in a sound tape of the audience reaction. Sometimes it was a recording from a packed Albert Hall, sometimes a few desultory claps, sometimes inane laughter and sometimes normal applause cut off abruptly. On one occasion, it was silence. I had to react to them all. One of the most difficult was when, after I had made my usual reference to our vast and excited audience, everyone heard a lot of dogs barking and howling. I responded with the only remark possible: 'For those who are confused, this programme is being performed before an audience at Crufts Dog Show.'

We had some marvellous guests throughout the show. Alice Cooper appeared on the first programme, produced a snake and handed it to me. I hate snakes and had never touched one before. I asked him to put it away or, better still, to eat it. He pretended to do so, which looked disgusting, then palmed it away. Katie Boyle brought her small dog with her. I think it became affected by the heat in the studio, because after the recording it attacked me. Perhaps it blamed me for the fact that Katie did not win.

The All New Alphabet Game remained on air until Christmas, and then it was decided to 'rest it'. The programme never returned, probably because it was realised that *Night Network* was now established and no longer required an item that demanded such a disproportionate amount of precious planning and recording time. Also, in spite of the success that Jill Sinclair and Dave Morley had achieved, LWT were not increasing their budget, so it was becoming embarrassing to ask those taking part in the quiz to work for such small amounts.

My popularity with the younger generation was probably due to the fact that I had become associated with their culture and also because I appeared to be sending up the image I had on *Sale of the Century*. I was, in fact, just enjoying myself. My exposure in the world of cult television was further enhanced a couple of months after the final broadcast of *The All New Alphabet Game* when *Mr Jolly Lives Next Door* was broadcast on Channel 4. It was part of *The Comic Strip Presents . . .* and proved to be very popular indeed, subsequently being released for cinema distribution. In it, I played myself and had the mickey taken out of me unmercifully by Adrian Edmondson and Rik Mayall.

The production company had sent me the script to read, and I thought it was outrageous and extremely funny. When they called to discuss it, I had the impression they were surprised by my positive reaction. It seems they had sent it out at the same time to one or two other well-known faces who had not liked the idea of being sent up.

From the work I had done with Arthur Haynes and others, I saw a way to play the part as a straight man to these two anarchic comedians, and in so doing I thought it would work well. I was happy to accept.

When filming began, I asked the director, Stephen Frears, whether he wanted me to act strictly as myself or as a pastiche of myself. 'Do it the way you think it will work best,' was his reply. I decided that as the whole show was over the top I should play up to my perceived image. Stephen directed the film superbly, and we had a highly talented cast. Peter Cook played Mr Jolly, a hit man who cut up bodies while singing along to jolly tunes. He had an office next door to two alcoholic incompetents, Rik and Ade, who ran a disastrous agency called Dreamytime Escorts. Dawn French and Jennifer Saunders, who were then just becoming well known for their comedy work, had small supporting roles. Rowland Rivron was some sinister character, and Peter Richardson played the deranged Mr Lovebucket, who, following a catalogue of misunderstandings, pays Rik and Ade £3,000 to 'take out' Nicholas Parsons. They naturally misinterpret the murderous implications of the request and blow the money on drink. On their way to Broadcasting House, they knock off the road a harmless couple who have won a prize of 'an evening with Nicholas Parsons'. Armed with this couple's ticket, Rick and Ade arrive to meet me. I think they are surprising winners but feel obliged to fulfil the conditions of the competition and take them to the Dorchester. From then on, chaos and anarchy reign as these two horrendous characters latch on to me and slowly begin to wreck my life, my home and my sanity. The Dorchester refused permission for filming to take place on their premises, so the production company hired the banqueting suite at the Café Royal, the management of which did not seem to mind that in the film they were referred to as the Dorchester.

Rik and Ade were easy to work with and, like a lot of comedians, took their comedy very seriously. Though the humour was wild, everything was meticulously worked out and, where possible, thoroughly rehearsed. Some of their comedy is so broad, however, that only certain elements can be planned technically, in the hope that the rest will fall into place in front of the camera.

At the end of the scene in the Dorchester where Rik and Ade have embarrassed me hugely with their vulgar behaviour, they decide we must all go back to my place. They get up from the table, turning it over in the process and scattering the contents in all directions, and make an outrageously drunken exit. The first take went well. Then Stephen Frears said he needed a shot from a different angle. The people sitting at the tables were all extras, members of Equity, and middle-aged and elderly – the sort of clientele the Dorchester would attract. One or two were looking a little apprehensive. They had never worked with anyone quite like Rik and Ade before. As one elderly gentleman said, 'It was never like this when I acted with dear Leslie Howard. I just don't know what they are going to do next.'

'Exactly,' said his companion. 'I never thought I'd be in a film where someone actually farted to get a laugh.'

'And then set fire to it,' added his friend.

The next take of the two rogues staggering between tables and dragging me towards the exit was fine. One more table was upturned as we went, a lady had her hat knocked off and one or two were accidentally buffeted a little. Stephen decided to go for one more. Everything was put back in its place, but I noticed that a few of the extras were not sitting in the same seats, which strictly they should have been to keep continuity. I tactfully said to one woman close to me, 'Weren't you sitting on the other side of the table last time?'

'Yes,' she replied, 'but I am not going to get near those two lunatics again. I might lose more than my hat next time.'

'Look what's happened to mine,' said another. 'And it's my best one, which I keep for posh scenes.' We did the take, and the fear on the faces of some of the diners who were close to the two stars as they stumbled by was very real. It was not all acting.

For the scene in my home, the film company had hired a private house just outside London. Being paid to let a film company have full use of your house, and being able to mix with celebrities, sounds an easy and pleasant way to make some extra money. However, unless the people concerned are used to having a film crew move in with all their cameras, lights and cables, they can be in for quite a shock. When, in addition, the scenes to be filmed concern two mad characters who systematically drink their way through a man's alcohol supplies and slowly wreck his home, the effect on the actual owners of the property can be traumatic. On this occasion, the family and some friends had gathered in the house, presumably hoping for a happy day watching gentle filming and talking with the principal actors. It was chaos throughout the whole of the elegant ground floor, which had been commandeered by the film crew. The watching party retreated to the stairs, and more than once the wife winced and put her hand to her cheek as she heard a loud bang or crash from below. The film company might agree to pay for any repairs or breakages, but it is your personal possessions that are suffering. During filming, I saw one small coffee table crushed, a cabinet dented, wine spilled, a settee damaged and a mirror knocked off the wall.

The success of *Mr Jolly* was quite amazing. After the cinema release, it came out on video, and it even spawned *Mr Jolly* fan clubs. One such group wrote and asked if I would like to come along to an evening get-together at which they had a few drinks, watched the video through twice, then re-enacted the whole story, playing all the parts. This was followed by pizza and more beer, and then they sat through the video again. It sounded a rather bizarre way to spend an evening, but it was good to have such devoted followers. I declined the invitation, saying that I did not think I would be much use in the performance part, as they probably knew the words better than I did.

I thoroughly enjoyed playing a version of myself in *Mr Jolly*, but I was also keen to undertake different roles, which I knew I could perform. Call it creative satisfaction, but I love being able to switch from stand-up to improvised comedy to dramatic roles. I had the chance to do this in 1988, in perhaps the greatest cult television series of all time, *Doctor Who*.

It was a four-part episode called *The Curse of Fenric*, and I played the Rev. Wainwright, a serious, emotional vicar. The plot is not particularly easy to follow, but it has proved to be one of the most popular stories for *Doctor Who* fans. My character was terrified because of the danger posed by runes he had discovered in the crypt of his church. The

Doctor had arrived on the scene, the Russians were not far away and MI6 were just round the corner. All kinds of weird things were happening in the village, and the vicar knew that if the runes were translated then further catastrophes could arise and all the villagers would start turning into vampire-like creatures called Haemovores, which they eventually did, myself included.

The director of the series was a lovely man called Nick Mallett. I was delighted he had seen beyond my supposed image and cast me in the part. I was chatting to him one day and said, 'It's lovely to have this opportunity to play a dramatic role again, because I have been doing so much comedy and presenting. I imagine you must have realised I am basically an actor who has branched out and done other things.'

'No, actually,' he said. 'I didn't know that.'

'Then what prompted you to cast me?'

'I happened to bring my children to see the panto at Bromley, and you were in it.'

'Yes,' I said, 'but I was playing the dame in that pantomime.'

'I know. It was the empathy you showed when you were talking to the children at the end,' he explained. 'That was the quality I wanted for my vicar.' This illustrates what a creative director Nick was, to make the connection out of context. I wish there were more like him. Not just for me but for other actors as well.

The regulars, Sylvester McCoy who played the Doctor, and Sophie Aldred who played his assistant, Ace, were great fun to work with and were so conversant with the non sequiturs in the plot and all the time-travel references, so beloved of the show's fans, that they took them in their stride. It was sometimes very confusing to a newcomer, until I realised it was best not to try to unravel the mysteries of the storyline but to play each scene as sincerely as possible and let the director and producer put it all together.

The filming was done on location. My chief memories are of working in an army training camp in Crowborough, Sussex, where the final scenes were shot out of sequence. It was April and bitterly cold, with the snow that had been missing all winter now in evidence. It soon melted, and the place was a quagmire. The film crew and technicians were wrapped in overcoats and balaclavas. The poor vicar, the good Doctor and Ace were in thin summer clothes. I was blue with cold. At one point, my teeth were actually chattering during a take. They had to break the filming to thaw us out over a Primus stove in an army hut. The rain, snow and slushy ground gave considerable atmosphere to the scene, and when I was overcome by the Haemovores and trampled to death in the mud I did not have to fake anything. I was in genuine distress as I lay in the squelchy mire.

The shooting was more enjoyable a week or two later in the now warm spring sunshine at Hawkhurst, Kent, where a beautiful old church was transformed into my rectory. We had a mobile wardrobe van in which we changed, but no dressing-rooms, and as a result I was frequently moving about the village in costume. On one occasion, I was standing beside the lych gate to the church when a lady came up to me and said, 'Oh, vicar, I am so pleased to have caught you. Can I come and talk to you about a christening?' I replied that she could, but I doubted whether I could help. She looked at me for a moment and then recognition dawned. 'Oh, I am so sorry. You are not . . . I mean you are . . . Oh dear . . . I recognise you . . . You're Nicholas Parkinson . . . I mean . . . the century man . . . Oh, I do feel a fool.' I quickly reassured her she was not foolish and had flattered me by mistaking me for the genuine article.

The Curse of Fenric was broadcast in October and November 1989 and was the second last story before the show was mothballed for a number of years, returning in 2005 to great success. At the time, the press seemed to have their knives out for the series, and when people like myself and Ken Dodd appeared in it they branded us as gimmicks, which I felt was a very simplistic attitude.

When you have acquired a degree of recognition on British television, you find yourself invited to make guest appearances on various programmes. In 1978, I appeared in *The Morecambe and Wise Christmas Show*, where I met ex-prime minister Harold Wilson, who was also taking part. He was amiable and chatty to the extent that my wife, who had accompanied me to the recording, presumed we had met before. In 1979, I appeared with Anna Dawson, Shirley Anne Field, Roy

Hudd, Beryl Reid and Eddie Waring on Terry Wogan's *Blankety Blank*, which was enormous fun. These are not acting jobs, however. You are asked to appear purely because you are well known. It is the same reason I have been invited to a number of *An Audience With . . .* shows, including Freddie Starr, Bruce Forsyth, Ken Dodd, Alf Garnett, Shirley Bassey and Céline Dion. I have enjoyed them all. Being a good friend of Ken Dodd, I asked one of the audience questions on that programme, and on Céline Dion's show I was disappointed to notice that she was miming. Shirley Bassey certainly was not when she sang on her show. Shirley's was a memorable *An Audience With . . .*, as was Freddie Starr's, for a different reason.

Freddie is an exceptionally talented performer and a lovely man. There is also something slightly manic about him. He has the ability to suddenly go off the deep end and do something unfathomable. That may be the reason why he has not continued in the high-profile position he once had. Producers are nervous to employ him.

His *An Audience With . . .* was going incredibly well and Freddie was getting lots of laughs when suddenly he produced a bowl of maggots to illustrate a story he was telling about fishing. At that moment, I sensed something was about to happen. Freddie can just snap and suddenly indulge in utterly eccentric behaviour. The next thing we knew, Freddie was hurling the maggots out into the audience. It was a very odd thing to do and naturally caused a stir, as people were trying to get them out of their hair and off their laps. Poor Faith Brown, who was sitting near us, seemed to get the worst of it, with a large clump landing on her ample bosom. She was such a trouper and pretended to take it in good spirit, although I do not think she enjoyed the incident at all.

QUIZ OF THE WEEK

The television role with which I am probably most associated is as presenter of the quiz show *Sale of the Century* or, as John Benson, the unseen voice for most of the series, used to introduce it, 'And now, from Norwich, it's the quiz of the week.'

For fans of quiz shows, *Sale of the Century* is one of the best known. It was so commercially successful, with a tremendously high profile, that my role in it is remembered by many people to the exclusion of all the other creative, challenging and demanding work that I have done. Being part of that success is something I have always embraced, although there was a downside.

At the beginning of 1971, I was going through a 'quieter' period in my career when, out of the blue, I received a phone call from Peter Joy, senior producer at Anglia Television. Peter wanted to know whether I would be interested in fronting a quiz show that they were planning to pilot. My only previous experience of this type of work had been in the early '60s in a local show at Westward Television, which I had left because of the ITV strike. Keen to accept the challenge and do something different, I agreed to meet Peter for an initial discussion.

At Anglia's London office, Peter showed me a video of a programme called *Sale of the Century* that was already doing well on US television. I watched as a laid-back American compère asked some rather banal questions and three overly excited contestants, continually applauding themselves, won fabulous prizes for giving the correct answers. I told Peter that if Anglia wanted someone to perform in the style of the American host, I did not think I was right for the job. He assured me he was perfectly happy for me to front the show in my own way and thought I was the ideal person to make this American-style quiz acceptable to the British public.

Peter and I worked well together, and he was happy to consider any suggestions I had that might help the show. Two in particular were adopted. As an actor, I was aware that any show needs to be paced, so I suggested that the quiz should start quite gently, with some fairly simple questions to put the contestants at their ease, and then move to slightly more difficult ones before increasing the pace – and the excitement – in the final session with some brief, quick-fire questions that relied more on speed of recall than depth of knowledge.

I also proposed that the contestants be carefully auditioned beforehand, not just to make sure that they would not dry up in front of the cameras but also to be certain they could answer general-knowledge questions to a good standard, which would make the show more interesting.

Nowadays, the contestants on quiz shows tend to be picked on the basis of their personality. In our show, we wanted it to be a fair, hard-nosed quiz in which contestants won prizes on merit, so the breadth of knowledge of the people taking part was more important than what they looked like. When the show became successful, Bill Perry, who succeeded Peter Joy after he resigned from Anglia in 1974, travelled up and down the country auditioning anyone who had written asking to be in the show. On one occasion, he went up to Carlisle to run the auditions and a woman arrived, looking rather smart, and said in a plummy voice, 'I've come for my audition. Where is Nicholas Parsons?'

'Well, I am afraid he is not here,' Bill replied. 'I am doing the auditions. I'm the producer.'

'Oh, in that case I am not staying. I expected to meet Nicholas Parsons.' At least it was one person fewer for Bill to interview that day.

Initially, *Sale of the Century* was to be transmitted only in the Anglia Television region. What I did not know when I went to Anglia's headquarters in Norwich to make the pilot was that Thames Television had previously made a pilot with Wilfred Pickles as host. It had,

219

apparently, failed quite dismally. Had I known, I might not have been so keen to accept the engagement.

The musical director at Anglia was Peter Fenn, who was asked to play the electric organ, which, it was decided for economy reasons, would be the instrument used at different times in the show for link music and to punctuate various moments. Peter was also commissioned to write a signature tune, which he orchestrated and called 'Joyful Pete', as a gesture to Peter Joy. I am sure he never imagined it would come to have such a long run and that I would still be frequently greeted by people who remember it fondly.

Prior to the pilot, Peter had sent me a bundle of questions that had been supplied by the American creators of the game and asked me to choose the ones I preferred. I told him there were very few that I liked. It was important that they should be interesting enough to hold viewers' attention, and those we had been given were all extremely boring and American-orientated. I ended up writing most of the questions myself.

I thoroughly enjoyed composing quiz questions. I believe there is such a thing as a good question and a bad one. A good question should immediately involve the viewers, so they say to themselves, 'I know the answer to that one', or 'I should know the answer to that one', or 'I don't know the answer to that one, but I would like to.' A bad question just leaves viewers cold or does not fire their interest or imagination. For example, 'What is the number of the motorway that links Glasgow to Edinburgh?' Answer: 'The M8.' A bald fact, and to many it is specialised knowledge.

Anglia Television was not a large company, and the only studio they had was really too small for the complicated set that had been designed for the show plus all the goods that had to be displayed. A considerable amount of rehearsal time was taken up trying to solve the technical problems posed by the size of the studio, which meant we were never able to have a complete run-through. If ever a pilot programme seemed doomed to failure, this was it. The game's creator, Al Howard, who had flown in from America, was so convinced that it was going to be a disaster that he rang up Heathrow to see if he could fly home that night rather than watch his creation being destroyed before his eyes. There were, however, no flights available. Al told me later that they piloted the original show in America for three consecutive days in the studio with different audiences, following a week of rehearsals. We were trying to do it in one afternoon and evening, in a studio that was all but inadequate for the purpose.

Al, however, was unaware of the skill of British technicians and the ability and professionalism of Peter Joy. The pilot went surprisingly well, and, although I felt as if I was making it up as I went along, the audience obviously loved it.

The format was simple. There were three contestants who had to answer general-knowledge questions, which got progressively harder as their value increased. The questions in the first sequence, worth £1 each, were relatively simple in order for the contestants to relax and gain some confidence. They would naturally be nervous. Following this first sequence of questions, an 'Instant Sale' would be offered, in which the contestants could buy quality goods at a fraction of their retail value. Throughout the show there were three such Instant Sales, which added an interesting dimension to the game: tactics. The contestants had to make the decision whether to spend their money or save what they had in the hope of ending the game with the most cash in the bank and therefore going through to the big prizes on offer in the final 'Sale of the Century'. I remember there was one contestant who bought various prizes in the Instant Sales but was so good at the game that he also won enough money to go through to the big finale.

Following the first Instant Sale, the value of the questions increased to £3, and after the second it rose again, to £5. After the final Instant Sale, the format of the questions changed. They were still worth £5, but here the quick-fire questions were introduced. I think I was the first person to adopt this style of rapid, succinct questions. This built up the excitement and tension, but at the same time it offered ammunition to those who wished to criticise the quiz. Part of my job was to ask as many questions as I could in this section, in order to allow the contestants to win as much money as possible. One journalist described me as 'spitting out the questions'.

In the first couple of series, there was an additional element: the 'Open Sale'. This came between the first and second Instant Sales. We would offer all the contestants the opportunity to buy a variety of goods at knock-down prices, which were rather crudely displayed on the screen. For instance, a cuddly toy worth £12 was offered for £1 or a Teasmade worth £15 for £2. This was rather downmarket, a little too 'bargain basement', and I believe this was responsible for some of the flak the show received. It was soon dropped.

The quick-fire sequence built to a dramatic climax, and when the gong sounded to announce the end of the game I would say, 'And now, who has the most money and is going to go to the Sale of the Century? It is . . .' The actual length of time spent asking questions was an important element of the show, as I had to be sure to leave sufficient time at the end for the Sale of the Century. In addition, it was vital that we were consistent from show to show, in order to give every contestant the same opportunity to accumulate money. The total question time was always between nine and ten minutes.

After I announced the winner, I would say, 'Now will you please take the money you have won and come with me and spend it in the Sale of the Century.' The music would start, the curtains would be drawn back, and we would proceed together to view the goods on offer.

The Sale of the Century segment had to run for two minutes, no more. This was quite a challenge, so when I arrived in Norwich for each recording, around 2 p.m., I would walk through the sequence with the producer twice, memorising the details of all the products on offer together with their actual value. That was the extent of our rehearsal. There was no autocue or notes to prompt me when it came to the real event. In fact, at Anglia there was no autocue for any section of the programme. I often had to thank my days with Arthur Haynes and my time at Bromley Rep for training my memory.

In the final Sale of the Century, if the winner had banked sufficient money during the game they would be offered the opportunity to purchase the star prize – often a car – at a huge discount, around one-tenth of the actual value. They had options, however. There were a lot of valuable products on offer, and a contestant could decide to buy two or three smaller prizes rather than spend all his or her money on the big one. On one famous occasion when I showed the winner the various goods on offer, at each item she said, 'No, I don't want that', 'No, I don't like that one', or 'No, I don't need one of those.'

I was a bit nonplussed, as this hadn't happened before, and said, 'Well, I suppose in this instance you keep the £95 you have won and I hope you find something to spend it on.' She bought nothing, which I thought a rather strange decision. With the huge price differential, she would have been far better off taking something away and selling it later.

Throughout the show, the goods were displayed by various glamorous and attractive hostesses. They all did an excellent job – I never thought it was easy to stand there and show off an alarm clock or a lawnmower, for instance, and not look foolish. As the show grew in popularity, the hostesses were changed at frequent intervals – Anglia obviously realised they received excellent publicity in the papers each time the new hostesses were announced.

The show was an immediate success when it was launched in the autumn of 1971, and other independent companies soon began to take an interest. There was, luckily, a vacancy on the ITV network for a new quiz show. At that time, in an attempt to maintain the overall quality of Independent Television, the Independent Broadcasting Authority had ruled that there could be only two high-reward game shows on the network in any one week and only three in any one region. This all changed when television was deregulated and was subject to market forces. Now we have quizzes and games all the time, some with huge prizes.

London Weekend Television was the first major company to take *Sale*, and by early 1972 a quarter of the network was on board. By early 1973 it was fully networked and had become so popular that it ran for nearly a year without a break, which is exceptional for a quiz show. *Sale* first went to the top of the ratings in 1974, and over the coming years it reached number one again on a number of occasions and was regularly in the top ten. The viewing figures for the 22 December 1978 show reached an incredible 21.2 million, the highest-ever rating for an ITV game show. Thereafter, the programme planners moved the show to different days and times according to the strength of opposition from the BBC. Consequently, the programme was regularly in the ratings but did not have the same consistently high viewing figures that it had had when transmitted at the popular 7.30 p.m. slot on Friday.

When the show became fully networked, John Jacobs, then senior producer of drama at Anglia, joined us as executive producer. Peter Joy continued to direct, and it was a happy team. John went out of his way to see that we worked in as relaxed and harmonious a way as possible, given the demands of the show. They were worried, however, when they discovered that I was writing most of the questions, because it was against IBA rules. I felt it was part of my responsibility to see that we had good questions, and up until then Peter had thought they came from the original bundle he had given me. All this came to light only when they engaged someone from Norwich, John Erskine, to write the questions following our migration to the full network. In my professional naivety, I had been doing something for nothing because I enjoyed it, when I could, and should, have been paid. I asked my agent to become involved, and Anglia agreed I would work with John on the questions but could not receive a credit. They said it would not sit well with the IBA if the presenter of the show was also the question-setter. I accepted the situation, received some money for my work and continued to enjoy thoroughly this aspect of the show. I thought up nearly all the questions and left John Erskine to research them and eliminate possible errors or ambiguity.

Another IBA rule was that the questions should be kept in a sealed envelope and only opened by the host once the quiz had started. This was designed to eliminate any favouritism or the possibility of cheating and, while understandable, made it difficult to pace the shows. In addition, it was hard for me to deliver the questions with confidence when I was seeing them for the first time at the recording. It was also helpful to be able to discuss the questions with the producer and adjudicator beforehand to decide what range of answers I could accept if the contestants' responses were not entirely accurate.

Anglia negotiated with the IBA, who relented over the sealed envelopes. John Erskine and I made a good team, and over the years we must have devised over 30,000 questions – I used about a hundred per show. John was later replaced by David Self, a writer and broadcaster who had worked a great deal at Anglia, and it was decided that I should no longer be involved with the questions. That was a great disappointment. Once again, it seemed that in this country if you have a reputation for doing one thing it is difficult for people to accept that you can do anything else.

Peter Joy was sympathetic to performers and always saw that anyone who worked for him was well looked after, but he could be impatient and raise his voice at technicians who did not measure up to his high standards. This never bothered me; I knew it was just Peter doing his job. There is a difference between a director who does not know the job and who shouts or bullies to cover inadequacies and a director who knows exactly what to do and is professional but perhaps has a short fuse. I remember one of the studio crew once saying to me, 'Doesn't it worry you when Peter starts shouting?'

I replied, 'I get more worried when he is not shouting. Then I think there's really something wrong, or perhaps something wrong with Peter.' I could understand, however, how the crew felt, and it is not the best way to direct or to get the best out of your team. Eventually, the technicians made representations to the management, who tried to persuade Peter to change his ways. That was why he resigned. He was so upset. The show lost a great talent, and I missed him sorely.

Bill Perry took over and was a capable producer, but he lacked Peter's flair, imagination and experience. From the start, he let it be known he would be making certain changes, the most significant of which, as far as I was concerned, was that he wanted to cut out any talk and ad-libs to the contestants and concentrate on getting through as many questions as possible. He said he recognised my ability to deliver questions quickly and he wanted to exploit this to create more excitement. While I could see that this would be good for the show, I explained that he would be turning me into a kind of automaton. I had to be allowed the occasional comment. He came back with what I considered an impossible request, which illustrated to me his lack of humour and inadequacies as a producer. 'All right, but if you ad-lib it must be only one line, and if it's not funny don't say it.' What a straitjacket in which to work.

He also decided that, although the show was recorded, it was to be performed like a live show, with no stops or retakes. There were two breaks in the recording, at the halfway mark and before the final Sale of the Century, when any errors could be discussed and remedied if possible. I realised it was important to keep the show moving at all costs but now felt under pressure to be fluent and make the correct decisions all the time. I believe these two changes were a major contributory factor in how I was later perceived on the show.

When recording game shows today, if there is a mistake or a fluff they just stop the recording, work out what went wrong and put it right. This wasn't possible on *Sale* following Bill's decision to go for straight run-throughs, and this led to some problems. Canon Peter Freeman was Anglia's head of religious broadcasting and was much loved by everyone at the studios. He was full of energy and produced five late-night items for the region as well as looking after his parish outside Norwich. He also acted as the adjudicator on *Sale of the Century*, and I got to know him quite well. His counsel on any subject was always wise, and no problem of whatever kind was ever too small. There were many occasions when members of staff at Anglia would seek him out for advice or comfort.

We had a system on the show that we used if there was any ambiguity over a contestant's answer. During the actual recording, I made instant decisions to keep the show moving, and I felt I had enough knowledge and experience to do this. If, however, there was an issue with a response not being clearly correct and I felt I needed support, I would say to the contestant something like, 'I don't know if I can give it to you. I think you've said almost enough.' This was the cue for Canon Freeman, who had been listening, to give me backup. He would pass his decision to the producer, who would press the appropriate indicator light on my desk. I could see two bulbs: green accept, red decline. On one particular occasion, I waited for the signal and when the green light came on I said, 'As I indicated, I think you have said enough,' and I gave the contestant the money and we proceeded with the show. In the interval, the floor manager asked me to go up to the control room to see Bill Perry. When I got there, Bill exclaimed, 'What the hell are you playing at? I gave you the red light!'

'No, Bill, you gave me the green light. I am not a fool. You gave me the green light. So I flannelled my way around the answer and gave him the money. I'll tell you what, let's check the lights.' We did just that and discovered that an electrician had wired them incorrectly. 'What do I do now?' I asked.

Bill's response was to the point: 'We go back and start the second half. You apologise, and take the money back off him.' I was to be the fall guy for someone else's mistake.

We started the show again, and I had to say in front of the camera to the studio audience, and to the television viewers when it was broadcast, 'I'm sorry. You remember that question just before the break when I thought I was quite rightly being generous and gave Contestant 2 the money? Well, our adjudicator has informed me that I was too generous. I am afraid I have to take the money back and deduct a further £3 for an incorrect answer. Contestant 2 now has £6 less.' I felt I had been made to look a fool and was very embarrassed.

Something similar happened later on in the series, and I was again called up to the control room. Bill told me, 'We've had a bit of a problem. Apparently there has been a mix-up in the answering of two of the questions. It seemed fine at the time, but now Canon Freeman has told me we can't allow it. Somehow we have got to fix this.'

I asked Bill to play the tape of the first half, during which the incident had occurred. 'Look, Bill,' I said, 'there is a way out. You see when Contestant 3 gives the answer? If you cut there, I can go back out and put the next question to Contestant 1, who got it right. We'll just ask him to do exactly the same thing again. When I ask the next question, Contestant 3 will press his buzzer and give his correct answer again, and then we can continue from there.' Bill was unsure of the intricacies of editing, and I don't think he liked the idea of the presenter offering him a way out of the problem.

He suddenly became angry and said, 'Oh, for God's sake, can you please leave the control room and let me get on with it.' I explained the cuts to the contestants, we agreed it was all fair and it worked fine.

There is a fundamental difference between the show-business attitude towards performers in this country and in the US. In the States, they have huge respect for the performer, but it is a much tougher business. So if they have a show that is a big success, whoever is fronting it will get a lot of credit, sometimes out of all proportion. They will say, 'Gee, we have a success. Aren't we lucky to have X presenting?' In this country, they say, 'We have a success. Isn't X lucky to be presenting it?' They believe the show is far more important than the artist, who is the public face of the programme.

I had a couple of first-hand experiences of this during the run of *Sale of the Century*. My initial fee for presenting the show was based on the fact that it was to be broadcast only in the Anglia region. At that stage, there was no indication that it was going to be networked. If *Sale* had been scheduled as a network show from the beginning, my agent could have negotiated a considerably higher fee. As it was, at that time the contractual arrangements with ITV – negotiated with Equity – were such that, if a show went out in one area and then progressed to others, there was a sliding fee escalation. For two areas, the fee would increase by 50 per cent; three and it would go up some more, and eventually the scale might get to four times the basic. In my case, that was four times a very modest fee. I think it was around £90. So after a year or two I was getting paid around £360 an episode for one of the most successful shows on television. My contract also forbade me to do any advertising.

My agent thought this was unfair and started to negotiate as we hit the top of the ratings, which did not seem unreasonable. Not long after the process began, I received a phone call from Peter Joy: 'Dear boy, before we start, I have to make one thing clear: we have not had this conversation. Do you understand? We have not had this conversation.'

'All right, Peter,' I said. 'We have not had this conversation.'

'Thank you. Now, it has come to my attention that your agent is negotiating for a higher fee for you. While I think it is entirely justified, and I am supposed to have final approval, it does not work like that if the executives want someone else or don't want to pay more money. Also, I have to tell you, they have already started. They have approached someone, and he has expressed an interest.'

I told my agent to stop the contract discussions immediately.

This wasn't the only time I almost lost my job on *Sale of the Century*. Sometime after the contract negotiations episode, my agent's office called me with a revised recording schedule from Anglia. I checked my diary and said I could do the first two dates but had a problem with the third: 'I have something planned for that day. It is not vital, but I would rather not have to cancel. If I have to, then fine, but could they possibly find another date?'

In the back and forth with Anglia, my willingness to cooperate seemed to have been lost, because a few days later I was informed that the recording was going ahead on the date originally planned. I suspected what had happened. It seemed to me that Bill Perry was using this as an excuse to exercise his control over the show: 'Well, if Nicholas isn't free, I'll get someone else.' I had to grasp the situation immediately to protect my position, rather than leave it to my agent.

I phoned up and said, 'Bill, glad I got you. Right, everything's fine. That doubtful date we had? I've managed to shift it. I have got out of the other engagement, and I am free. It's in the diary. And I'll be with you.' I heard him catch his breath on the other end of the line.

Apparently he went to see the controller and said, 'What do I do?'

The controller replied, 'I'm sorry. He's available. You can't recast it.'

When I next saw him, Bill put the blame firmly at my agent's door: 'Your bloody agent. I am never dealing with them again.'

For all the occasional behind-the-scenes goings-on, I had a wonderful time on *Sale of the Century*. Some of the funniest moments came directly from the contestants. All the work I had done as a straight man for Arthur Haynes and Benny Hill had taught me to think on my feet, and that certainly helped when dealing with nervous participants. Most of them had never been on television before, and it was my job to help them relax and enjoy being on the show. I always met the contestants beforehand, to get to know them so that they would not be inhibited when I put on the pressure later in the show.

On one particular occasion, the three contestants were an attractive young woman, a quiet, self-effacing middle-aged man and a friendly, voluble cockney character. I spoke to the woman first and discovered a little about her. I then turned to the Londoner and said, 'On the card I have here, it says you are a pawnbroker . . .'

Before I could go any further, he jumped in to explain rapidly that, while he did that kind of work, his main source of income came from working off barrows in the market, where most of his money was earned in cash: 'Mostly back-of-the-hand stuff, you understand, Nicholas, nothing declared. What the eye don't see, the heart don't grieve over, if you get my meaning, Nicholas. I couldn't put that down as my living for obvious reasons, so I thought pawnbroker covered a multitude of sins, without raising any suspicions . . .' He carried on loquaciously for a time and then said, 'Oh, look at me, I'm talking too much.' Turning abruptly to the third contestant, who had been listening quietly, he asked, 'And what do you do for a living?'

The man replied dryly, 'I'm an income-tax inspector.' I had never before seen anyone actually turn white in an instant. Needless to say, our cockney contestant did not do well on the show.

The best-ever response came one evening when a lady pressed her buzzer to answer one of the early £1 questions: 'According to the proverb, what should people who live in glass houses not do?'

'Take a bath,' came the reply. She received a huge laugh. I told her the correct answer, 'throw stones', and said I would love to give her a bonus, but as it was a serious quiz I had to take the money away from her total.

A different kind of embarrassment, this time over prizes, occurred after the show had been running for some time. The IBA had strict rules about the value of prizes that could be offered in a quiz or game show: the top prize could not be worth more than £1,000. The star prize on offer each week in *Sale* was usually a car, and when the show first began there were about 20 small cars on the road for under £1,000. Within six or seven years there were only three, and they were all foreign makes. The IBA refused to change the rules in line with the cost of living, and the programme was taken to task by the press for being unpatriotic. One week, to try to ring the changes, we had on offer one of the new Lada cars that were just coming on the market. During the rehearsal to time the Sale of the Century section, I arrived at the car, extolled its virtues, then went to open the door. It came off its hinges.

Anglia used the bad press we had received about the cars we were offering to reason with the IBA, and the Authority conceded. As the price of a small British car increased over the years, further adjustments were made. By the time *Sale* ended its run in 1984, the rules had changed again. It was possible to offer a major prize up to £1,750 to cover the price of a new car, but not every week, and all this was conditional on the total money given away in a four-week period not exceeding £4,500.

In 1981, I appeared as a contestant on the show. It was one of our Christmas specials, and I took part alongside the comedian and presenter Tom O'Connor and the host of Border Television's *Mr & Mrs*, Derek Batey. We were each raising money for our individual charities. My charity was the Lord's Taverners. Tom and Derek are both lovely fellows and personal friends. The DJ Steve Jones was brought in as the host. I was nervous beforehand, because I felt I was on a hiding to nothing. The man who presented himself to the public as having all the answers could now be shown up. There wasn't much I could do but try my best. My general knowledge has always been pretty solid, perhaps helped by the fact that I used to write some of the questions, and I won. At the end of the show, I think I had one of the highest scores any contestant had ever had. I would have done even better, but I slipped up on a question to which I knew the answer: Where does Ken Dodd live? Ken is a good friend, but for some reason I just couldn't remember 'Knotty Ash'. This was a reminder to me of how well many of our contestants did under pressure. It is easy to let your mind slip and give a wrong answer when you know the correct one. Having accumulated enough money to purchase the star prize, I decided that the Lord's Taverners would be better off with a range of products that they could use as raffle prizes to raise funds, and accordingly I bought as many products as my winnings allowed in the final Sale of the Century and happily sent them on to the charity.

Derek Batey and I look fairly similar, and people often greet me on the street and mistake me for him. Derek says the same happens the other way round. I remember once a terribly nice chap approached me on the street and warmly shook my hand. 'So lovely to meet you,' he said. 'You are one of our favourites. We've seen all your shows. All your shows. The family, we all love you. And I'll tell you the one we loved most of all: *Mr & Mrs.*'

'But I didn't do that show,' I replied.

'Come off it, Nicholas. We saw you. We know. You did it. Is your memory going?'

'No, that was Derek Batey. He was the host of *Mr & Mrs.*'

He looked puzzled. 'Who?' And then he obviously realised the error. 'Oh, you've got yourself mixed up, Nicholas. Derek Batey did *Sale of the Century.*'

When *Sale of the Century* was on air, it was at a time when the press were very pompous and condescending about quiz shows. They considered them downmarket entertainment; the television companies shouldn't be putting such things on our screens. They should be lifting the aspirations of the general public and broadcasting quality shows. Quizzes are much more accepted today. The general criticism has gone, and the only debate you hear or read in the press is whether a particular show is a good quiz or a bad quiz. The attitude in the '70s was very different. Quiz shows were naff and, therefore, according to the press, so was I for presenting one of the most popular ones.

The Goodies constantly poked fun at me on their television series. They needed someone to ridicule, and I fitted the bill. They went about it in often quite bizarre ways – in one episode they tried using Nicholas Parsons masks to scare Eskimos and fish. Nearly every pantomime at the time also contained a joke about me, as did many radio and television shows. Benny Hill performed a funny parody of the show in his television series. I never minded when fellow artists made these jokes at my expense, because it was always done to raise a laugh, and when it was funny I would laugh as much as anyone.

The press also had a field day during this period. Every newspaper, from *The Times* to the tabloids, had a go at the show – and me – in different ways. Each time it happened, the show's ratings went up, which I am sure is not what the press intended at all. It came as a shock, however, when the show-business columnist of *The Sun* went so far as to run a campaign to have me taken off television. She said the time had come to get rid of 'the great switch-off' personalities on television, and her particular 'switch off' was Nicholas Parsons. She encouraged all her readers to join together and try to have me removed from their screens. Again, during the 'campaign' our viewing figures went up, so we must have been doing something right.

The press also had a way of twisting things and taking them out of context. When *Sale of the Century* ended in 1984, we threw a party to mark the many years of success we had all enjoyed. I thought it would make a fun photograph if a couple of the hostesses poured a bottle of champagne over my head, to celebrate our 'launch in reverse', as I called the party. We did the shot, it was a lot of fun and everyone was happy. In one of the papers the next day, the photograph was written up as if the crew were giving me two fingers.

I learned to live with the comments and criticism, but when it began to have an impact on my family it did upset me. Both my children, Suzy and Justin, admitted later that they were embarrassed at the time to have a well-known father who was often portrayed as a figure of fun. Suzy, I think, coped better, because she was more of an extrovert and her girlfriends made much less of it. Justin, however, did have a hard time at school and faced a lot of teasing over the things that were written about me. I felt particularly sad one day when he admitted he would rather I did not attend a school open day because of how the other pupils might react. The press don't always realise that innocent people can be hurt by what they write.

All the ridicule also had an impact on my career. When I was first asked to do the show, I assessed what was required of a quizmaster and did what they wanted. Many performers stick to one thing, but I enjoy being versatile and engaging in different and varied performances – comedy, straight roles, presenting, compèring, pantomime. This approach can lead to the press being dismissive of you. They see you as being a Jack of all trades but a master of none. I consider it being professional and responding to the discipline that each job demands.

Prior to *Sale of the Century*, I had done a lot of very good work; then suddenly I had done a quiz show, and when it eventually came off air my career slipped into a bit of a lull. I had to re-establish myself, as the feeling seemed to be that once I had become a presenter I had sacrificed whatever talent I might have had.

My great friend Peter Jones, with whom I have worked on a number of shows and plays, made a good point to me during my time presenting *Sale*. He saw that I was unhappy that the public might remember me solely for *Sale of the Century* and said, 'Don't think like that. The public have their perceived image of you, and that's what you have to accept and build on if necessary. Don't disillusion them. That's what they want to go with, and you should be proud of that.' He was right. A year or two later I had just finished a recording of *Sale of the Century* and arrived back at Liverpool Street Station from Norwich quite early in the morning. I jumped in a cab, and just as we pulled up outside my house and as I was paying, the driver decided it was time to show off some of his show-business jargon. 'Well, Nicholas,' he said, 'I suppose that's another one in the can is it? What do you do now? Go in, put your feet up and lounge around until next Saturday is it? Then up again to Norwich?'

I thought, 'Is that really the only image the public have of me? If it is, then I should try out what Peter said and have a bit of fun. He obviously thinks I am extremely high profile. I should be pleased about that and build on it.' So I said, 'Heavens, no. I'll go in and wake up my man-servant, we'll get the Rolls out and we'll drive down to Lydd Airport, where I have a helicopter. Get the old chopper out and head over to Le Touquet, where I have an interest in a casino. Then I'll head down to Paris: I've got some business to attend to there. Then I'll fly down to the south of France, to see about my boat and check with the captain to make sure everything is shipshape and have a little sail. Then I'll fly back, probably just in time for the show next week.'

I waited, and he looked at me and said, 'Yes, Nicholas, that's what it's like in your business, isn't it? All go.' He was happy that I had lived up to his image of someone on the television. When he got home, though, he probably said to his family, 'I met that Nicholas Parsons today. Bloody hell. He's got a Rolls-Royce, a boat in the south of France. And all he does is ask a few quiz questions. He's a lucky sod!'

For all the press sniping, there was a huge amount of fondness for the show from the public. I used to have a Mini that I drove around London, because it was so easy to park back then. When I was working in town, I would grab a cab and ask to be taken to wherever I had left the car. I remember once getting in and the driver recognising me: 'Right-o, Nicholas, just let me know when we get there.'

When we approached the spot, I looked out of the window and said, 'Slow down, slow down . . . There it is.'

'Where?' he said.

'There,' I replied and pointed at my Mini.

'Blimey,' he said, 'a bleedin' Mini.'

'Yes, they are wonderful little cars. What did you expect?'

'Well, a man in your position, Nicholas. A Roller or a Jag or a Bentley or something. But not a mini. Can I ask you a personal question, Nicholas, if that's all right? Has something happened? Has the show come off or something? My missus will be right upset if it has. Are you reduced to having bleedin' Minis now? That just doesn't seem right.'

I have a lot for which to thank *Sale of the Century*, despite some of the negative reactions. It gave me a good income and the chance to explore my other interests – I developed my one-man shows, I built up my production company and I evolved as a producer and director.

I am proud of what we achieved. The show ran for a record 14 years, and everyone involved did their job well. When I think about the number of viewers who regularly watched it, the people who can still quote the opening lines and remember the theme tune, and the fact that we awarded over 500 contestants more than £500,000 worth of prizes, we obviously made a lot of people happy. I am delighted to have played a part in that.

THEATRICAL
SUPERSTITIONS, SAYINGS
AND CHALLENGES

People in the world of show business are some of the most superstitious you could meet. Perhaps the nature of the industry, the precarious and unpredictable world in which we work, helps to foster the unusual beliefs that abound. These are found mostly in the theatre, where traditions stretch back a long way. The worlds of film and television are too transitory for superstitions to arise and take hold effectively. For instance, the colour green is considered very unlucky. You should never wear green clothes on the stage. In the late '60s, I was appearing in a series on television, *The Very Merry Widow*, starring that lovely actress Moira Lister. It was the technical run for the episode, in which we appeared in the clothes the costume designer had planned for us. As this was television, perhaps the designer was not aware of the anxieties and superstitions that exist in the theatre.

On set, one of the actresses suddenly walked on in a green dress. Moira, who was theatre-trained, almost went berserk: 'No, no, we can't have it. Take it off. Take it off. She must wear something else.' The poor young actress did not understand and in a panic fled to her dressing-room. Moira explained the old saying to those less knowledgeable: 'Wearing green in a show will bring disaster.' As with all superstitions, no one knows the exact origin of this. It is believed that over a period of time theatre managements observed that whenever a play failed there was always someone in the cast wearing green. Once a superstition begins, word of mouth increases its potency and people do not want to tempt fate by ignoring it, especially when there is usually an alternative. *The Very Merry Widow* was successful, but it was never revived after the series in which the green dress momentarily appeared. Those who believe in these things will probably say it was significant – but then the actress never performed in the dress.

The mention of green reminds me of an anomaly in our profession. The room where actors and others meet and socialise, in both the theatre and in television, is called the Green Room. Did this arise as a denial of the superstition surrounding green?

I do not like to be affected by superstitions, but it is difficult to tempt fate and ignore them. I bought a smart green blazer, which I still occasionally wear. I decided to put it on for a recording of *Just a Minute*. It was without doubt the flattest and least entertaining recording of the show we have ever made. Coincidence? One will never know. I have never worn the jacket for a professional show since. This is how superstition preys on the mind, seeping through to our primitive belief in magic.

There is another theatre superstition that states you must never open a show on the 13th, proverbially the unluckiest of numbers, and Friday the 13th would be inviting instant disaster. Incidentally, my daughter was born on Friday the 13th. She was our first child and brought tremendous joy into our lives, and since then I have adopted that date as my lucky day and 13 as my lucky number. It is an interesting coincidence that whenever Friday the 13th arrives in the calendar invariably something pleasant occurs in my life, usually of a show-business nature. It is good to have the confidence to ignore accepted superstitions, but until you have actually done so it is an uncomfortable thought to consider deliberately tempting fate, especially in show business.

There are other superstitions that have no logical explanation, like whistling in the dressing-room. It is easy to think of explanations. Someone did this on a first night, and the show flopped. It probably would have flopped anyway. In the theatre, some people prefer to find mystical reasons rather than look for common-sense answers.

Real flowers must never be used on the stage. This superstition could have arisen quite logically, theatre managements not wishing to pay for fresh flowers two or three times a week. On a film or television set, it is quite a sensible policy to adopt, as there may be a retake that occurs some time after the first take, and if the flowers have wilted it would not be good for continuity.

The best-known superstition in the theatre is the one surrounding Shakespeare's *Macbeth* – there, I have said it. Will this book fail? Most actors would not dare utter the title of the play, let alone a full quote from it. The work is always referred to by those affected as 'Shakespeare's Scottish play'. I often wonder how the actors who rehearse and later perform in this marvellous work feel as they speak the words. Are they flying in the face of fortune? Has our patron saint, Saint Genesius, given them a special dispensation? Or are they waiting for catastrophe or disaster?

This superstition arose around the early part of the last century, possibly before, when touring companies were travelling the country presenting a sequence of plays in different towns. This was the period of the great actor-manager, people such as Frank Benson, who revived many of Shakespeare's plays that had not been staged for years. The most recent actor-manager was probably Donald Wolfit, who toured his company to various theatres around Britain in the pre-war days of the late '30s. I remember seeing him in Glasgow in *The Merchant of Venice* in the early '40s. He was very theatrical in his performance – some would say 'hammy'. He assumed the style that he obviously felt the great Shakespearean actors of the past would have adopted. He was successful but not always admired by his fellow thespians. I remember a classic line delivered by that incomparable actress Hermione Gingold in a revue entitled *Sweet and Low* at the Ambassadors Theatre in London in the late '40s. She was talking about great personalities in the news. Her companion in the sketch mentioned Laurence Olivier. 'Ah,' she said, 'as an actor, he is a tour de force.'

'And Donald Wolfit?' asked her companion.

'Oh, he's just forced to tour.'

The superstition about *Macbeth* took hold when one of the touring companies of the early 1900s decided to introduce a new play into their repertoire. If a production was not well received by the audience in a particular town, they quickly replaced it with their rehearsed production of *Macbeth*, a play that never failed, and their fortunes were revived. There is another strange anomaly here. The disaster was the other play, and *Macbeth* brought them success, yet the curse has passed onto the Bard's masterpiece. Perhaps all superstitions are illogical, and yet it is amazing how they rule some people's lives.

I had reason to be grateful to this play when I was working in weekly rep in 1949 with Ronald Kerr in the New Theatre, Bromley, which is now called the Churchill Theatre. When Ronnie staged his yearly Shakespeare production, those playing the major roles were given time off the previous week to memorise the demands of the verse. The production was *The Merchant of Venice*. I was playing Gratiano, friend of Bassanio and Antonio the merchant. Portia, dressed as a lawyer, has successfully defended Antonio against Shylock's charges and has returned to her home at Belmont in Padua with her handmaiden and companion, Nerissa. Both now dressed as women, they are talking in the courtyard when suddenly in burst the three men with tales of what happened in the courtroom. On this particular evening, however, three men did not rush on stage. Two of them missed their cue. I was the only one waiting in the wings. There was a pause on stage that turned to silence as the two women looked despairingly in my direction. Something had to be done.

I whispered to the stage manager, 'Quick, get the others,' and then, with an air of supreme confidence based on blind ignorance of what I was going to do, I walked on, bowed to the ladies and launched into what can only be described as Shakespearean gibberish. Keeping the rhythm of blank verse and using Shakespearean phrases and words taken at random from other speeches, I ploughed on in a continuous and meaningless monologue. The two actresses on stage, Jocelyn Parlane and Ann Castle, were at first transfixed and then got the giggles, for which I then took them to task in more stylised unintelligible nonsense. They were unable to respond. I had, through necessity, moved the play into an area in which they could not participate. The other two actors still had not arrived. I had studied *Macbeth* as part of my English literature course for my School Certificate, similar to GCSEs, and had been obliged to memorise four or five of the soliloquies. When you commit something securely to memory at a young age, it invariably stays with you. In desperation, I plunged into two of these soliloquies.

For those who know their *Macbeth*, the speech towards the end of the play that begins, 'Tomorrow and tomorrow and tomorrow,' all about the futility of life, fitted very nicely here. I delivered it with as much style and panache as I could and seemed to carry the audience with me; some even clapped at the end. I carried on improvising for what seemed an age but was probably no more than five or six minutes. That was long enough in the situation. I was into my second soliloquy when suddenly onto the stage burst Antonio and Bassanio. They stopped, nonplussed, naturally not recognising any of the dialogue. I endeavoured to harangue them with cod Shakespearean oaths, and somehow we got back to the correct text and moved the play forward. I think some members of the audience never realised anything was wrong. The more observant, who knew *The Merchant of Venice*, obviously guessed what was happening; some even clapped again. I do not know whether this was to applaud my ingenuity or my downright cheek at trying to ad-lib our national poet. The unforgivable sin I had committed, according to some of my fellow thespians, was that I had quoted from Shakespeare's Scottish play. As I pointed out, the disaster had occurred before I spoke the lines and *Macbeth* helped to save the day: a reprise of the convoluted way the superstition had arisen.

In addition to superstitions, there are certain theatrical sayings that resonate with most actors. One is 'Never work with children or animals.' I believe the phrase was coined by the great American comedian W.C. Fields. He delivered it in that amazing vocal style of his, and the recipient replied, 'Don't you like children?'

'Oh, yes,' he said. 'But preferably parboiled.' The phrase, however, has stuck, and you can understand why. Children and animals are both naturals on the stage. They can be intuitive or unpredictable even when rehearsed, so the audience's attention is usually firmly on them. If you are in a scene with a child or a dog, you make them look good. Unconsciously, you use your talent to help them shine, because the audience are not watching you. Their attention is on the youngster or the little dog, to see what they may get up to.

I have worked a lot with children in pantomime, and the audience always love them. They are usually from an acting school and are experiencing for the first time what it is like to perform on a big stage. They will vary in age from eleven or twelve down to five or even four on occasions. If there is a tiny tot, he or she will catch the audience's eye. They are probably not as skilled as the older ones, but they have great appeal as they endeavour to keep up with the other children.

One of my favourite activities when working in pantomime is talking to the children you invite to join you on the stage towards the end of the show. I have had this responsibility in a number of pantomimes. The task is usually undertaken by the Buttons or Idle Jack character, but unusually I have done it when playing dame, my favourite pantomime role. I was never a conventional dame. Instead of being an unattractive, vulgar and perhaps even a forbidding creature in the traditional style, I was saucy and over the top with glamorous make-up and a flamboyant wig.

I find it easy and fun to talk to young children, and you often receive wonderful spontaneous responses. When I was in *Dick Whittington* at Sunderland Empire, I had all these little ones on stage, and they were delightful with their broad Wearside accents, although sometimes I was not sure what they were saying. On one occasion, I understood the child perfectly well. It was just that he did not say very much. 'Where's your home?' I asked.

'It's oot there.'

'I know, but where is oot there?'

'It's a long way away.'

'Has your home got a name?'

'Oh, aye.'

'Well, can you tell me?'

'No. Me mam told me not to talk to strangers.'

On another occasion at Sunderland, after asking one or two children where they lived, I turned to the next little boy, who was about five, and said, 'And where do you come from?'

With that wonderful logic that children possess, he pointed to the stalls and said, 'I've come from doon there.' The audience love these moments.

In the same pantomime, I asked a rather knowledgeable little lad what he liked best in the pantomime. 'I'll tell you what I didnae like,' he said. 'That cow.'

'Why not?' I replied.

'It's a fake. It's no a real cow.'

'It's make-believe,' I tried to reassure him. 'We have to pretend it's a real cow. For instance, I am not a real woman.'

'Oh, don't give me that. I can see you are. You've got boobies an' all.'

This was going very well with the audience, so I said, 'Would you like us to have a real cow?'

'Oh, aye.'

'But real cows can make a mess on the stage.'

With perfect logic, he replied, 'Well, you could do what me da does and put the stuff on your garden.'

There is no answer to that. I gave him his prize and a hug, and he went back to his seat amid much laughter, of which he was completely unaware.

One of the classic responses in this situation was told to me by my dear friend Leslie Crowther, who alas is no longer with us. He assured me it was true. It concerns Lionel Blair, a great pantomime performer and a good director of these happy Christmas shows. Lionel was talking with the children at the end of one show, which he always did extremely well, and had spotted a real character among the youngsters who had come up on stage. His professional instinct was to save this one for last. It is usually a boy, and on this occasion the lad was really enjoying the experience, even playing up to the audience. Lionel had asked the others the conventional questions and then turned to this little show-off and said, 'And now, what have you got to tell me?'

He immediately replied, 'You touch my dick, and you're a dead man.'

It was a time before the audience laughter subsided. How do you follow that? Lionel, being a great pro, coped amazingly and soon had the show back on track. You cannot script these moments.

Working with animals is an entirely different proposition. One little dog can sometimes be unpredictable, but a whole pack of them can be almost impossible. In the '60s, I was filming a television commercial for a dog food called Stamina. The storyline had me appearing on a desert island, incongruously dressed in a black jacket, pinstripe trousers and wearing a bowler hat, saying, 'Alone at last! Now I can tell you all about Stamina...' As soon as I mentioned the brand name, innumerable dogs of all shapes and sizes were to appear from every direction and leap all over me to try to get at the dog food. That was the idea anyway.

I went to a small studio in Bushey, where I met the director and was introduced to a canine trainer who had brought a large collection of dogs. I changed into my suit and spent some time getting to know the animals. The handler assured the director, and everyone else concerned, that the dogs would respond to his commands and, on a given word, rush forward as required.

We attempted a rehearsal. The dogs seemed more interested in exploring the studio. We tried more rehearsals, with the handler exhorting his animals to 'Attack' and 'Go fetch him, Boy.' The director then pointed out that, as they wished to record only my dialogue and the dogs' barking, the handler would have to keep quiet. It was then decided that I should have some food smeared over my hand, in the hope of luring the dogs towards me.

Before the next rehearsal, the dogs were given the scent of the food, after which it was hoped they would all leap forward for more of the mushy stuff, which was now oozing out between my fingers. Two or three of the more intelligent dogs got the hang of it, but the remainder continued sniffing around the far corners. After many more rehearsals, for which dog food was smeared on my clothes as well, and a few attempts at actual takes, it was decided to abandon the filming and try again the following morning.

When I arrived at the studio the next day and put on my City suit, which now smelled of stale dog food, I was told that a different group of dogs had been brought in. I was introduced to their trainer, a tough-looking character with a strong cockney accent who did not inspire confidence. 'Don't worry, Nick. I've been starvin' them since last night,' he said. 'They'll be ready to 'ave a go as soon as I give 'em the word.'

More dog food was smeared over my suit jacket, along the arm, round my hand and underneath the tin of Stamina. The director decided to try a take right away in the hope that, with the dogs fresh, it might all happen. It was not much better than the previous day. The dogs were affected by the atmosphere and the lights, and while most of them could smell food they were puzzled as to where to find it. More dog food was applied to my jacket, which was now becoming saturated and rather evil-smelling, and we tried further takes. Some of the cleverer dogs were now getting to know their part and jumped up to lick my clothes. I decided the best way to act the scene was to pretend to fall down when the dogs jumped up, so they could crawl all over me and appear to be licking the tin of Stamina in their excitement. I would then shoot up from the midst of the canine melee to proclaim the virtues of the brand.

One of the crew then mentioned that dogs went mad for aniseed, and someone went in search of this dog-provoking substance while we broke for lunch. I was not hungry, and no one wanted to sit next to me because of the stench that was issuing from me. After the break, I climbed back into my suit, now stiff as cardboard, and the aniseed was added to the already pungent smells that were issuing from the ruined material. Being black, at least it still looked quite presentable.

We tried another take. More dogs got the idea. This encouraged the trainer and the director to smear more aniseed on me and cover me from top to toe with dog food. It was pushed down my collar, behind my ears, around the rim of the bowler, on my trousers, into the pockets of my jacket. Some was even put under my hat so that it got in my hair, in the hope that, when the bowler fell off, the dogs would lick my head. With me in this revolting state, we began the next take. By now, some of the dogs went for me on cue, while others could still not understand that I was 'food'. They barked loudly but refused to leap.

The director was now desperate. More food, more aniseed and

now bacon fat was added to the mix. I will never forget the next take. I stepped into camera shot and spoke my opening line. The dogs were released, and more than before came bounding towards me. I fell to the ground as if knocked over by the rush. All seemed to be going well, and I tried to tell the viewers about the quality of Stamina. Just then, two of the animals that had not yet had a lick, or a bite, leaped forward for their share and landed full force on my lower regions. They began a dog fight for the food that was clinging to my trousers. I leaped to my feet before the two ferocious creatures could cause me irreparable damage. In the true tradition of show business, the director simply shouted, 'What's wrong? Why did you run away? It was going so well.' I explained, and, while he was mildly sympathetic, he asked if I would mind doing it again right away because the dogs were obviously in the mood. I said I was not very happy about the particular mood of one or two of them and asked if anyone had a cricket box I could wear. In the end, I had to settle for two jockstraps that I put on for my protection.

Now feeling very nervous, I lined up for another take. More food and aniseed was once again forthcoming, and this time, for luck, they also put chocolates in with the food so that once the dogs had discovered the source of supply they would continue to enjoy themselves. Gritting my teeth, with my hand barely able to hold the tin of Stamina, yet trying all the time to look happy and relaxed in front of the camera, I called upon my professional skill and instincts and stepped forward on the word 'Action'. This time it worked like clockwork, and the ordeal was over. The commercial had taken two days to shoot, had cost a small fortune in film stock and was 30 seconds on the screen.

Perhaps W.C. Fields was correct all along. I am certain Arthur Haynes would have agreed with him when we employed a dog trained by Barbara Woodhouse to take part in one of our sketches in *The Arthur Haynes Show*. This was Barbara's first taste of television. She went on, of course, to have her own highly successful series about training dogs, but at the time she worked with us she had only one animal, a Great Dane called Juno.

We were performing a sketch in which I play Father Christmas in a large store. Arthur, together with his wife, played by Patricia Hayes, and son are queuing to see me. When his turn comes, Arthur says to the boy, 'Go on, kick him,' which he does.

I wince and whisper to Arthur, 'What was that all about?'

'That's for last Christmas. You didn't give him the train set he asked for.' It was a lovely line created by Johnny Speight.

I then take Arthur aside and say, 'I am not really Father Christmas. I am just an actor doing a job. It is up to you to give him the present he wants.'

'Oh,' Arthur says, 'trying to spoil the little lad's illusions, are you? You're not Father Christmas. Just an actor pretending to be him, is that it?' He goes on in this vein for some time and then arrives at the pay-off, which involves him calling on his dog, which turns out to be a Great Dane, and threatening that it will attack me if I do not cooperate with the gifts his family want this year. Juno is supposed to snarl and start barking at me, and I am to be so frightened that I give Arthur the train set his boy wanted.

Barbara arrived for the rehearsals with Juno (a male dog with a female name), was told what was required and nodded confidently. She had presumably advertised her dog as fully schooled to undertake any situation required. However, since she had never been on television before, during the run-through she proceeded to shout instructions to Juno from behind camera, which was completely inappropriate, as the dog was supposed to be obeying the orders of his master, Arthur. It was explained that she would have to keep quiet and Juno was to follow Arthur's instructions while the sketch was in progress. She pleaded ignorance and then assured us that everything would be fine by the evening.

The time arrived for transmission. When we came to the sketch – the last one in the show – everything was going well and we were getting good laughs and building to the pay-off with the dog. Whether it was the atmosphere of the studio or the fact that he could not hear his mistress's voice, we will never know. Arthur shouted at his dog, which he had assured Father Christmas would obey his every command. The dog wandered around looking extremely docile and started to sniff everything in sight. Arthur tried to get Juno to bark, but instead the dog started to lick him affectionately. Arthur was getting desperate, and the audience loved every minute of it. They had realised things were not going according to plan. The technicians were also laughing, and I was wondering how I could help. At this point Juno spotted the Christmas tree, which was close to me, and, overcome with excitement, went up to it and cocked his leg. Most of the spray hit Arthur, who, acutely embarrassed, began to shout at the dog and try to get out of his line of fire. By this time, the audience were falling about. It made a good ending to the sketch but was quite the opposite of what was intended. For once, I was not on the receiving end of the discomfort or embarrassment.

In our profession, awkward moments arise frequently, and it is up to the performer to have the experience and skills to cope with them. They are always a challenge, and there are others of a different nature that can occur on cruise ships.

Many of the passengers on cruises are from the older generation and tire easily and doze off. They are also the ones who like to get to the shows early. It is not uncommon, fifteen minutes into a performance and in full flow, to glance down at some nodding heads. The show can be going well, and you know the bulk of the audience are listening and enjoying themselves, but it is a little disconcerting to see two or three of them fast asleep. Why do they always have to sit in the front row?

I have been performing my one-man show on liners for long enough now to know what works best, and I enjoy doing it. You are encouraged to socialise with the passengers. In fact, some contracts actually state this, and as all passengers fill in a questionnaire at the end of the cruise and are asked to comment on the entertainment it is in your interests to be friendly and also circumspect in what you say in your show. When I am telling my tales of working on Clydebank, I have to wrap some of them up carefully: 'Now I am going to tell you a story that involves lavatories. Actually, they used a much cruder word, but I am not going to tell you what it was. If anybody is sensitive about this word, "lavatory", I do apologise.' All the cruise liners put a lot of faith in the passenger feedback, and if your material is deemed to have been upsetting or inappropriate it can be fatal. One company's contract actually says that they will be asking passengers to rate you on a scale of one to six, and if you fall below four you will not be engaged again.

You meet some lovely people on cruise ships, and some interesting characters. On one trip, I was talking with a rather vivacious and charming woman in her 70s who was travelling alone, which is not uncommon. She had clearly taken quite a shine to a chap who was probably 80 years old and also on his own. I noticed they were becoming quite friendly and one evening saw them leaving the ballroom after the show hand in hand. Next day, when I came across the lady on deck, I could not resist it. 'I saw you with George yesterday,' I said. 'Did you have a nice time?'

'Oh,' she said, 'it was terrible. Absolutely terrible. I had to slap his face three times.'

I said, 'Really? Did he get fresh with you?'

'No, he kept falling asleep.'

You also hear of people who are not quite au fait with what it means to be on a cruise ship. One chap, having settled himself into his cabin, appeared at the reception desk to complain: 'I am not at all happy with the view I have been given. I was promised some wonderful sights, and all I can see are cranes and ships.'

The receptionist replied, 'But, sir, we haven't sailed yet.'

On another occasion, a passenger enquired at the reception desk, 'Where do the staff go at night? How do they get ashore?' The receptionist politely informed the passenger that the crew actually had their own quarters on board.

Cruising has become a growth industry for travel companies and, as a consequence, also for the world of entertainment. It is as though there is a new style of variety circuit. On the larger ships, resident groups are engaged for three months or more to put on regular evening shows, sometimes twice nightly depending on the size of the ship. These entertainers are often supported by solo acts, who may perform for a four- or five-day stint before disembarking and moving on to another ship. I have friends who make a good and happy living out of this. In addition to these solo acts, there are also the guest entertainers who take on less regular engagements. I probably fall into that category. I usually go with my wife, Annie. We treat it as a working holiday and have visited some spectacular locations. On a fortnightly cruise, I will perform three hour-long shows and two shorter ones, all of which require minimum preparation after the initial tech run. I am well looked after, with a nice cabin, and earn a modest fee. The food on all ships is first class and plentiful. In fact, it can be far too much, but it is one of the attractions of cruising and the restaurants are an absolute haven for foodies. If you are not careful and take advantage of all that is on offer, you can end up many pounds heavier when you return from your cruise. You have to discipline yourself in order to resist all the temptations on offer. There is breakfast, where you can have a full English, elevenses, a five-course lunch, if you so desire, tea with cakes and scones, an à la carte dinner and then, believe it or not, after 11 p.m. a full buffet if you are still hungry. Annie and I have not had a midnight feast yet, but it still astonishes me what is available.

The ships are so well appointed, with every facility and form of entertainment you could wish, that I am told there is a new culture developing, particularly in the US. Families seem to be sending their elderly relatives on cruises for a whole year, visiting them at various different ports. It can be more economical than a care home and certainly more enjoyable. It makes sense if you can afford it. There will be like-minded company on board, opportunities for exercise, libraries and medical facilities, and in the unfortunate event of a death the cruise company can even perform the burial at sea.

Compared with the travails of touring around the UK and performing in different towns every evening, cruise work makes a welcome change and is an option that a number of entertainers have embraced. The wonderful Norman Wisdom was one of them. In the years before his dementia became serious, he was experiencing some memory loss, which meant he was not able to appear in the theatre. He decided to take bookings on cruise ships, where he could put on a show, meet the passengers and be himself. He loved cruising, and the cruise operators loved having him on board. He would wander around the deck, chatting to everyone. People naturally warm to Norman. On the cruises, rather than a stand-up routine, Norman would be interviewed about his experiences in show business. Sometimes he would forget the stories he had already told and start to repeat himself until the audience shouted out, good-naturedly, 'We've heard it!' Norman did not mind. He had already created a bond with them through his personality and his natural friendliness, and he was enjoying himself.

The first cruise I joined was back in the '80s with the Lord's Taverners, on the *Canberra*. Nowadays I confine myself to a couple of trips a year, travelling on average for two weeks on each. Cruise ships seem to be getting larger, with some carrying over 2,000 passengers. I prefer the smaller ships, which are more personal. I used to perform a lot on the Fred Olsen line and have been recently engaged on the Saga ships. They are a delightful company for which to work. Annie and I were on the final cruise of the lovely *Saga Rose* before it was retired, a ship on which I enjoyed working and knew very well. The old saying goes that 'strange things happen at sea', and that was certainly true on one trip on that lovely ship.

I split my one-man show, *Just a Laugh a Minute*, into two halves, performed at 11 a.m., three or four days apart. It is an ideal slot for me, and the pre-lunch audience respond extremely well to my brand of entertainment. On this cruise, I had a packed house for the first performance, but as I started my second show the number in attendance was considerably reduced. It was not a surprise, however. There was a huge drama unfolding on deck. We had intercepted a boat in some difficulty that contained illegal immigrants from Algeria, probably bound for Spain. In fact, there were two boats, but one had sped off at the sight of the *Saga Rose*. Presumably that vessel contained the people who had been paid to take the immigrants across the sea. Our captain had drawn the *Saga Rose* alongside the small boat and was overseeing the removal of the passengers, who were then safely transported back to Algeria. I perfectly understood why my audience had decided to watch the dramatic incident on the lower deck rather than enjoy my theatrical stories.

One of the pleasant problems with cruising is that there are so many different functions to attend, with perhaps five formal evenings in a fortnight, plus various other events. This requires a lot of clothes, not necessarily for me, as I can wear my dinner suit on most occasions, but poor Annie has to pack numerous different dresses. As a result, we do not travel light, which is fine if you join the cruise at the start of the voyage and stay with it for the full duration. In such cases, your luggage is whisked away from you on arrival at the quayside and taken to your cabin, and when you arrive back at port it is once again taken off your hands and delivered to you once you have disembarked. The issue of weight allowance arises if you join or leave the cruise part-way through and have to fly.

On the last *Saga Rose* trip, I found a way to handle the problem of excess luggage. We were on board for two weeks of its six-week voyage and were flying home from Corfu. On a previous engagement, I had been on a ship that sailed up the Amazon. In certain countries, there are strict rules that state you cannot work on board unless you are a member of the crew. This applied on the Amazonian trip, which meant that before I joined the cruise I had to apply for a rather unfortunately named Seaman's Discharge Book. This was a fairly straightforward process, and once I obtained these papers I was legally entitled to sail with the ship and perform. I have since taken the book with me on every cruise. As our bags were being weighed at the Corfu check-in desk, it became clear we were going to have to pay a baggage fee. I produced my Seaman's Discharge Book and said, 'By the way, I've got this,' handing it over to the woman behind the desk. She did not even bother to open it to see whether it applied to the cruise on which I had been engaged.

'Oh, you are all right then,' she said. 'You don't have anything to pay.' It seems seamen travelling the world are looked on favourably. I may not have been fit enough in 1944 to actually set sail with the Merchant Navy, but over 60 years after I had been accepted into the service I was at last officially recognised as a crew member.

Another challenge in our industry is after-dinner speaking. It is something that has only evolved into a business over the past 20 or 30 years, and there are now a number of agents who specialise in booking entertainers for this purpose. There are artists I know who regularly undertake such engagements, and some of the larger corporate clients can pay handsomely. These particular performers have the ability to relate to their audience in whatever environment or mood they find them and tailor their act accordingly. I find the whole experience one of the more stressful areas of work in which I am involved, as you can never know what conditions you are going to face until you arrive. The acoustics may be awful, the lighting poor and the audience drunk or uninterested. I remember on one occasion I was speaking in the Banqueting Suite at Old Trafford football ground. The layout of the room was unusual, with the audience separated on either side. They were obviously not familiar with how to behave when there was entertainment laid on. Not long after I had begun my speech, as I was mid-story, a chap got up from his table and walked across the room, straight in front of me. He was heading towards the Gents. It was very off-putting and distracted the audience. I realised I had to think quickly, or I would lose them. I took my hand-held mic and followed him, continuing with my tale. The audience seemed to enjoy this, and when I reached the loo I gave them a running commentary as to what he was up to. I emerged a few moments later to a round of applause, and the situation was recovered.

Unlike a normal show, where you arrive, perform and leave, for after-dinner speaking the people who have engaged you not only look forward to your speech but also want to chat with you from the reception all the way through the meal. I find this draining. By the time the moment comes for me to stand up, I can be mentally exhausted by the conversation, I may perhaps have had a glass of wine or two to be sociable, which can slow me down, and I have a stomach full of good food. Hardly ideal preparation to be energised and funny. At that moment, I fall back on all my experience of working in clubs and hope that I can entertain them. Mostly it comes together and the evening ends well, with the audience happy and the atmosphere upbeat, but that is no guarantee that the same will happen next time. There are so many variables that you cannot rest on your laurels just because you have had a couple of good nights on the trot. This adds to the pressure.

I think Willie Rushton summed it up best in a lovely story that Barry Cryer tells. Willie hated doing after-dinners. He did not regard himself as a 'joke man'. He always resisted offers unless they were too good to refuse. On one occasion, he was experiencing all the challenges of after-dinner speaking that I find difficult but was trying his best to be engaging. He was sitting next to the company MD and making all the right noises – 'Yes, I agree. Oh, fancy that' – while the man chatted away. After a while, the MD suddenly said, 'Mr Rushton, I hope you are going to be funny. We are paying you a lot of money.'

Willie's reply was succinct: 'Yes, and most of it is for sitting next to you.' Whether the story is true or not I cannot confirm, but I am certain anyone who has done a few after-dinners will recognise Willie's sentiments and probably wish they had the courage to say the same thing on occasion. Of course, more often than not, even if I have found the evening tiring, there has often been delightful company and I have had an enjoyable time.

Willie Rushton was one of the most engaging and delightful people you could ever meet, an amazing wit, a wonderful cartoonist and someone to whom you naturally warmed. He was also a great cricket enthusiast, and that is where our paths crossed. I got to know him well through the Lord's Taverners, where we often turned out together in cricket matches. Before Willie died, at the all too young age of 59, he had expressed a wish for his ashes to be buried at Surrey County Cricket Club's ground, the Oval. I wondered why Willie had not chosen Lord's, the home of cricket and the place where the Lord's Taverners began. Barry Cryer, who knew Willie very well, said to me, 'Willie could not stand Lord's. He found them all far too stuffy. He was a Surrey cricket man, and he loved the Oval.' Willie's was an exceptional request, but the club were happy to grant permission because of his commitment to Surrey CCC. The day of the ceremony arrived, and a number of us, friends and family, gathered on the edge of the boundary for the laying to rest of Willie's ashes. I was interested to see a rather modest-sized hole had been dug, and after someone said a few words in emotional tribute to Willie, his son, Toby, then in his early teens, stepped forward with a canister. I assumed Toby was going to place the container in the hole, which would then receive a final blessing and be buried. To my amazement, however, he had clearly been instructed otherwise. He opened the canister and began to tip dear Willie's ashes into the hole. Unfortunately, there was quite a breeze blowing, which caught some of the contents, scattering them across both the boundary and the mourners. We all remained in respectful silence, not wishing to laugh at such a solemn occasion. The blessing was made, and the hole was filled in. Whenever I visit the Oval, I like to think that Willie would be happy to know his remains are buried there and also scattered round the boundary.

I have been a supporter of Surrey cricket from a young age. When my brother and I started to take an interest in the sport, he said to me, 'You have got to have a county. I am taking Sussex. You can have Surrey.' I looked up to my brother then – he was older and more authoritative – and did as instructed. I have faithfully followed Surrey and their fortunes ever since. Some of my fondest memories from the age of ten or eleven include the long walk across Clapham Common, which was near to where we lived at the time, to the Oval, carrying a little case containing my sandwiches and a drink, with the prospect of a whole day of cricket ahead. I can still recall the team I watched: Sandham, Gregory, Squires, Barling, Fishlock, Parker, E.R.T. Holmes (captain and an amateur, hence the use of his initials), H.M. Garland-Wells (vice captain, amateur), Watts, Brooks, Gover. I could never have imagined then that years later I would actually meet Alf Gover, Surrey's fast bowler who also played for England. After he retired, Alf ran a cricketing school in Battersea Rise, and I attended for some coaching when I was turning out for the Lord's Taverners. Meeting Alf was wonderful, but my treasured memories of that period are of playing alongside some of my cricket heroes, such as Denis Compton, John Edrich, Godfrey Evans, Colin Cowdrey, John Price and Ken Barrington, for the Taverners. Such moments are one of the great joys of my involvement with the charity, and it has been a great privilege to have had these opportunities.

If show business produces challenges, then so does sport. I have followed Surrey since the '30s, through their heyday in the '50s, and I am as passionate about them now as I was then, even though as I write this book they are languishing at the bottom of the Second Division. A challenge is not something to be feared but to be embraced. That is an attitude I have adopted throughout my career, and I am confident Surrey County Cricket Club will find a way to overcome the challenges facing them and fight their way back to the top.

COMEDIANS:
A SPECIAL BREED

When I was young, the 'legitimate' theatre received respect and the variety theatre was looked down upon, almost as a second-class art. If any honours were being given out, they would invariably go to actors playing serious drama and not to those specialising in comedy, let alone comedians. That has all changed now, and I am pleased to say that comedians and comics receive the respect they are due. As a general observation, I see a subtle difference between 'comics' and 'comedians'. Comics are naturally funny, and comedians make things funny. There are also clowns who indulge in physical comedy, stemming from the days of the silent films, but there are few of these around today, as public preference has moved to mostly verbal humour.

There has been a huge upsurge in solo comedy performance in recent years, with comedy clubs springing up to cope with demand. In the old days of variety, comedians told jokes – some still do – but today most express themselves in observational humour, drawing on incidents in their own lives or on the activities of people around them. These performers are what we call 'stand-ups' or 'stand-up comedians'. I have worked in all areas of comedy and am aware of the different disciplines required in each category: as a comedy actor in plays and farces, in smart, clever revue and in sophisticated cabaret and, of course, as a stand-up. There are many people who attempt stand-up, but to become successful requires courage, bravado, skilled comic timing and an innate instinct for what is funny. This cannot be taught, and I have particular admiration for anyone who attempts it.

Straight actors are different. However talented they are, most find it a challenge to walk on the stage as themselves and make even a simple announcement. Actors are used to getting into character. I was once compèring at a big charity event at Drury Lane, and a famous actress from the Royal Shakespeare Company was about to go on stage and introduce the next act. She was shaking with nerves, and I asked her what was wrong. 'Well, I haven't done this before,' she replied. She would have been absolutely fine if she had been playing a role, but having to walk out there and be herself was difficult.

On stage, actors not only have their character written for them but also have the support of those around them. They are part of a team and have someone to help them cover if something goes wrong. Kenneth Williams's story of appearing in an Agatha Christie thriller is a classic example.

Kenneth originally saw himself as a serious actor, and he was very good, but even in those early days he demonstrated an incredible ability to improvise. His character was shot quite early on in the play, and Kenneth was supposed to sink to his knees, fatally wounded in the stomach. When using guns in plays, there is always a standby in the hands of the stage manager, so if the one actor is holding fails to fire the spare is used from the wings. It never sounds realistic, as the shot is heard after the actor has pulled the trigger, but at least the audience is aware of what is supposed to have happened. On this occasion, both guns failed to go off. Silence.

The actors on stage were transfixed. The audience were whispering, and some were beginning to laugh. Kenneth saved the situation. He whispered to the actor with the gun, 'Throw it at me.' In desperation, the actor did as he was told, and Kenneth caught the gun and held it against his stomach. Falling to the floor, he went into his full death scene: 'Oh, I'm going, I'm going . . . This is it. You never told me the gun was poisoned.' It was a brilliant ad-lib, and it brought the house down.

It is my belief that every performer, whether it is an actor or a comedian, exhibits a degree of insecurity, which is one of the reasons they strive to be on the stage. They need the acclamation of the audience to satisfy something in themselves about which they are not confident. A positive reaction is reassuring and reaffirming. Performers, myself included, can be quite shy. Their public personae may appear to be outgoing and confident, and in some cases this is genuine, but often the reality is quite different. Recently Annie and I appeared on *All Star Mr & Mrs*, presented by Phillip Schofield and Fern Britton. One of the questions asked revealed this side of my personality publicly. Out of earshot of Annie, who was sitting in a soundproof booth, I was given three possible answers to a question and asked to identify which one of the three I thought Annie would choose when the question was posed to her. The question asked was quite clever: 'When are you most likely to fall foul of the *Just a Minute* rules? Would it be: a) Repetition of an anecdote? b) Hesitation when entering a crowded room so that Annie decides to go ahead of you? Or c) Deviation from your usual afternoon nap?'

Annie, who knows me so well, matched my answer in an instant: 'Hesitation.'

If I go on the stage, I know what is involved. It may be tough and tense, but I go out there with the hope that my concentration levels will be high and I will be able to interact positively with the audience. If I go to a social function where I don't know anybody, I am more anxious. I do not know why, but I do think it is a common trait amongst performers, even if they do not admit it.

Of all performers, I believe it is the comedians, in particular those who stand on stage on their own and have to live and die by their talent and nothing else, who are the most insecure and require the biggest boost from the audience reaction. This need for acclaim might explain a certain character trait I have noticed. A lot of comedians seem to have a distinctive attitude towards money. Most of them find it difficult to put their hands in their pockets. Some of them are downright mean. I put this down to the possibility that the much sought-after positive audience reaction is ultimately expressed in the income they earn. It is hard to part with that.

The stories about Max Miller are legendary. It is said that Max never bought a drink for anyone. Barry Cryer recounts a story that Roy Hudd told him when he was on the same bill as Max. There were two performances a day, and between houses Max took Roy and another young performer to the bar. The young man said, 'Max, I must get you a drink.'

Max replied, 'No, no. You two sit there and just wait. Just wait.' The first house finished, and towards the warm-up time for the second house some of the audience entered the bar.

On spotting Max, one of them cried out, 'Maxy, Maxy. You want a drink, Maxy? What about your friends?'

I first met Max after he was retired from theatre work and living in Brighton. The radio producer Bill Worsley booked him to do a ten-minute slot in *Midday Music Hall* in the late '50s. It was transmitted from the Playhouse Theatre at the end of Northumberland Avenue, which the BBC then owned or rented. What was unusual about his performance was that he appeared on the radio in his full stage regalia of multicoloured jacket and trousers as well as the saucy hat he always wore. As it was an audience show, perhaps there was some logic. That is how his public expected him to dress. Bill was taking a big gamble having a comic of Max's reputation on a live show, but Max was a true professional and did not go over the top with his material. It had all been passed by the producer in advance, but you could never be sure with a comedian such as Max, who always responded to his audience's reaction. To be sure he kept to his time on a live show, Bill arranged for him to have a light when there was 60 seconds and then 30 seconds to go. He was wonderful on the show and a lovely, kind man.

Arthur Haynes was occasionally known to fall into the category of being cash-shy at the bar. He would sometimes buy a drink, but he had a wonderful system of getting them bought for him. I was on the receiving end of it once. It was when *The Arthur Haynes Show* was being transmitted from the Hackney Empire. During the lunch break, a lot of us went to the pub, including the technicians. I arrived a little late. Arthur was already there, and he had obviously asked, 'What you having?' to the people around him. Then the producer walked in, and Arthur said, 'Dicky, what you having? Lovely. Jim, Nick, what you having? Pint for you, OK, lovely. Have you got all those, barman? Right, that's all. Nick's paying.' I do not think Arthur had necessarily planned it, but a comedian cannot resist the opportunity to get a laugh.

Arthur entertained everyone with his great comic timing, and I was presented with the bill, which I paid.

Tommy Cooper was another one. It is probably an apocryphal story, but it was said of him that on one occasion when he was getting out of a taxi and paying the fare he reached across and slipped something into the driver's top pocket with the words, 'Have a drink on me.' It was a teabag. Tommy was my favourite comedian from the point of view of being physically funny. There was something instinctively humorous about this large man with large feet who had a funny face and a funny walk. He made you laugh the moment he appeared on stage. He was wonderful and was much loved within the profession and outside. Tommy enjoyed a drink, but you never saw him put his hand in his pocket when he was standing at the bar. He had a lovely technique that he used on me once when we bumped into each other in a pub. 'Tommy, how good to see you.' I said, delighted at the chance meeting.

'Let's have a drink,' he suggested.

'Thank you. What are you drinking, Tommy?'

'A double whisky. That's very kind of you. Thank you very much.' With that I was left ordering and paying.

When I was at the Palladium in *Swing Along* with Arthur Haynes in 1963, if Tommy was around he often came backstage for a chat – and a free drink. He knew I always kept some booze in my dressing-room for guests who might come by after the show. Towards the end of our long run there, if he could not see a bottle of something on my dressing-room table when he popped his head around the door the first thing he would say was, 'Where is it?' and he would go searching. I really think he had hollow legs on him.

I never worked with Tommy on the stage, but I got to know him during my summer season with Arthur Haynes in Blackpool in 1962. Back then, Arthur was top of the bill at the Winter Gardens, and at the adjoining theatre, the Opera House, Ken Dodd was the headline act, with Tommy Cooper starring on the Pier. At the Grand Theatre, there was a play with Thora Hird and Michael Medwin, who was a big name then. There were also shows in other theatres, plus the Tower Circus. They were packed out every night.

You would have very different audiences from week to week. We'd ask, 'What's the audience this week?'

The management would reply, 'Oh, it's the Oldham Wakes week.' So all the people who worked in factories and firms in Oldham would come. Another week it might be the Glasgow Fair. There would be a different influx of people depending on which part of the country was having its annual fair or holiday, and with each new audience the reaction to the shows would be subtly different. The laughs were never quite the same, which always made things interesting and kept everyone on their toes.

There was a group of us who would often go to the Stuart Hotel after the shows. Tommy was regularly there. He may even have been staying at the Stuart. Mike Medwin and Thora Hird often made an appearance, and Arthur Haynes would sometimes go down. We would gather, have drinks and chat. One evening I was talking to Tommy. He was the most natural comedian. I don't think he always knew where his laughs came from. There was a delightful routine he used to do in front of the stage curtain. He would begin a story and then slip his hand behind the curtain and swiftly produce a hat, which he put on, and he then continued as a different character. Throughout the story he would use eight or nine hats, and sometimes they got mixed up. It was hilarious. Simple, and yet it required great deftness of touch. It was perfect for Tommy, and he executed it brilliantly.

Tommy was telling me a story about working in America. 'Oh, it was terrible,' he said. 'They started laughing, and then they started booing and jeering. Like that, booing and then jeering. Awful.' The more he described how dreadful the experience had been, the more I laughed. Eventually he said, 'It's not bloody funny. I was suffering out there.' He was explaining a serious story about an upsetting event, but because of his natural delivery it was very funny.

Tommy suffered a heart attack on stage during a broadcast of *Live From Her Majesty's* and died shortly afterwards. It was very sad, and many people were shocked at the manner of his death. He had not been well for a time prior to the show, and he probably wasn't feeling well when he took to the stage. When you perform, however, once you go out there and the audience responds to you, the adrenalin overcomes all the stress you might be feeling and you give a performance, but it puts a lot of strain on your body. That is what I think happened to Tommy. He loved his profession, worked hard and was in his element when the audience were laughing. It was a terrible loss, but for someone like Tommy it was probably a wonderful way to go.

Tommy might not always have known exactly why he was getting the laughs, but Frankie Howerd certainly did, even if outwardly it all seemed to be a bit haphazard and stumbling. That was his great skill.

Frankie had something of a roller-coaster career. In the early '50s, he had been riding high on his radio successes, reaching a peak in *Variety Bandbox*. Then suddenly he was no longer the flavour of the month, and only a few years later he had hit a low. Around that time, I met him by chance walking near Holland Park. He was wearing a shabby old coat, looking forlorn. We talked, and he was soon bemoaning the fact that he had no work and no offers. I tried to reassure him by saying that show business was going through one of its upheavals because of the arrival of commercial television and the changing styles in comedy.

Frankie was a law unto himself, lovable and insecure in real life. He was a lugubrious character at the best of times, but he was at a particularly low ebb in the early '60s, when he secured an engagement at the successful Establishment Club in Greek Street, Soho. The club had been started in 1961 by Peter Cook and a fellow member of Cambridge Footlights, Nicholas Luard. On the wave of the satire boom that had begun with *Beyond the Fringe*, and thanks also to the fact that the censorship of the Lord Chamberlain's Office did not extend to private clubs, the Establishment was where all the new young comedians were presenting modern revue and political comedy. It was a huge success.

Frankie courageously stepped into an environment that was totally new to him, and he was an immediate hit. I will always remember the opening line of his act at the Establishment. To me it represents the essence of comedy – the unexpectedness. He stepped out, or rather ambled out, to the centre of the stage of this club for the young, smart set and said, 'If you have come here tonight expecting a lot of crudeness and rude words, I am sorry, but you won't get it from me. So you might just as well piss off now.' Big laugh, and he was launched. From then on he had his audience with him all the way.

Frankie was a partner in the writers' agency Associated London Scripts, together with Spike Milligan, Eric Sykes, Johnny Speight and others. Following his appearances at the Establishment Club, Frankie was invited by Ned Sherrin to appear on the cult late-night satirical television programme *That Was the Week That Was*. Johnny and Eric wrote Frankie's script for him, and he went down a storm. Suddenly he was back.

Frankie was a thinking-man's comedian who worried things to success, though his style rarely gave that away. To me, he never appeared to be confident in what he was doing, but it was all carefully worked out. Every hesitation had been meticulously planned.

I worked with Frankie in one of his last engagements, a commercial for R. White's lemonade in the early 1990s. The company had decided to revive the famous 'Secret lemonade-drinker' adverts from the 1970s and '80s in which a man in pyjamas creeps downstairs in the middle of the night to sneak some lemonade from the fridge. We had both been asked, as recognisable faces, to appear in separate commercials based on the original format. The campaign featured a number of celebrities of the time, including Ronnie Corbett, Jimmy Greaves, Ian St. John and John McEnroe.

Unlike the confident comedian most people thought him to be, Frankie had a worried expression when I arrived at the studio. He said immediately, 'Have you read the script? It doesn't work. Not for me.' He then went into an animated conference with the producer and writer, revamped what he had to do, by changing his clothes and working out every pause and facial expression, and made it very funny for himself while keeping the essence of what the client wanted. I did the original version of the script, which worked for me. The two commercials were shown initially in one television area but were never transmitted nationally because of Frankie's sudden and sad death.

The insecurities that seem to go hand in hand with comedic talent show themselves in different ways. In the case of Tony Hancock, he felt he could not share his success with anyone else. The applause and laughter had to be all directed towards him.

Tony Hancock was an exceptional comedian. I admired him greatly. His comedy timing was superb. Working with the brilliant writers Ray Galton and Alan Simpson, who understood him very well, he was able to get laughs out of simple situations. Away from centre stage, however, Tony was a melancholic character.

I worked with him in 1963 at the Palladium when he stood in after Arthur Haynes had his first heart attack. I used to go to his dressing-room sometimes to have a chat, and he would often just sit there, like some contemplative Buddha-type character. I had great difficulty getting through to him. Admittedly, by then, which I did not know, he had his alcohol problems, although he was not drinking while he was performing at the Palladium. I found it impossible to develop any off-stage rapport with Tony. He was not interested in socialising outside of work, although that was not uncommon in show business. Eric and Ernie did not spend a lot of time in each other's company away from the television studio or theatre, and Arthur Haynes and I rarely went out together. What we would do, however, was go for a quick drink in one of our dressing-rooms after a show to discuss the performance and look at ways we might be able to improve it.

When Tony arrived at the Palladium, the idea was for us to do some sketches together, but after a few days he dropped those and basically did his solo act. He was always happiest on his own, although some of his best work came when he was supported by Kenneth Williams, Hattie Jacques and Bill Kerr. The problem was that they were very talented and got lots of laughs in the Hancock shows, and in Tony's eyes that meant they had to go.

Sid James lasted the longest: you could never feel threatened by Sid because he was so laid-back and couldn't care less. He was completely unassuming, with no edge. Sid wasn't interested in pushing himself, like so many people were. He got on with his job, did it properly and went home. Tony was comfortable working with him, but he saw the others as a threat and got rid of them. He even broke up with Galton and Simpson.

Many British comedians share that same sense of insecurity: they never like to feel they owe their success to anyone else. In America, comedians will happily assemble the best people to support them, because they realise that having a talented team strengthens the show and increases their own prestige. Jack Benny was the best example of this; he used to have regular sidekicks, like Eddie 'Rochester' Anderson and Phil Harris, but it was still *The Jack Benny Program*. Eddie and Phil sometimes got some of the biggest laughs, but Jack never resented it. He played up to it. If Phil Harris had done one of his fast comedy numbers and the audience called him back, Jack might walk on waving his hands to indicate enough was enough and say, 'Well, personally, I don't get it.' He too would get a big laugh, but he was not looking to steal all the glory for himself. The secret was that Jack knew it was the quality of the whole cast that brought the bigger success.

There are some British comedians who do not mind sharing the limelight. Paul Merton is one of the best examples. He demonstrates his generosity in many ways. In *Just a Minute*, as I explained in a previous chapter, he always puts the show first and will hold back his challenges if he thinks he has been dominating proceedings, to ensure we have an evenly balanced programme and the other players have their fair share of airtime. He does not try to dominate. He also continues to work with the Comedy Store Players, with whom he has been associated since long before he became well known. Now, when they go on tour, or appear at the Edinburgh Festival, the show is billed as Paul Merton and his Impro Chums. This is not because he is seeking star billing. He recognises that by trading on his name the show will attract larger audiences to the benefit of everyone, and I understand the money is shared equally between all of the performers. On stage, he does not look to grab all the laughs for himself but performs as one of the ensemble. He is naturally one of the most self-effacing comedians you could ever meet.

I liked Tony Hancock, but you could never completely warm to him. He was too distant. In a way, his own melancholy got the better of him. He tried to do it all himself. He wrote his own film script, which was a disaster, and eventually everything he had slowly slipped away and he ended up committing suicide. It was dreadfully sad.

I asked Kenneth Williams once about what happened when he had been written out of the *Hancock* radio show after several successful seasons. He said, 'Well, Tony told the writers, "I don't like this character. It is a caricature."' That was it. Kenneth was not invited back even though he was very humorous in the programme. I still find the 'Test Pilot' sketch extremely funny. It is classic comic radio. Tony plays a pilot who is testing a new plane, and Kenneth is a mechanic who was working on the plane when it took off and ends up with Tony on the flight. The sketch is full of the clever voices and catchphrases Kenneth had developed – 'Don't be like that' and 'Stop messin' about' – which were natural to the character and not inserted deliberately to get a laugh.

Kenneth was one of the most humorous, gifted men I have ever known, combining strange characters, wonderful voices and outrageous stories that made you laugh. He was a very funny man, but he did not admire that aspect of his talent. He denigrated it because he wanted to be accepted as an intelligent, erudite character actor. He was proud of the success he achieved playing the Dauphin in Bernard Shaw's *Saint Joan*. I saw him in that play, and he was wonderful.

He then went on to great fame in the *Carry On* films, which became highly commercial. I think he enjoyed them because he enjoyed being with his chums. He worked well with other performers, and in the *Carry On* films he liked others getting a laugh on screen. At lunchtime in the canteen during the filming of *Carry on Regardless*, I would see him holding court. He had everyone roaring with laughter. It was a great family party.

However much he enjoyed the experience of making the *Carry On* films, Kenneth never respected his success in them. If anything, he was embarrassed about it. He regarded the roles he played as merely requiring broad character interpretation and little subtlety. It was not what an actor did, which was how he saw himself.

Kenneth's attitude reminds me of two men about whom I have developed one-man shows: Edward Lear and W.S. Gilbert. Lear had an incredible ability to write wonderful nonsense verse and stories, and to draw amazing pictures, which children loved, but he never regarded that as worthy talent. He saw himself as a landscape painter, but he worked at a time when landscapes in watercolours were not appreciated. Everyone wanted oils. So he struggled and sold them for a pittance: a far cry from what these beautiful paintings are worth today. W.S. Gilbert saw himself as a serious dramatist, and he did write plays, which received modest success, but he had a gift for writing wonderful songs, which Sullivan put to music. For him, this was just a facility, something he could do, not something to be proud of and respect. Kenneth was similar.

To some extent, that applies to me. There are aspects of my career that I would like to be remembered for more than others, but to a certain section of the public there will always be one show that made the biggest impression. I was in a taxi recently, and the driver said, 'Nicholas, it is lovely having you in the cab. You know, I can still remember the signature tune to that show.' At which point he started to hum the *Sale of the Century* theme.

The question of Kenneth's sexuality is often discussed. I maintain he was an aesthete to some extent and did not have a private sex life. In one of Kenneth's obituaries, it was pointed out he was friendly with flamboyant homosexuals. That says nothing about his sexual proclivities, since he was also friendly with flamboyant heterosexuals. I do not think he had or wanted an intimate relationship with a man or a woman. He did once propose to Joan Sims, however. He was very fond of her, and the feeling was mutual. He said that if they were married they would have separate bedrooms and bathrooms and that there would be none of that embarrassing 'sex stuff'. She told him that was fine for him: he was getting what he wanted, a companion and someone to cook and clean the house, but what about her? The proposal was gently but firmly refused. His best friend was his mother, Louie, who lived close to him in London and came to every recording of *Just a Minute*, sitting in the front row and usually watching her clever son throughout.

The thought of physical intimacy, I believe, repulsed Kenneth. He was very nervous about close contact with people and would rather keep his distance. He did not like people going to use the lavatory in his flat. He could not bear to think of someone sitting on his loo seat.

In fact, when he met the *Round the Horne* team at his home, he used to make them go to the Great Portland Street station toilet, which was just around the corner from where he lived.

In public, it was a different matter. He liked to show off and make a strong connection with those around him. I used to observe this when I introduced him on *Just a Minute*. He would come on the stage, stick his little bum out, do a humorous walk and smile that Kenneth Williams smile. The audience loved it. He was having a relationship with them, and that was satisfying to him.

Kenneth's last professional job was a recording of *Just a Minute*. He had been booked to do two more recordings but phoned at the last moment to say that he could not take part. He had told me previously that he had been suffering from a stomach complaint, and, knowing him as I did, I realised there must be something seriously wrong. I wrote to him, and, not being a natural letter-writer, I kept it simple and to the point: 'Dear Kenny, so sorry you could not be in the show. We missed you very much. It is not the same without you. Hope you are soon feeling better.'

Kenny was extremely punctilious and wrote back immediately: 'Dear Mate, I did miss the show terribly. But I have been trying something new, and I was taking the tablets. I've still got the pains in my stomach. I think if it doesn't go away it will be the dreaded surgeon's knife.' I believe that last remark demonstrated how such a physical invasion was too much for him to handle.

Kenneth had always said to me that he was not worried about the passing years or troubled by the thought of death. He once mentioned that he thought 65 or 70 was a good time to go. 'Why hang about?' he said. Sadly, he did not 'hang about', falling considerably short of what he regarded as an acceptable age.

Not all comedians find it hard to part with their money. There are some for whom money does not mean anything. Benny Hill was an example. He was very generous and always threw a lovely cast party at the end of the last recording of *The Benny Hill Show*. Benny made a considerable amount of money throughout his career, and the sad thing is that the only will he left was so old that he named his parents as beneficiaries. They had long since gone when Benny died, and as a result his estate was not transferred to named individuals but instead went to distant relatives with whom I understand he had lost touch. Perhaps this would not have mattered to Benny, as money never seemed important to him. When he died, cash and numerous unbanked cheques were found stuffed haphazardly into drawers in his flat.

I first met Benny in 1952 when he was compèring *The Centre Show*, which was transmitted on television from the Nuffield Centre in London. Troop shows had been staged there during the war, and servicemen still came to watch entertainment in its theatre. *The Centre Show* was one of Benny's first major engagements after the war, and all the acts that he introduced at the time were making their television debuts. When I appeared, I reverted to the material with which I had begun in show business and did impersonations, taking off all the current sports commentators.

During the late '50s, I deputised for Benny in his summer show while he was in hospital having his appendix removed. I next met him in the '60s when he appeared in a charity show at the Prince of Wales Theatre, performing his popular *This Is Your Life* sketch, in which a little man is surprised by an Eamonn Andrews-style presenter carrying a big red book. Benny played a number of unlikely characters, male and female, who were supposed to be associated with this man's life. The actor whom Benny had used before as the link man was not available. We shared the same agent, Richard Stone, and he suggested that I might be a good choice for the role. I did an impersonation of Eamonn Andrews, which got laughs at the beginning of the sketch. Apparently this had not happened before, and Benny, being a true comic who felt only the funny man should have the laughs, said to me afterwards, with a lovely smile on his face, 'I was standing in the wings at the beginning, and I heard you getting laughs. I said, "This isn't on. He's the straight man. Get him off."'

Apparently he was pleased with the way the sketch had gone, and in 1967 he asked me to work on his series, *The Benny Hill Show*, and decided to revive the sketch. By then I had taken the hint, however gently he had conveyed it. I loved him dearly, but he held definite ideas on the role of his straight man and never liked me playing for laughs in character, as I did with Arthur Haynes. He had a charming way of letting me know: 'Oh, Nicky, Nicky, don't go for the laugh there, darling boy. Just play it straight.' Benny Hill started his career as a straight man to Reg Varney, and he respected the skills required to play the foil and feed the gag lines. Benny told Richard Stone he loved the way I interviewed his character, Fred Scuttle, and was very complimentary about the energy I brought to those sketches. The only other person in his shows who was allowed to get laughs was Bob Todd. Benny never minded that. He gave Bob some funny characters. I think it was a similar situation to that of Hancock and Sid James. Bob was very amiable and utterly different from Benny, so he never felt threatened by him. Everyone else was expected to toe the line.

Benny was a lovely man to work with, but, like Arthur, he could be insecure. I remember a journalist writing an article in which he said, 'Benny Hill was once the straight man to Reg Varney, and Nicholas Parsons is now a very good straight man to Benny Hill. One day, will Nicholas be as successful as Benny?' I wish it had never been written, because it slightly undermined our relationship. Benny showed the cutting to our producer and said, 'Look at the rubbish they write.'

Benny had worked hard for his success. In his younger days, he had accepted every engagement that came along: stage, radio, television. Once he was famous, however, he ceased to work obsessively and did just four or five shows a year, for which he wrote all the material. These shows would be made over a four-month period, and in between Benny would travel around Europe. I enjoyed four seasons on *The Benny Hill Show*, which ended when *Sale of the Century* took off and went fully networked. I think that once my show began to be successful he thought it best not to use me any more. I would have been happy to carry on working with him, but I respected his point of view and we remained good friends. He did a wonderful skit of *Sale of the Century* in his show a few years later. The episode was called 'Sale of the Half-Century', and he did a wicked impersonation of me. I was asked if I felt insulted. Of course not. If you cannot laugh at yourself, you do not have much sense of humour. I thought it was very funny. In fact, I telephoned Benny and told him he should take over my show!

When Benny went travelling, no one knew how to get hold of him. People would telephone Richard Stone to enquire whether Benny was available for jobs, and Richard could not find him. Occasionally, Benny contacted the office, and Richard would discuss the offers with him, but Benny at the time was not interested in doing additional work. He enjoyed seeing shows in other countries and formulating ideas for new sketches and songs. I asked him one day, 'When you go travelling and people see you, how do you cope? You must be recognised everywhere.'

He replied, 'There is a simple way round it, Nick. I can be sitting in Barcelona Airport in the midsummer, the peak of the holiday season, with hundreds of British people around, and all I have to do is take the teeth I use for the Chinaman in my show and put them in. It changes the shape of my face, and I am incognito.'

Thames Television cancelled *The Benny Hill Show* in 1989, and there is no doubt that Benny was surprised and hurt by the decision. Quite why the show was axed is unclear. Whether it was a decline in viewing figures or someone at Thames bowing to external pressure when it was pointed out that Benny's shows were not always politically correct in the way they depicted women, it is impossible to say. If it was the latter, Benny would have been mystified. His style of humour had been popular for generations. It was broad, basic and at times in the style of old-fashioned variety and seaside postcards. Any innuendo was no more overt than in the *Carry On* films. Benny loved and admired women, and he never understood why he was criticised for the way they appeared on his show. He would point out that it was the men in his sketches who were made to look foolish.

The producer for the last ten years or so of *The Benny Hill Show* was Dennis Kirkland. Dennis, who was originally the floor manager, became a great friend of Benny. He probably understood Benny better than anyone else. Dennis was hurt and angry when the show was dropped, and although he did continue to do some work the cancellation upset him so much that it marked the start of the decline of his career as well as Benny's.

On 18 April 1992, Frankie Howerd died. As is common in such sad circumstances, the media looked to contemporaries for tributes and quotes about the deceased. Benny was high on the list of the people the press wanted to speak to about Frankie, but unfortunately no one knew where he was. Dennis Kirkland was contacted, and, as he knew Benny well, and was fully aware of Benny's views on Frankie, he was happy to give a few quotes on Benny's behalf, which appeared the following day in the newspapers. Dennis grew worried when he could not contact Benny and decided to check on him. Receiving no answer at Benny's front door, Dennis fetched a ladder and climbed up to the living-room window, where he saw Benny slumped on the sofa, dead. Benny had been very low over the previous year or so, and by all accounts he had an eating problem and was over-indulging, especially for someone who had received a warning from his doctor about the state of his heart.

Benny died alone in his flat. It was a sad end for a great comic and a gentle, loving man who brought pleasure to millions across the world. Benny's shows are still being shown across the globe, particularly in the US, where they remain popular. The only British comedian to have more success outside his own country than Benny was Charlie Chaplin, which is a great compliment to his talent.

Benny had a warm and lovely personality that came across on screen and stage, and the public adored it. Certain performers have this quality naturally. You cannot put it on. It is part of their secret and creates an empathy with the public, which often accounts for the longevity and success of their careers. Eric Morecambe had this quality in spades.

Eric was wonderful, generous with his time and his humour and lovable in the extreme. In private, he was absolutely the same as we saw on television: a warm, bubbly personality who exuded humour. He was also a perpetual performer, always on show. He loved an audience, whether he was on the stage or in a restaurant with friends. When he was president of the Lord's Taverners, he gave a huge amount of his time and energy to the charity. At events he would spend an age at the autograph table, laughing with all his fans and showing off, sharing his talent endlessly.

I sometimes wonder whether this constant desire to entertain contributed to Eric's death in 1984. He had a heart attack in 1979 and underwent bypass surgery. He was given a clean bill of health and did take things a little easier. He continued to record his television show with Ernie but stopped undertaking so much theatre work and went fishing to relax. Whenever there was an audience, however, he switched on immediately. That was one of the many things that made him so wonderful, but given his health it might have been better to take things even more slowly than he did. He suffered his fatal heart attack after taking part in a charity show for a friend at the Roses Theatre in Tewkesbury. He made a number of curtain calls and then walked into the wings and collapsed. As with Tommy Cooper, Eric died in the environment he loved, and he is much missed by his family, his friends and his public.

Along with Eric, Norman Wisdom, Ken Dodd and Bruce Forsyth also exhibit this natural warmth. Norman Wisdom is the most delightful person you could ever meet, and that quality came across whenever he was on stage. He glowed. I had the pleasure of working with Norman in the Children's Royal Variety Performance in 1990 on a sketch he wrote – 'The Decorator' – which he originally performed with Bruce Forsyth. The sketch was pure slapstick, similar to the Eric Sykes classic 'The Plank'. We come on stage as two workmen to decorate a room, and things go wrong – wallpaper peels off the walls and paint is splattered. In writing the sketch, Norman had worked out every movement precisely. If he had not, it would not have been funny and it would have looked crude. Norman is a natural clown, a great tumbler, and has the unique ability to win over an audience completely and make them laugh at his misfortune, which he so brilliantly expresses in comic terms. Working with him was tremendous fun. During rehearsals he paid me a compliment, which meant an awful lot to me. We had been working on the sketch for a little while when he said, 'You are one of those people who are what this business is about. You are just lovely to work with.' I treasure that comment, coming from Norman Wisdom.

When you consider the difficult and impoverished lifestyle from which Norman came – he slept rough on the Embankment in London for a time – it astonishes me that he did not end up a bitter man, feeling hard done by. It demonstrates his lovely nature. Norman eventually joined the army. They did not really want him, but he managed to bluff his way in because he was desperate for food and a bed. He was grateful to the army and has said that he felt it saved him. Perhaps his upbringing has something to do with his ability to create pathos and endear himself to an audience.

Ken Dodd is another exceptional comedian, and I am very fond of him as a person. I first worked with Ken in the '50s when I was introducing *Midday Music Hall* from the Midlands, and he was on his way to becoming the inimitable comedian he is today. Ken is devoted to comedy. His principal nourishment in life is derived from the applause and laughter of audiences. For this reason he is much more successful in the theatre than in the mechanical media of television and radio. Failure to elicit a positive response from an audience is difficult for Ken to handle. There was an occasion in the late '60s when I was compèring a cabaret at the Hurlingham Club in London. It was a charity ball in which all the performers had given their services free, and the audience were a rather smart, young, monied crowd that one would not automatically associate as being fans of Ken Dodd. I had been informed that Ken, who was then starring at the Palladium, was arriving after his second show just to draw the raffle. It was emphasised to me that he was not permitted by his contract to do more than that. The young audience were mostly sitting on the floor and had enjoyed more than an hour's cabaret, which included Joan Turner performing quite a long act. After this, I went on and introduced Ken. A number of the audience had left the ballroom by this time, and Ken walked out to at best an average reception, which probably in itself made him feel he had something to prove. He immediately began to tell a few jokes before drawing the raffle, but he did not receive the laughs he expected. Ken proceeded to try to win them over. He worked on them, he persisted, he coaxed them and he would not give up until he had them roaring with laughter. I can think of no other comic who would have risen to that particular challenge, let alone succeeded so magnificently.

Ken has become known for the length of his shows. He trades on that. 'I hope you've brought your sandwiches,' he will say right at the outset of the evening, 'because you are here now and you can't leave.' I think it has become almost a challenge for him to keep going. Fortunately, he has a wealth of material to sustain the act.

When Ken was a regular guest on *Midday Musical Hall*, his girlfriend at the time would sit in the audience with a notebook and annotate every joke and gag Ken told, how well they worked and the variations in audience reactions. She did this everywhere he performed. Slowly, Ken has accumulated a vast store of comedy material. Nearly all comedians keep a joke book, but Ken has taken this to a new level. He categorises the gags under various headings, which allows him to build his routines around almost any subject he wishes. Over the years, he has stored all this in his brain. He is almost a walking computer of jokes. He can produce gag after gag, for as long as he wants, and the audience loves it.

Where Ken is the consummate stand-up, Bruce Forsyth is the exceptional all-rounder with universal talent. He can sing, dance, tell jokes, play the piano and present shows. This is a long way removed from what Vivian van Damm, the manager of the Windmill Theatre in London, thought of him when he first appeared solo at that venue. Van Damm lacked a certain sense of humour, insisting, for instance, that everyone call him by his initials, 'V.D.', without recognising the obvious connotations. Van Damm may not have been a great spotter of comic talent, but he was a shrewd businessman.

He had marketed his theatre all over the country in a most imaginative way. As a result, the Windmill had a nationwide reputation as the home of a very saucy, provocative show with lots of pretty girls, scantily clad and, sometimes, it was said, not clad at all. To millions throughout the British Isles, the Windmill was the best-known theatre in London. There was a running joke I told in the '50s of a lad who is warned by his father never to set foot inside the Windmill: 'If you go in that place, son, you will be shocked. Inside those four walls lurk sights that you should never see.' Unable to resist the temptation, the lad bought a ticket, went to the theatre, and he did see things he should not have seen . . . his father. The Windmill's famous motto was 'We never closed', referring to the fact that it was the only theatre that stayed open continuously throughout the war, even during the Blitz. This slogan was soon twisted by comedians to 'We never clothed.'

This image of the Windmill as a Mecca of sexual naughtiness, however, bore little resemblance to reality. The problem was that censorship ogre, the Lord Chamberlain, and because of him van Damm had to walk a difficult professional tightrope. On the Sunday night before a new show opened, he would invite the Lord Chamberlain to a special performance. It was always a full house, attended by relatives and friends of the cast and backstage staff, and other invitees. The fact that the Lord Chamberlain never delegated his responsibilities to an underling on these occasions suggested he did not find the visits irksome. It also meant that van Damm had won the first hand. For his second hand, he dealt out the hospitality in no small measure, so that, by the time the curtain went up, the Lord Chamberlain was in an amenable mood. Van Damm's ace followed. Girls who would normally be rather economically clad would be covered in yards of tulle and flimsy lace. Whatever disappointment 'His Lordship' was feeling inside, outwardly he had nothing but praise for the show and went away saying how absolutely charming it was, and giving it his complete approval. It would be six weeks before he would be seen again at the Windmill. It would also be six weeks before the tulle and flimsy lace were seen again.

To see female flesh naked in the theatre was one thing. To see it move was another, and it was this that was strictly ruled out by the Lord Chamberlain. The girls, if unadorned, had to remain completely motionless. In the words of a well-known revue number of the day, 'It's all right to be nude, but if it moves, it's rude.' Even van Damm did not break this rule. The period of total exposure in the show was, in fact, very brief, and, again, much out of proportion to the image that had been created.

The scene so many of the gentlemen in the audience wanted to look at took place during the fan dance. As the dancer performed, her nude form hidden behind two giant fans, another girl would stand totally naked in a delicate pose on a pedestal at the back of the stage. On one memorable occasion, the girl on the podium was suddenly taken with a fit of coughing, which got progressively worse. Everything began to move, and the fan dancer was forgotten when the poor girl turned full frontal. Nothing like it had ever been seen on the Windmill stage before, and there was a thunderous round of applause. The stage manager too became highly disturbed, but for a different reason. The nude's uncontrollable oscillations were in strict contravention of the censorship laws, and, in desperation, he brought the curtain down, or they would have lost their licence.

In addition to the regulations laid down by officialdom, the Windmill had its own house rules, which were displayed for the audience at each performance. Failure to abide by these would result in expulsion and blacklisting:

> The use of cameras is strictly forbidden.
> Customers must not survey the goods through binoculars.
> Customers must not climb over seats to get nearer the stage when places become vacant.

This last rule had little impact. The Windmill was run like a cinema, with continuous performances throughout the day. Customers sat wherever they chose, and many stayed on, hoping a seat might become free nearer to the front so that, should a fan slip or a nude statue inadvertently move, they would have the perfect view.

The shows ran along set lines. There would be the opening music, with girls singing and dancing, followed by a speciality act, booked for a six-week period. A tap-dance routine would follow, after which a girl would sing some corny song as best she could. After another speciality act and dance routine, it would be the interval. After the break, the ever-expectant customers were entertained by another song, followed by the famous fan dance. This was normally performed by one of the more experienced dancers, and here van Damm could be rather devious. From time to time he would ask one of the newer girls to do the dance, thinking that she might make unplanned errors with her fans and briefly reveal all.

Between the fan dance and the closing song and dance routines came the comedian. It has been said many times that the Windmill was the birthplace of up-and-coming comics. To those who had to go on and perform immediately after the fan dance, a more apt word might be 'graveyard'. Many did go on to achieve great things, but it was in spite of their experiences at the Windmill.

The resident comedian slot was for a six-week stint, and Bruce Forsyth followed one of my three residencies there. As the comedian, you just longed for the later performances, because they drew a mixed crowd, with some women in the audience. At the early shows, you were confronted with a group of men who had not come to enjoy a laugh, so as soon as you appeared, after the fan dance, some of them would pick up their newspapers and read. As you finished, you would walk off to polite applause and the sound of newspapers being refolded in anticipation of the next display of womanhood.

Bruce had already been performing on stage for a number of years when he took up the residency, and I believe he may even have performed at the Windmill previously, as part of a dance act. His solo act was more a song-and-dance routine, with soft-shoe shuffles and an impersonation of Tommy Cooper. He did a very good impersonation of Tommy, and it was the main plank of his performance. He was funny and had a lovely personality on the stage, with tremendous warmth. I remember talking to van Damm one day and commenting, 'That chap Bruce Forsyth is good. He has a lovely quality that comes over.'

Van Damm's reply was succinct: 'A one-trick comedian – he'll never come to anything.'

Bruce is a pleasure to have around – he is jokey, warm and giving. Eric and Benny were the same. Bruce also has a unique quality. He can build a rapport with the contestants on his game shows to the extent that he can actually almost insult them and get away with it. No one else could make the facetious, outrageous remarks that Bruce does and not offend. Bruce makes the contestants laugh, which is his great gift. For me, Bob Monkhouse was the best technical game-show host and Bruce the best comedy host. People like him immediately, and that is why he has survived at the top of his profession for so long.

Two other comedians made a particular impression at the Windmill. Jimmy Edwards was perhaps the theatre's most successful resident. He knew how to deal with that strange audience, many of whom might be sitting through three or four performances waiting to see the girls each time. If Jimmy was not getting a positive reaction to his material, he was happy to deviate from his set routine. He would take on a bluff, aggressive manner with the audience. In some ways, he adopted an early version of the character he played in *Whack-O!* a few years later. If he insulted anyone, he always did it in an amiable way, and they took it in good spirit. He would sometimes sit on the stage with a newspaper himself, making cracks at those whom he had seen in the audience during the previous performances that day.

The other resident comedian who stands out is Arthur English. He was not well known when he first appeared at the Windmill, but he quickly made a name for himself there with his brash spiv character, complete with kipper tie. He used to ad-lib with the audience and mock them. He would also try to involve them, giving them the opportunity to come back at him. If someone in the audience did, he would put his victim down with a quick one-liner, much to the amusement of the rest of the theatre. He had a quick-fire style that built and built with sheer vocal aggression and bravado before he would deliver his catchphrase: 'Play the music! Open the cage!' and he would exit.

Arthur was a lovely chap and a huge success at the Windmill. He went on to do *Variety Bandbox* but eventually exhausted the spiv routine, and that seemed to be all he had. The same applies for a lot of comics. Arthur, however, came back as an actor. He had never trained as such, but I believe that, with rare exceptions, all people who can play comedy can act. In this country, we breed great comedy character actors.

Bernard Cribbins is a perfect example. He is a brilliant character actor, wonderful in whatever he does. Ronnie Barker was the same. Ronnie was one of the finest comedy character actors you could ever imagine. His performances, in particular in *Porridge*, were incredible. He had the rare gift of subtlety in his comic timing. Of course, in *The Two Ronnies* Ronnie Barker was ably partnered by Ronnie Corbett, who is also a huge talent. Between them they generated those all-important ingredients of warmth and charm.

The wonderful slapstick comedian Charlie Drake also exuded a delightful warm quality on the stage, which the audience loved. I once took over from his straight man for a couple of weeks on a summer season, and we performed sketches together. I got on well with Charlie, but he did have a reputation for being difficult. I believe that is one of the reasons he did not go on to become an even bigger star. Charlie had a self-destruct button. Tony Hancock had a similar trait, but he showed it in a different way. Charlie had struggled to make it for years, so when he eventually achieved success I think it went to his head. He used to rub up the backstage people the wrong way, and they did not enjoy working with him. He became rather big-headed, and that does not go down well in this country. In America, they are more tolerant of that type of behaviour, provided there is talent there.

In Britain, you have only to whisper the desperate magic words, 'He's difficult,' and that is the kiss of death. In the US, you might say to a producer that such-and-such is 'difficult', and the response would be, 'I don't mind. I'll find a way to handle him.' Here they think, 'Oh, we'll steer away from him.' That is what happened to Charlie. He began to antagonise and irritate the crew. On one of his shows, it seems they even took a degree of revenge. Charlie's talent was in performing madcap stunts, and it was very funny. At the end of this particular sketch, Charlie had to dive through a bookcase made of collapsible balsa wood. Normally all went smoothly, but on this occasion the balsa had been replaced with a piece of real wood. Charlie tried to hurl himself through the 'wall' and bounced straight back. He hurt himself quite badly, and I think he went to hospital.

I am sure the label of being difficult hampered Charlie's career, and although he found success as a straight actor later on he never reached the peak that his talent merited. I was fond of him, but he was not easy.

Another comedy actor whom I did find difficult was Terry Scott. Many comedians have some personal neurosis that can make them delightful, a bit eccentric and off the wall or else they can be bloody

281

difficult. Terry Scott was one of the latter, as far as I am concerned. We did a play together – a comedy *The Mating Game* – and he used to prompt me on the stage, muttering under his breath, 'Give me a pause. Lift it up. Now the cue.' It was irritating and the last thing any actor needs when he is performing. During the interval of one performance on the tour, I was in my dressing-room preparing for the second half when the door flew open and Terry burst in. He was ranting and raving, but I cannot now remember what it was about. I ignored him, and he continued to shout loudly. The stage manager and his assistant obviously heard the commotion and rushed in to see what was happening. They could not stand Terry and were concerned for my well-being. 'Are you all right, Nicholas?' they asked. I said I was fine and that it was Terry they should be worried about. He was clearly having some form of brainstorm. Terry eventually got rid of me. I have no idea why, and even though he later admitted to Richard Stone, our mutual agent, that he had made a mistake, it was no consolation. The 'difficult' tag did not stick to Terry, however. The difference between him and Charlie Drake was that Terry did not act difficult with producers and directors, only with fellow actors and the stage management.

In many ways, show business is a crazy profession, and you have to be a little mad to want to go into it. This is never more true than with comedians. They are a special breed, some quite eccentric, some even slightly touched. It takes a particular kind of skill, courage and talent to step out onto a stage alone. I have huge respect and admiration for all those who are prepared to accept this demanding professional challenge.

THE ROCKY
HORROR SHOW

It was June 1994, and I was signing copies of my newly published autobiography at a luncheon organised by Waterstone's bookshop in Birmingham when my telephone rang.

'Nicholas,' said my then agent, Susan Shaper, 'I've just taken a call from Turnstyle Productions. They want you to take over the role of the Narrator in *The Rocky Horror Show*. It is currently on tour and coming to London on the 26th of this month. At the Duke of York's Theatre.'

Amid the noise around me, I was not sure I had heard her correctly: 'They want me in the remake of *Rocky*? I haven't boxed since I was at school.'

It is true that in our profession sometimes you receive a call out of the blue with an enquiry about a possible engagement. It is often something you had never thought about, which can turn out to be a delightfully enjoyable job. This was one such occasion. I am an actor who has adapted to many different areas of work, and I can truthfully say that I have rarely been out of work for more than a few weeks. Many actors never seem to explore new areas, and they confine themselves to what they assume they do best. They seem nervous to test their talent and accept the challenge of something outside their professional comfort zone. I am regularly casting my professional bread upon the waters, in the proverbial sense. A lot of the time it comes back soggy, but I am always busy.

I believe strongly in the motto 'Work breeds work.' Do not turn down any engagement just because you are worried it is not your 'thing'. You have no idea how one performance can open the door to other opportunities. It happened with me time and time again. For instance, as I have previously mentioned, my *Doctor Who* role came as a direct result of playing the dame in pantomime.

I had seen Richard O'Brien's *Rocky Horror Show* a few years previously at the Piccadilly Theatre. I enjoyed it but was not exactly carried away by the production. I was tentative about accepting the offer Susan was outlining. She went on to explain further: 'It is the 21st anniversary revival of the show. They have put together a wonderful new set and a lavish production. It is on at the Forum in Kentish Town next week. Why don't you go and see it? They would like a quick decision.'

The Forum is primarily a rock venue and attracts a raucous audience. They had even taken the seats away in the stalls, so the audiences could sing and dance along to the bands appearing there. Fortunately, the dress circle still had seats, and that was the place for me. I do not know why the management had decided to take the show there. It was hardly an ideal venue. Admittedly, the theatre was packed, but the audience in the stalls treated the whole experience as a concert – a concert in which they were an integral part. They sang, danced and shouted, hurling encouragement, obscenities and outrageous comments in equal measure throughout the performance. You could barely hear the dialogue above the noise. They did seem to enjoy the songs, however.

I telephoned Susan the next day. 'I couldn't handle a part in a show like that. It is not my scene, and the audience showed no respect whatsoever for the actor playing the Narrator. You could barely hear a word he said.'

'Nicholas, you saw it under the worst possible conditions. It won't be like that in the West End,' said Susan. I was still far from convinced that I could blend into the production. 'They are very keen to have you, Nicholas. They recognise you have quite a following now among the younger generation. That's the main audience for *Rocky Horror*. And you haven't been in the West End for quite a while. I think you'll enjoy it. I've also got you nice billing and a quite a good salary.'

'You've talked me into it! When do I begin?' If you are sensible, you don't argue in show business. You know you are lucky to be working when there is so much unemployment and good performers are queuing up for every job.

I was given the script on the Monday and told there would be one day's rehearsal with the cast on the Friday. As they were working every night up to then, that was the only time available. I would just have to slot into the show. The director, Christopher Malcolm, must have had confidence in me, because in the end the rehearsal period turned into no more than half a day. This leap of faith was all the more surprising because putting on the best possible performance meant a huge amount to Christopher, not only because he was the director. He owned the stage rights to *Rocky*. He had been in the first production in 1973 at the Royal Court Theatre in Sloane Square, playing the juvenile lead, Brad Majors. Christopher obviously saw the long-term potential for the show and acquired the rights. I do not think even Christopher could have predicted that, after its short season at the Royal Court, where it received critical acclaim as a one-off original piece of musical theatre, the show would evolve into an internationally successful cult musical.

I assured them I was a quick study but was worried about the entrances and exits. They put my mind at rest by saying the resident choreographer, a lovely girl called Stacey Haynes, would be in the wings to nod me on and off and, if necessary, prompt me if I lost the words.

On his first entrance, the Narrator carries a huge book in which the outline of the story is written. This is the scene in which the character has most dialogue, and this meant I could, if necessary, glance down at the words during this sequence of the show. This was a comfort, but I did not think it would be necessary thanks to my years of experience in weekly repertory. I had taught myself to commit to memory copious dialogue against time while performing in a different play at night. The limited number of lines I had to handle here would be securely in the memory bank by the opening night on Monday. With the Narrator's elegant crushed-velvet blue evening jacket having been tailored for me by the costume fitters, I was prepared. First, however, I had to negotiate my way through a rather feisty cricket match. I had agreed to turn out for the Lord's Taverners in a charity game on the Sunday, the day before opening night.

The match took place in the beautiful Buckinghamshire village of Penn Street, on the picturesque green in front of the village pub. You could not imagine a more traditional English setting. As was usual in Taverners charity cricket, there was a lunch beforehand in a specially erected marquee, during which a certain amount of fundraising was conducted by selling raffle tickets and an auction. On these occasions, the Taverners team is made up of actors and other entertainers and supplemented with ex-professional cricketers. These games tend to attract a good-sized crowd, and the local team are naturally thrilled to have such a large and appreciative audience, especially when they usually play to only a few local supporters.

There can be a downside to this, however. When a well-known face goes into bat, a young, keen bowler can become fired up, too fired up sometimes, at the prospect of dismissing a celebrity and perhaps getting his name in the local paper. In Penn Street on that June afternoon, the 'face' under fire happened to be mine.

In my youth, I had played for my school and university and could put up a reasonable show with the bat, but now I was middle-aged, out of condition, and I had not had a moment to get my eye in with a net in the lead-up to the match or even snatch a second or two with some practice balls that afternoon. In a match such as this, I would always rather face a retired professional cricketer who understands the ethos of a charity game than a keen club player. I have faced many well-known English bowlers in charity matches, and they could probably have bowled me out quite easily if they had put their mind to it, but they had nothing to prove and were not embarrassed to be struck to the boundary by an out-of-form, ageing thespian. They recognise the public want to see the celebrity do something with his bat before being dismissed. They can even make you look good by bowling a comfortable half-volley or just pitching the ball on the spot, so that you can hit it. Then, after you have had a bit of fun at their expense, they decide your time is up at the crease. You might have convinced yourself you were cutting a rather dashing figure in the middle, striking the odd boundary, until, suddenly, the quality of the deliveries changes and before you know it you are back in the pavilion. That is how it should work. The crowd have enjoyed it, the celebrity has not disgraced himself and the charity has gained from the entertainment.

It was not quite like that at Penn Street. The first ball I faced was, quite accidentally, what we call in the game 'a beamer'. It went straight, full toss at my head. We do not wear helmets in charity games, but fortunately I was sufficiently agile to duck out of the way. I received a profuse apology from the bowler after the match, but at the time it certainly shook me.

The commentary was being conducted by the late Bill Frindall of BBC's *Test Match Special* team. Bill was a good friend of whom I was very fond. It was a terribly sad day indeed when he died in January 2009. The contribution he made to cricket and to the Lord's Taverners was evident from the wonderful turnout at his memorial service in the lovely setting of Devizes, Wiltshire. It was a beautiful, crisp day, and the picturesque church was full with people wishing to pay their respects to Bill. He is greatly missed.

On that afternoon in Penn Street, it was Bill who immediately drew the bowler's and their captain's attention to the fact that the batsman at the crease had turned up to help the cause, not be killed, and could everyone please take it easy and play within the spirit of a friendly game. The match settled down after that, and I think I went on to make a few runs, but on the way home I realised that perhaps it had not been my wisest decision to turn out at all. I had come within a few inches of ruining my chances of a return to the West End and, as it turned out, of making an impression in a role in which I subsequently had some success.

Most contracts that actors sign for film, television and other work have a clause that forbids them to take part in any potentially dangerous sport or activity. I do not think I have ever seen cricket included in the specified list. Perhaps the lawyers who draw up these agreements have never played the game. I was on the Council of the Lord's Taverners at the time this incident occurred and raised it at the next meeting, only to discover that, had I been injured, they had no insurance against such an occurrence. I proposed they rectify this situation, and I am pleased to say that the necessary cover is now in place.

I arrived quite early on the Monday afternoon of the opening night and settled into my dressing-room. With the production having moved to a new theatre, it was essential that everyone was there considerably earlier than normal to allow for a technical run-through. I was hoping, as the newcomer to the cast, that I might find some additional rehearsal time, but as it turned out no one seemed particularly concerned about going over my scenes. This was, in many ways, a compliment. There was the usual checking and balancing of all the sound equipment, and the various principals tried out their major songs, but I was given only one opportunity to run through the 'Time Warp' number, in which the Narrator joins in with certain other characters in the show. Towards the end of the afternoon, Christopher Malcolm took me through all my entrances and exits. I quietly went over my dialogue to be sure I was fluent on the night. Stacey Haynes, who had instructed me in the dance movements for 'The Time Warp' – a jump to the left, and then a step to the right – told me where she would be backstage to guide me if necessary. A first night is always quite nerve-racking, and everyone is tense, especially as the critics from the various newspapers are in the audience to review the show, and here was I going on under-rehearsed and with no experience of the special kind of atmosphere *Rocky Horror* creates: audience participation in dress, song, dance and the odd verbal assault. I was nervous, but my years of stage work gave me the confidence on which to fall back.

In the Narrator's opening dialogue, there are certain sections where the audience shout out standard comments or insults. Most of these are repeated every night, so the producer was able to mark my script and warn me where the interjections would arise. As I had done stand-up comedy in many different venues, I was used to raucous reactions and heckling, so I was reasonably confident I could take this in my stride.

By the time I appeared in the show, it had become traditional for the regular fans to shout at the Narrator on his entrance, 'Boring, boring, boring,' probably because, to be fair, he is fairly boring, certainly in contrast to the other colourful characters in the show. Some more vociferous individuals would go further and shout, 'Get off, get off, get off, piss off.' Not exactly how an actor likes to be greeted on his first appearance on stage.

What amazed me most was looking out at the audience and seeing so many people dressed as characters from the show. This is the power that *Rocky Horror* has exerted over its faithful fans and followers. I used to enjoy talking to some of the fans at the stage door after the show, which gave me an insight into how involved and committed they are. There was one charming man who lived in Brighton and had booked the same seat in the front row of the stalls for both performances on the Saturday for every week of the six-month season. He was always dressed as the principal character, Frank N. Furter: black fishnet tights and suspender belt, basque and long, fingerless gloves. I asked if he travelled on the train in his costume. 'Only if I have friends with me,' he replied. 'Otherwise it's the Gents loos at Leicester Square.'

That sounded a risky operation to me, knowing the reputation of some of London's public toilets. He said he had been known to use the Gents at the theatre but had been asked to stop this on the basis that, if all the fans who dressed up did the same, the place would be so crowded there would be no room for those who wanted to use the lavatories for their normal purpose. Not unreasonable, I thought. Cinema usherettes, tail-coated hunchbacks and men in stockings and suspenders could put anyone off their business.

Having taken a deep breath, the moment had come to make my entrance. Clutching the Narrator's cloth-covered book, I stepped out. 'Boring, boring,' came the chant. This was regarded as subdued by comparison with some of the audiences the production had faced.

I instinctively paused, absorbing the atmosphere, and fell back on a professional skill I had honed on many appearances in front of student audiences and in rowdy comedy clubs. 'Thank you,' I responded, smiling at them and trying to gain their attention with a little charm. I then moved swiftly on to my first line of scripted dialogue. 'I would like if I may . . .'

It had now become standard practice that the regular fans shout back, 'You may!' It all sounds rather banal, but if you appear to enjoy their reaction it diffuses a potentially volatile situation.

'. . . take you on a strange journey.'

The fans: 'How strange?'

The Narrator: 'Very strange.' I was now building a rapport with the audience, and here I slipped in an ad-lib: 'Stranger than most of this audience.'

I felt I was beginning to win them over. Certainly there were no more 'Borings' being hurled from the auditorium. I am pleased by the fact that throughout the London run I rarely heard that particular chant again. I had weaned the fans away from seeing the Narrator as a figure of fun to be insulted. He was now someone to be enjoyed. As I grew familiar with the dialogue, I developed some regular ad-libs, which I worked into the script. I discussed these additions, which always received a laugh, with our producer, pointing out that they helped me make a connection with the audience and probably helped the show overall, as they calmed some of the more unruly audience members. I agreed that I should ad-lib only on my first entrance and from then on was completely disciplined and did not deviate from Richard O'Brien's original.

The Narrator: 'It seemed a fairly ordinary night when Brad Majors . . .'

The fans: 'Arsehole!' Brad is somewhat naive and comes across later as the fans describe him.

I paused, reacted and ad-libbed back: 'That is a side of him I don't know.' Not a great line, but the audience loved it. The script goes on, '. . . and his fiancée, Janet Weiss.'

The fans: 'Slut!' Once again, this is their response to how they see the character behave later in the show.

The Narrator: '. . . left Denver that late November evening to meet up with a Dr Everett Scott'. This is a character who turns out later to have Nazi sympathies.

The fans: '*Sieg Heil, Sieg Heil.*'

One evening, I tried an experiment that illustrates something about audience psychology once you have built a relationship with them. I looked at the members of the audience who had shouted out, one or two with hands raised in a Nazi salute, and said, 'You fascist bastards.' They roared with laughter; they enjoyed being insulted. On another night, I added, 'How did you get in?'

They replied, 'Through the back door.'

'Oh, another arsehole job.' They loved this, such is the explicitness of much of *The Rocky Horror Show*. That was the limit of my deliberate ad-libs in this opening scene, and I make my sincere apologies to Richard O'Brien for adulterating his dialogue.

On that first night, I had engineered one last surprise for the audience, a surprise that, I am delighted to say, was so successful that it has been retained for almost every production since. Not all Narrators feel entirely comfortable with it.

In the finale, called the 'Floor Show', which arises naturally out of the big final production number, most of the cast take part wearing fishnet stockings, high heels, suspender belts and basques. The soberly dressed Narrator then joins them for the final curtain. At the rehearsal on the Friday before we opened, I had tentatively suggested to the producer that as a throwaway gag it might be fun if the 'boring' Narrator was seen to embrace the mood and dress in the same manner as the rest of the cast. I remember Christopher looking at me incredulously. 'Nicholas, would you really? he asked.

'Yes, I think it might get quite a laugh.'

'I think it will bring the house down. Let's do it.'

The costume designer, Sue Blane, a very talented and experienced exponent of her art, made a creative suggestion. I should keep the jacket on, as this was symbolic of the Narrator, but go for the 'sexy' look on my lower half. My jacket had already been made, and the fishnet stockings and suspender belt were available because they formed part of the costume for the rest of the cast. I thought finding patent-leather high-heeled shoes to fit me at such short notice might be a problem. I need not have worried. The next day a number of pairs were produced for me to try on. I was intrigued as to where these had been bought and was told the wardrobe mistress visited shops that catered for transvestites. They may have been having a bit of fun at my expense, however, because I noticed that the programme credit went to Gamba, who supply most of the shoes for theatre productions.

I had thought my change of costume would be seen as a bit of fun. It might get a laugh, and that would be it. Christopher was right; my entrance was such a contrast from the formal way I had been dressed throughout the show that it received a huge reaction from the audience.

One of the most surprising things about my appearance in this amazing show occurred as a result of my cross-dressing in the finale. Apparently, my legs could be described as 'shapely', and in fishnet stockings and high heels it seems they are shown to their best advantage. This was something, as an average male, of which I was not aware. More than one person said to me after seeing the show, 'I've got to congratulate you . . .' and I waited for some kind remark on my performance, '. . . you've got very good legs.' As a performer I am never one to shy away from a compliment, but a passing nod to my timing, my contribution or even my 'pelvic thrusts' during 'The Time Warp' would not have gone amiss before my pins received top billing. Naturally, all the photographs of me that appeared in the newspapers promoting the production showed my nylon-encased legs from the few minutes in the finale. I am sure a lot of people who read these reviews thought that was how I appeared throughout the show. I hope they were not too disappointed.

My new look produced one or two other amusing moments. One was when the *Rocky* fan magazine referred to me as their 'sexy-legged Narrator'. I rather enjoyed that, as well as all the compliments from the huge crowd of fans who gathered at the stage door after every show. Some of the girls, dressed as different characters, were very flattering and provocative, and some were even flirtatious. I realised that, had I been younger and unattached, I could have made some interesting, perhaps even intimate, liaisons. As it was, I just chatted to them, signed their books or programmes and went home to the comfort of my flat and the warm embrace of my wife.

The mention of my wife in connection with *Rocky* reminds me of one particularly memorable evening. It is a great show to go to with a group of friends. My wife, Annie, who loved the show, planned a hen party one night. She and a group of her girlfriends went for an early dinner and then on to the theatre. It is an ideal way to enjoy *Rocky Horror*. They all came round to my dressing-room afterwards. They were in high spirits, helped no doubt by a little alcohol and the euphoria the show can engender. They were fascinated by all the clothes, particularly the old-fashioned suspender belt and the high-heeled shoes. I said how difficult it was to wear them and move naturally. I do not know exactly how long it takes to master standing and walking elegantly in such footwear, but it is certainly longer than a couple of turns round a tiny dressing-room. On my opening night, when I bowed to the audience in the final line-up, if I had not been holding on to the hands of the actors on either side of me, I would have gone head first into the orchestra pit. My legs were like jelly, and I completely lost my balance. One of Annie's girlfriends picked up one of the shoes and, examining it, said, 'Look at those heels. They must be at least six or seven inches.'

'Yes,' I said, 'I call them "tart's shoes".'

Another of her friends said, 'I wear them all the time.' What can you say to that? There was a slightly embarrassed silence as I tried to flannel my way out of the mess I had made. I rather suspect the ladies were enjoying my discomfort, as absolutely no offence was taken and Annie and I remain good friends with the person who made the remark.

The continuing success of *The Rocky Horror Show* is not surprising when you analyse what the show has to offer. It is all there: wonderful characters, unusual costumes, great songs, dramatic scenes, a lot of sexiness and even some underlying morality, all performed with such style, panache and sophisticated wit that the audience get caught up in the mood. A talented cast conveys all this on the stage, and, with a fine production, there is something infectious about the show. The audience feel they are present at a party in which they are very much involved.

The starring role of Frank N. Furter is an exceptional part for any actor if he has the talent to make an impression and captivate the audience. In the 21st-anniversary revival in which I appeared, Frank N. Furter was played by Jonathon Morris, who had made an impact in the television situation comedy *Bread*. The role of Frank could not have been more different from that of Adrian Boswell in the sitcom, but Jonathon's professional experience was wide and he grabbed the chance with both hands. He was most certainly one of the best Frank N. Furters with whom I worked. Every actor brings something special to a role, and Jonathon managed to give his interpretation an innocence that brought a different dimension to the part, while not losing all the other elements necessary for a successful portrayal of a complex character.

When *Rocky* was revived a year later for another six-month season, also at the Duke of York's Theatre, I was invited to return to the show, but it was the casting of Frank N. Furter that proved a little unusual. The part was played by Robin Cousins, the champion ice skater. I do not know what acting experience he had, but he was surprisingly good, with a strong singing voice. As a natural athlete, the way he moved on the stage, particularly in the dance numbers, was most impressive. He left before the end of the run, and Anthony Head took over. Anthony is an accomplished actor, and, while displaying a good singing voice, he was particularly outstanding in the more theatrical and dramatic scenes. Anthony was only filling in, and Darren Day, who had made a name for himself as a singer and presenter, moved into the role.

Darren did very well, exuding a lot of charm with an excellent singing voice. I found Darren delightful, almost a 'little boy lost', but unfortunately he became unreliable, which can cause considerable problems, particularly in the theatre. He was going through a well-documented troubled phase in his private life, particularly in his relationships with the opposite sex. On one occasion, he even failed to turn up for a show, though I believe he did warn the management he was not able to appear. Eventually he left the show and was replaced by Howard Samuels. Howard was not as well known as his predecessors, but what he lacked in stature and 'star appeal' he certainly made up for with a strong stage presence, a powerful singing voice and the ability to project a lot of sensual aggression.

Howard stayed with the show for the tour that followed. The following year, another production was mounted, with the same interesting set and a new touring cast. I was unable to commit to the full year, but the management were very helpful and agreed to slot me in on certain dates when I was free of other professional engagements. This was a great compliment and a genuine pleasure, as I loved working in *Rocky* and all the buzz it generated at every venue we visited. Having guest Narrators is now fairly commonplace whenever the show tours.

The role of Frank in this tour was played by the delightful Jason Donovan, and we became good friends. He has great charisma on the stage and is utterly charming in real life. He brought a vibrancy to his portrayal of Frank that was individual. He gave the character a slightly dangerous quality, which was exciting. He made you feel that Frank was a little unstable, and with the natural warmth he exuded his was certainly my favourite interpretation of the role. I treasure an unusual compliment Jason paid me when he was being particularly effusive: 'When I am older, I want to be like you, Nicky, and wear a cravat.'

I was naturally very flattered and said, 'Jason, never fear. I will be sure to leave you some in my will. By that stage, you might just be old enough to carry it off.'

The management and producers of *Rocky* have always taken great trouble in their casting, and this production was no exception. It is sad to think how many actors and actresses are always out of work; it is such an overcrowded profession. This tour of *Rocky* provides an example. Each performer was excellent in his or her respective role, yet few have gone on to significant work since, with a couple of exceptions. One is Laurie Brett, who played Magenta and the Usherette at the opening of the show and is now in *EastEnders* as an established character. Long may she remain there. The other is Mike Neilson, who took on the roles of Eddie and Dr Everett Scott. Mike is a wonderful impersonator and has put that skill to great use playing Dean Martin in *The Rat Pack Live From Las Vegas* at the Strand Theatre and abroad.

When *The Rocky Horror Show* was first launched in June 1973, the original cast were all talented. I suspect they sensed the potential of the show and were pleased to be appearing in a production that was different and creative. They certainly were not doing it for the money. It was originally staged at the Royal Court Theatre Upstairs, which had only 60 seats, and the price was under £1, with half-price concessions for students. Even if they happened to attract full houses, there would not be much income to pay realistic salaries. Tim Curry was already quite well known, but his performance as Frank N. Furter certainly advanced his career. Julie Covington, who had done a considerable amount of excellent television and theatre work, appeared as Janet. The author, Richard O'Brien, played the part of Riff Raff, a truly eccentric character who is described by Frank at one point as his handyman but is actually much more. Jonathan Adams was the Narrator, and the parts of Magenta and the Usherette were played by the lovely Patricia Quinn, who went on to reprise the roles in many successive productions over the years. She was playing both characters when I joined the 21st anniversary season in 1994. The director for the first production was Jim Sharman, and he clearly made such a successful job of bringing Richard O'Brien's writing to life that his interpretation has in many ways remained the blueprint for successive stagings of the show.

The reviews were very complimentary. Critics love to discover something new and exciting and gave the show unqualified praise. Barry Humphries, who was then the critic for *Punch*, praised all the cast. 'None less than excellent,' he wrote, adding, '*Rocky* is a lewd and lovable show, reeking with grime, gunpowder and gusset, and laughter flows with haemophilic abundance.'

On 14 August, eight weeks after its debut, *Rocky* moved to the dilapidated Classic Cinema in King's Road, Chelsea, which boasted two hundred and seventy seats, and on 3 November it moved on again to the King's Road Theatre, also in Chelsea, which had three hundred and fifty seats and where it remained for six years. There were changes of cast over the years, but it slowly built a cult following and dedicated fans would make frequent pilgrimages to this small venue to enjoy the show. It arrived in the West End in 1979 and on 6 April opened at the Comedy Theatre in Panton Street, which seated 800. The show finished there on 13 September 1980, ending a run of almost 3,000 performances.

The interest generated by the early reactions to the show led to a production opening at the Roxy Theatre in Los Angeles on 24 March 1974, with Tim Curry reprising the role of Frank N. Furter and Richard O'Brien again as Riff Raff. It was a success, but when a Broadway production opened in March 1975 it failed and finished after 45 performances. Sometimes the world of theatre is inexplicable.

A film was made in 1974 with Tim Curry and a number of the original stage cast, including Richard O'Brien and Patricia Quinn. To try to capture the American market, an up-and-coming American star, Susan Sarandon, was brought over to play Janet. It was a modest budget and made in six weeks at the old Hammer Studios in Bray. The film was less explicit than the stage version and titled *The Rocky Horror Picture Show*. It was a commercial failure but has since become a popular midnight matinee show in American cinemas. Audience participation is still much in evidence, with the addition of water pistols to spray when Brad and Janet get caught in the rain and rice to throw during the scene with the cod wedding between Frank and Rocky. Those fans who have seen the film but are new to the stage version often indulge in the same tactics, and announcements have to be made before the curtain rises to request that the audiences resist the temptation. A wet stage or, even worse, a stage strewn with rice makes dancing extremely dangerous.

While in the US it is the film that is more popular, in this country it is the theatre show that takes precedence and is frequently revived. This seems to illustrate a cultural difference between the two nations. Where the American entertainment tradition is more movie-based, Britain's is rooted in the theatre and all the magic that goes into creating a live production.

In this country, audience reaction varies in different towns and cities, particularly towards comedy and humour. These differences are especially marked when it comes to *The Rocky Horror Show*. I have first-hand experience, especially as the insults and heckling the Narrator experiences are often very personal. In London, the audiences are perhaps more theatre-minded, with the interjections and participations friendlier in nature and more in tune with the show. In the provinces, there can be an element who are not regular theatregoers and who have come out to enjoy themselves at the expense of the show, often behaving in a loutish fashion and spoiling the entertainment for the rest of the audience. The worst experience of this I endured was in Leeds.

The show was playing at the Grand Theatre, which seats over a thousand. The audience had been extremely vocal most of the week, shouting a lot and drawing attention to themselves, but on Saturday night the noise they made was unbelievable. The cast were disciplined and carried on, trying to ignore the clamour. When I walked on and took up my position at the side of the stage, looking immaculate in my velvet jacket, the place simply erupted. I have never heard anything like it. In front of me was a wall of noise, and I was genuinely frightened. It was as if a thousand people had waited for this moment and were now going to destroy the lone figure on the stage. Nothing in all my professional experience had prepared me for this. I was unsure what to do and so followed my instincts. I stayed silent, looking at them with a smile on the basis that, if they continued shouting and I didn't respond, they would eventually tire or run out of vocal steam. I had to summon all my courage to do this. It is not a pleasant experience facing a howling mob.

As the volume subsided, I began to speak. They immediately erupted again. I stopped and waited patiently, but I was far from confident inside. I tried this three times. Each time I started to speak, the noise returned, but it did seem they were getting tired of shouting at nothing. After a while the howling eased sufficiently for me to deliver a sentence. They reacted again, and so the battle continued, but I was slowly gaining some control. Eventually they began to realise I did have interesting dialogue to deliver, and they began to react to that and not just to me. I managed to finish that opening solo scene with a reasonably attentive audience. For me it was professionally satisfying and certainly helped the performance, as the audience were more attentive from then on while still actively participating in the show.

I thought perhaps I would be thanked by the stage management. Instead, I received heavy criticism for adding ten minutes to the running time. I did understand their reaction though. On a Saturday night, they need to strike the set and load everything into a large pantechnicon for delivery to the next town or city on the tour. This is always a long and demanding evening, stretching into the early hours of the morning. Their thoughts were on finishing up, not on how 'clever' one of the actors had been on stage. We all wanted a similar thing, I suppose. They were looking to get their job done and return to their digs. I had been looking to do the same, but in one piece.

THE EDINBURGH FESTIVAL

I love Edinburgh and the Festival Fringe. It is the best place to be in August, especially if you enjoy performing and watching first-class entertainment. Naturally, there are also a lot of duff or indifferent shows, but it is wonderful that such an amazing festival exists, where established entertainers can, as Shakespeare put it, 'strut their stuff'. More importantly, new and aspiring comedians and actors have a shop window to display their talent.

The Edinburgh International Festival began in 1947. Britain was still suffering from the aftermath of the war; there were shortages, rationing of many food items and other necessities and a general atmosphere of psychological inertia after years of intense struggle. The people needed something to help them forget the stresses and harshness of life around them, some positive excitement. The Festival of Britain had been a success in London, and a number of enterprising and creative individuals north of the border realised that nothing gave a bigger lift to the spirit than entertainment, and the truly beautiful city of Edinburgh offered the finest backdrop to organise an annual festival of theatre. Described as 'the Athens of the North', its centre is dominated by Princes Street, with the magnificent castle on one side and elegant Georgian buildings and fine squares on the other. The historic Royal Mile stretches from Edinburgh Castle to the grandeur of Holyrood Palace. The city had not suffered from the bombing in the way that Glasgow and the industrial cities of England had, and with its fine theatres it was a perfect setting. Theatre companies and artists from abroad were invited, providing the public with the opportunity to see performers who had been denied to them for over six years.

I had just finished touring in a play and had returned to Glasgow, where I had spent most of the war, and decided to visit Edinburgh and sample this new festival. Each major theatre featured an exciting production, and in spite of all the post-war drabness there was a real buzz in the air. You felt that was what people wanted to lift their spirits. All branches of the arts were represented, and there was even a variety show at the King's Theatre featuring that fine Scottish comedian Jimmy Logan. Successive Festival directors have seized the baton from their predecessors and have not only kept the Festival alive and dynamic but, with imagination and great initiative, have expanded and developed it. They encouraged everything that brought diversity to the festival and more people to the city. There is now an independently run Book Festival, a Film Festival, a Jazz Festival, and a television symposium with lectures on the media and all branches of the visual arts.

One of the most amazing features of the Edinburgh Festival, which was not initially planned or even catered for, is what is now called the Fringe. Small companies or groups of individual performers, realising there was a theatre-minded audience looking to be entertained, hired halls or small venues and presented avant-garde shows or little revues. This grew and expanded until established producers rented premises and hired out venues to anyone who wanted to present a show, large or small. In terms of the number of shows and performers, the Fringe is now far larger than the main festival and has its own box office, brochures and Fringe director. What started as some delightful and modest entertainment on the outskirts of a big international festival has now become larger and to some more popular than its original progenitor. You could say it has become the proverbial tail that wags the dog.

There were two shows, more than any others, that acted as the catalyst that changed the ethos of the Fringe. The first, in the early '60s, was the famous Cambridge Footlights show *Beyond the Fringe*, starring Peter Cook, Jonathan Miller, Alan Bennett and Dudley Moore and which later came to a London West End theatre and made stars of them all. The rest, as they say, is history. The other show arrived in 1966 and was an altogether more serious proposition. Tom Stoppard's *Rosencrantz and Guildenstern are Dead* drew considerable acclaim, establishing its author as one of our top playwrights, and later achieved huge success in the West End and elsewhere.

For four weeks, finishing August bank-holiday Monday, the whole centre of the entertainment industry moves from London to Edinburgh. Almost everyone who is actively involved in the creative arts visits Edinburgh at some time during the Festival to see new shows, view some of the new talent searching for a big break and reacquaint themselves with some established performers hoping to be rediscovered. There is so much talent on display during the Festival, particularly on the Fringe, that it has become a work of art going through the programme to discover which shows you most want to see. There is a performance at some venues nearly every other hour, so it is possible to plan an itinerary and see three or even four shows in one day and still find time to eat in between and, of course, drink.

I first performed at the Edinburgh Festival in 1990. I was booked to present my show on the life and work of the great nonsense poet Edward Lear in the Royal Museum of Scotland Theatre as part of the main Festival for two weeks.

My adult fascination with Lear was sparked in the early '70s when I was asked to perform the narration in an opera written by Edwin Roxburgh. It was going to be broadcast on the BBC's Third Programme, which became Radio 3, and was recorded at the Golders Green Hippodrome. It was a terribly clever production, with music composed to accompany a lot of Lear's nonsense verse. I rehearsed a great deal, as I always struggle with musical pieces and I wanted to get this absolutely right. 'The Owl and the Pussycat' was fairly easy because of the rhythm of the poem, but some of the others were quite a challenge. It worked very well, however, received considerable acclaim and was a big success.

My father used to read some of Lear's nonsense poems to me when I was young. He had two great passions, Lewis Carroll and Edward Lear, both of which I have grown to share. I found *Alice* quite frightening when I was young, but Lear I adored. My father was a busy doctor, and only occasionally did he find the time to come up and read a bedtime story, but when he did it obviously lodged in my subconscious.

After we completed the opera, I wanted to find out more about this amazing man and read a wonderful biography, *Edward Lear: The Life of a Wanderer*, by Vivien Noakes. I discovered that Lear had led an extraordinary life, and this gave me the idea of putting together a stage show to reflect that. The success of *Sale of the Century* gave me the opportunity I needed. While that show was running, I had a degree of financial stability that allowed me to explore other interests: after-dinner speaking, film production and Edward Lear.

How Lear survived after the deprivations he encountered is astounding. He was the youngest of 21 children, many of whom died as infants. When he was four, he was given away by his mother to his eldest sister, Ann, to be brought up. He was a delicate child, suffering from epilepsy, asthma and bronchitis, yet despite all of these drawbacks and difficulties he evolved into a lovely human being with a gift for writing the most wonderful verbal nonsense. His other great talent was as a graphic artist, which landed him his first job, illustrating macaws and parrots at the Zoological Society of London. Some of them are still there, beautifully drawn but so delicate they cannot be brought out to the light of day to be displayed.

Lear then became a landscape painter, which just about generated a living for him. His salvation came when he acquired a patron, the 13th Earl of Derby, who wanted Lear to illustrate his showpiece, the menagerie at his stately home of Knowsley, near Liverpool. This became a blessing for future generations, because Lear used to escape to the nursery and entertain the children with wonderful nonsense poems and lovely illustrations. Later, he published a book of these verses, but it did not make much money for him. It was successful, but he was not much of a businessman. His second book of poems, produced a number of years later, took off and established him as a writer.

I took the name of my show, *How Pleasant to Know Mr Lear*, from a poem Lear wrote about himself in which he depicts the somewhat eccentric character he had become. It is not one of his nonsense verses, but it does create a delightful picture of this much-loved and talented man in his later years. Throughout the show's hour-and-a-quarter duration, I tell the story of Lear's life and relate it to his nonsense verse.

I see his poems not just as a means of escapist humour but also as his way of coming to terms with the trials and tribulations of a terribly difficult life.

I love performing the show and working with the nonsense verse. I have always adored surreal humour. When Paul Merton goes off into a world of the abstract on *Just a Minute*, I think it is absolutely fabulous and demonstrates Paul's huge gift. I end my show with Lear's longest poem, 'The Dong with a Luminous Nose', which is quite dark in sections and reveals a great anxiety in his nature. On many levels, it is hardly a poem for children, but the genius of it is that you can enjoy it on the surface, with the clever words and rhymes, without having to explore the darker aspects if you do not want to.

I was a little apprehensive when I first performed it at the Festival, as there had not been a lot of advance publicity. The show had the right cultural content for the main Festival, but no one seemed to know where the Royal Museum of Scotland Theatre was situated. It was actually in the museum itself, and while the curator was happy to be part of the Festival he was forbidden to place any advertising beyond the museum walls for a show that was taking place inside. There were no posters or any indication that there was a theatre within the museum, and once inside even I had great difficulty finding where I was actually working. What hope was there for the public? All this was brought home to me one evening when I was accosted in the street outside the museum by a rather agitated gentleman. 'Excuse me, can you help?' he said. 'I am looking for the Museum Theatre.'

'It's there,' I said and pointed to the building. 'The theatre is inside.'

'How very confusing. Actually, I've come to see Nicholas Parsons. He is doing a show there.'

'I know. That's why I'm here.'

'Oh,' he said, 'are you going to see him as well?'

Rather naughtily, I replied, 'I don't need to. I know the show.'

'You've seen it before, have you? Is it any good?'

'Excellent,' I replied, and thought the penny must have dropped by now.

He looked at me with curiosity. 'I hope you don't mind me saying, but you bear a remarkable resemblance to Nicholas Parsons.'

'I know,' I said. 'A lot of people have told me that.'

'I wouldn't worry. You're obviously a lot older than him.' With that he went inside, presumably to enjoy the work of my young double!

In spite of the difficulties, my two-week show was well attended and received excellent reviews. This is one of the joys of Edinburgh during the Festival. The whole city is given over to entertainment, the public, both local and visitors, search for shows and names that appeal to them, and word of mouth, as well as newspaper write-ups, rapidly spreads the information about the quality of a performance, or lack of it.

Over the years, I have performed my Edward Lear show at many festivals, including the prestigious Hay-on-Wye literary event. I recorded it for Radio 4, and the show was subsequently transmitted on Radio 2. I have presented it in South Africa and on many cruise ships. It is incredibly well received by American audiences, and I have a theory as to why. There is something essentially English about Lear's verse. It does not sound the same with an American voice, so when it is performed with an English accent it gives the words a different dimension. There seems to be a great love of the man in the US, where many Lear societies have been established. It is sad to think that we have no equivalent in this country. It seems to be another example of the British taking their literary heroes for granted.

In 1991, I was booked by Mark Goucher to present a one-man comedy show I had developed at the Queen's Hall in Edinburgh. It was anecdotal in format, based on my many experiences in and out of show business, drawing on my ability as a solo performer and giving myself another string to my professional bow. It is a good idea in our fickle business to be able to undertake many different engagements.

The show at the Queen's Hall went very well, especially as the venue is away from the main entertainment centres at the Fringe. What was particularly enjoyable was the reception I received to my experiences working on Clydebank. The fact that as an actor I could recreate the stories by bringing the characters involved to life was a great asset. The incongruity probably helped as well. The audience obviously had difficulty believing that someone with the image I project could have worked and survived with all the tough characters I depicted, with their basic use of the English language.

There is one anecdote that illustrates this and which I always include in my act. If you are a young, new apprentice, the senior skilled workers always enjoy having fun at your expense by taking advantage of your ignorance. It happened to me quite early on in my time at the engineering yard where I worked. I was assisting an engaging character called Davy Mitchell, who turned to me one day and said, 'Nick, what I think we need now is an arse wrench.'

I said, 'What on earth's that, Davy?'

'Oh, come off it, Nick. Ye know a monkey wrench. Well, this is a wee bit bigger. Go down to the store and say to Big Wullie that Davy Mitchell needs an arse wrench.'

In all innocence, I went to the store and found the senior man, Willie. In my English public-school voice, I said, 'Oh, Willie, Davy Mitchell says can he have an arse wrench?'

There were sniggers from all in earshot. Willie looked at me and, stabbing my chest with his forefinger, said, 'Ye go straight back to Davy and say if he sends ye on another wild goose chase I'll come straight to his bench and wrench his arse right aff him.'

I tried to look nonchalant and ignore the laughter of those around. The important thing in these situations is to try to look as if you are not embarrassed. I returned to where I was working with Davy and said, 'Oh, Davy, Willie said fine, but what size of arse wrench do you want?'

Everyone in the vicinity laughed, and Davy slapped me on the back. 'Ye're OK, Nick. Ye handled that well.'

It is stories such as these that always receive the best reaction, particularly in Scotland, where the audience can identify with the characters I describe and mimic. When I first put the show together, I had assumed it would be the show-business tales that would be most popular, but audiences all over the country seem to respond with most enthusiasm and laughter to the experiences outside my profession. This is not to say that the anecdotes from working in repertory in

Bromley or recording live with Arthur Haynes are not equally funny in a different way. The public always enjoy hearing about professional clangers and hiccoughs.

Most one-person shows follow the same line. The stories and anecdotes are told in a chronological order, and to begin with I called mine *An Evening with Nicholas Parsons*. After a while, I realised I might increase the business at some venues if the title conveyed more of what the show was about. I have done such a variety of work that I think some members of the public were confused as to what they could expect. This was made clear when I was asked by someone who had seen the show advertised, 'What do you do in your act? I know you best from your quiz *Sale of the Century*. Do you ask questions?' To help clarify the situation, I changed the title of the show to *An Evening of Comedy with Nicholas Parsons*. The box-office business at the various venues where my show was advertised remained much the same. Sometimes capacity, others times reasonably full. When trying to attract people to the theatre, you have to overcome a number of obstacles to win their support – the price of the seats, what is on television the night you are appearing, the weather, how much they have already spent on other activities – so I realised that I had to attract as broad an audience as possible and try to capture some instant recognition. Accordingly, I have changed the title once again, trading on the programme with which I have been identified for over 40 years. My show is now called *Just A Laugh A Minute*.

Since those early beginnings at the Queen's Hall, the show has evolved and developed. Every time you perform solo entertainment, you draw on your experience and professional creativity to polish and improve wherever you can so that the content becomes better and the humour sharper. This is the only way to achieve any kind of longevity in our profession.

The next time I worked in Edinburgh was 1993. David Johnston and Mark Goucher, enterprising young impresarios, engaged me to present a stage version of *Just a Minute*. I was a little anxious about this, as I was not sure how BBC management would react to having their popular game show exposed on stage. Ian Messiter had agreed and was keen to see how the public would respond to a run in the theatre. I was booked for three weeks, and the show was staged at an unusual venue called Calton Hill. It is at the east end of Princes Street, and you have a long, uphill walk followed by a large number of steps in order to reach the summit. We put the show on at noon in a tent, which in the evenings housed the *Jim Rose Circus Sideshow*. The whole venture was fraught with problems. First, the BBC were indeed unhappy and threatened to take the show off the air if we went ahead. In the end, it turned out to be a hollow threat, and if anything it increased the programme's popularity, as it reached out to a wider, non-Radio 4 audience. Then the circus, which was very explicit and violent, upset one or two of Edinburgh's more staid councillors. One in particular, Moira Knox, a Mary Whitehouse character, was so offended by the content that she agitated to have the tent closed. I never saw the circus so cannot comment, but it must have been pretty outrageous to have created such passion when one considers the verbal explicitness of some shows you can see on the Fringe. Mark Borkowski, who was doing the PR for the circus, exploited this situation and received a lot of publicity, some of which rubbed off on us.

Our show was efficiently produced, but it was all a little haphazard, even hairy on occasions. They had organised buzzers and a control box so that I could gauge who had challenged first, and I had the assistance of a lovely girl called Chantel, who was the PA in David and Mark's office, to run the stopwatch. Unfortunately, the technical aspects sometimes failed, and I was left to improvise on who had challenged by asking them to raise their hands: not the most efficient way to run the game.

We had one resident player, Tony Slattery, who had appeared in the radio version a few times and was very skilled and funny. The other players were performers who were working on the Fringe in their own shows and came on principally to plug what they were doing. Some of them knew nothing about the programme and were struggling, but not as much as I was as I endeavoured to bring them into the show or twist the rules so they appeared to contribute. Tony Slattery was generous and always played along when we had a contestant who was floundering. The big surprise, and, as it turned out, a huge asset, was a young comedian who was hardly known at the time. He was performing an off-beat solo show, *Mother Teresa of Calcutta*, in which he appeared with a tea towel wrapped round his head and presented a pastiche of the iconic saintly woman. Another show he did was called *Graham Norton and His Amazing Hostess Trolley*. Unfortunately, I never saw either of them, but knowing Graham as I do now, and admiring his skilled professionalism, I would love to have seen his early beginnings. He was friendly with David and Mark, and they had engaged him for the season to be the standby contestant in the event that one of the performers did not turn up, which happened frequently. The artist had slept in, could not find the venue or had forgotten, so Graham made many appearances and was very good. In fact, I think the experience he gained in those Edinburgh shows was probably valuable when he began to appear regularly in the radio series. I warmed to Graham immediately. He was great fun, unassuming and full of natural charm, which he has used since to woo audiences in the many programmes he now presents on television.

It says a great deal for the strength of Ian Messiter's idea and format that even when it is technically not running smoothly we can improvise and ad-lib around it so that the audience are still entertained and find it funny. This happened frequently up on Calton Hill, and, with the talented support of Tony and Graham, we had a successful run. Not successful enough for Ian Messiter to want to stage it again, however. Perhaps he felt he wanted to concentrate his energies on the radio version. There are those who feel that is the best medium for the show, and Ian's two subsequent attempts to take it to television seem to support that view in some people's eyes. Personally, I am all for it reaching a broader audience. We could not now go back to Edinburgh as a stage show, since the BBC record two episodes for the autumn series every year at the Pleasance. We perform in a big venue, and it is flattering to report that the shows are booked out within an hour or two of the announcement that the tickets are available.

In 2000, I developed a different show to take to the Edinburgh Fringe. It was to be basically a chat show, but I wanted something different, so I combined audience participation, which is always successful at Edinburgh, with some personal stand-up comedy. The Pleasance, which was then run by a great theatre man, Christopher Richardson, was keen to present it. Christopher and his successor, Anthony Alderson, have built up their organisation into one of the most successful names on the Fringe. I agreed a joint production with the Pleasance and decided to try it out at their sister theatre, the Pleasance in Islington. I asked my friend Chris Neill, who is an experienced director and was the producer of *Just a Minute* for three years before returning as a panellist, to help me stage the new show.

The Pleasance had booked me to come on at 6 p.m. in a disused church-hall venue situated across the road from the main theatre and venue complex. I thought it apt that a Parsons was working in a church building and made some gags about that when the show was running. I still had no title, until one day I was describing the format to my wife, Annie, and said it was being performed at 6 p.m. 'That's the happy hour,' she said.

'Thank you, darling. You've given me the title: *Nicholas Parsons' Happy Hour*.' It is still running successfully at the Fringe under that title ten years later.

When we launched the show, it was very laid-back and casual, a little like an old-fashioned chat show, with a sofa for the guest or guests and an armchair for myself. We added a charming touch: a trolley with a collection of drinks from which to offer a tipple before we began talking. Slowly, I dropped all this embroidery and concentrated on what makes the show work: the comedy and rapport I could generate with my guests. In these days, because of the pace at which people lead their lives and the speed at which some shows are now edited on television, it is essential from a production point of view to concentrate on the core elements that make a show work and eliminate any unnecessary frills, however entertaining they may be.

We were helped in the first year by an advertising gimmick thought up by a delightful and attractive young person at the PR agency working for the Pleasance, Mary Gleeson. She had a life-size cut-out made of me that stood in the booking hall to encourage people to buy tickets. Before the show opened, it was stolen by a group of students, who requested a ransom for its return as a means of raising money for their student rag. They also sent a series of photographs of the cut-out appearing in a number of strange and ridiculous places, including being taken on a taxi. The most bizarre was one of N. Parsons apparently relieving himself in a public toilet. The photographs were tremendous fun, so instead of giving in to their ransom request we blew up the photos to life-size and displayed them on the stage. I started the show by describing each one as if the moment depicted had actually taken place. It was a great way to open, and the annoyance at having the cut-out stolen was compensated for by the fun and jokes I was able to extricate from the pictures they sent me. The cut-out was eventually returned at the end of the Fringe season. It was then stolen at the beginning of the next season and no note left. The mind boggles as to where it now resides and what vicarious thrill it is affording some disturbed individual.

Mention of Mary Gleeson reminds me of an incident the following year for which I will be eternally grateful to her. It was something she did that was way above the call of any duty that her professional responsibilities asked of her. I was staying in a flat in Jeffrey Street. It was on the second floor of a typical solid Scottish house, with 42 stairs to climb to the front door. The furnishings were sparse, but it was clean and comfortable and, most importantly, was within walking distance of where I was working, at the Pleasance. There was a mini-market shop opposite where I could buy all my groceries, and my favourite restaurant in Edinburgh, Iggs, was a few yards away. It is Spanish, with an adjoining tapas bar owned and run by a delightful Spanish fellow of the same name. It was all very practical, not least because the changing areas at the various venues are cramped beyond description and, as they are used all day by successive shows, it is unwise to leave your stage clothes backstage. The dressing-rooms are best described by an old music-hall joke: 'My dressing-room! That's a laugh! A nail on the wall.' With my accommodation so well located, I was able to change in the flat, descend the 42 stone steps, walk down the hill, then up the other hill, do the show, retrace my steps, ascend the 42 stairs, change go downstairs again, go out to see another show, return and go up the 42 stairs, hopefully to bed. Sometimes I went up and down those forty-two stairs three or four times a day, and with all the hills in Edinburgh, and not always having time to eat properly, I usually lost weight during my season in that fine city.

One morning I had slept in until 9 a.m. The phone rang in the kitchen. I leaped out of bed, my feet hit the small rug on the polished floor and I went down like a ninepin. As I fell, my head hit the sharp corner of a small bedside table, causing a nasty, deep wound on my forehead. I was lucky the impact was not two inches lower, or my eye would have taken the full force of the fall and my show-business career would probably have been over. There was blood everywhere. It seemed to gush out across the floor and onto my pyjamas. I tried to rise, but I was too dazed from the force of the impact. I crawled on my hands and knees into the bathroom, pulled a towel off the rail and applied it to my head to try to staunch the blood. I sat there for a minute or two assessing the situation.

When I eventually rose to my feet, I did not dare look in the mirror for fear of what I would see. In moments of real crisis, you turn to the one closest to you. I staggered into the kitchen and telephoned Annie, who had been on holiday with her daughter and grandchildren but had now returned. It was absurd to think that she could do something from 400 miles away, but I needed to speak to someone. She was very concerned and, as always, thoroughly practical: 'You must phone 999 and get an ambulance to take you to the hospital.'

She was right, but on an impulse I telephoned Mary Gleeson first. As luck would have it, she was in the office. I told her what had occurred and said I needed to go to the hospital to be patched up. She went straight into action, saying, 'Stay there. I am coming round. I'll take you to the hospital.' I now summoned enough courage to look in a mirror at the damage. It was not a pretty sight. I somehow managed to get out of the blood-soaked pyjamas and into some trousers and a shirt and sweater. Mary was soon ringing the buzzer downstairs. I let her in, and she came up to the flat and then helped me down to the street, holding another towel to my head, and into the waiting taxi. It all seems a little vague, as I was still quite dizzy, but I remember on arriving at A&E the receptionist waving us through as if we were expected. I was soon on a hospital bed in Outpatients, having the wound inspected by a doctor, a young Australian. He had a strong resemblance to a brilliant young comedian called Adam Hills, with the same features and voice. Adam had guested on my show more than once, and in my dazed state I had the illusion – or delusion – that he was moonlighting at the hospital and was about to apply the sutures. I was going to be stitched up by a stand-up comedian. I need not have worried. He was a real doctor and did an excellent job: two lines of nine stitches along the eyebrow and above. Nowadays, you can see only a faint scar.

Mary's kindness did not finish there. She asked for the keys to the flat and told me to wait until she returned to take me back. After I had been repaired and had the necessary dressings applied, and with my head swathed in bandages, I sat and waited for her return. She had gone back to the flat, cleaned up the blood on the floor, put my pyjamas and towels in the washing machine, changed the sheets and made up the bed. What a wonderful woman. She was not employed by the Pleasance to nurture the sick and wounded. She returned, took me back to the flat and said, 'Now, about tonight's show. You obviously cannot go on. What do I say?'

I replied, 'Mary, people have paid good money to attend. I am an old pro. The show must go on. Warn the stage management. Somehow I will get through, even looking like this.' I rested until close to curtain up, phoned my wife to say I was not irreparably damaged, had a snack and waited for the taxi. I was still a little unsteady on my feet, but I held on to the furniture on the stage while explaining to the audience what had happened. I was not as fluent as usual, but it all went well and the audience were most sympathetic.

My final guest that night was an old friend, Sandi Toksvig. You can imagine how she capitalised on my injuries: 'Come off it, Nicholas. Tell them the truth. You were out with the boys, drank too much and finished up in the gutter.' With Sandy's impeccable timing, the audience laughed, but I probably received more sympathy.

I took Mary some champagne and chocolates the next day, but it was a small reward for her amazing act of kindness and brilliant organisation in a difficult situation. I cannot imagine what would have happened to me if she had not been on hand to help.

In 2002, we moved the show to the Cabaret Bar venue in the main Pleasance Courtyard, where it remains to this day, and brought the start time forward to 5.15 p.m. This turned out to be a shrewd move. The timing was right and the venue ideal, small and intimate. The only drawback is that it can be very warm if we have a hot summer, but I cannot remember one of those in Edinburgh for a few years. There is no air conditioning in many of the venues in Edinburgh, but that is part of the fun of the Fringe: intimate, compact, sympathetic places to perform, with the audience close. The Cabaret Bar holds just under 200 people. There is a bar but no service while the show is in progress. Everyone in Edinburgh works on a percentage of the profit your venue can make. You negotiate and hire a location from one of the four major organisations – the Pleasance, the Assembly Rooms, the Gilded Balloon or the Underbelly – or from one of the smaller ones. There is no question of what your show is about, no censorship. You are on your own to make your mark. The overheads can be high, so no one makes a good living. Most of the youngsters who are experiencing Edinburgh for the first time go home out of pocket. Some find success later through the exposure they have received. Others leave deeply disappointed and disillusioned. This is the tough reality of show business, and in Edinburgh it is displayed in all its glory, glamour and heartache.

Established performers and those who have built up an audience over a number of years take a large venue and run for four weeks, but they have to play to full houses every night to justify their gamble. I would rather be sure of a packed audience and go home with a reasonable income than take the risk on a big venue. My production costs are minimal, as I am my own director and producer and do not employ a PR agency to push the show. I have one assistant, a lovely person called Maria Hanna, who has been with me for eight years. Together we plan each show, organising and booking the guests and ensuring everything runs smoothly. Maria is very conscientious, seeing each guest arrives on time and arranging transport if necessary. We don't pay them; they plug their shows. Maria also fixes tickets for me to see their acts in advance so I can engage with them better when they come on my show and thereby establish that all-important rapport. This can be demanding, and sometimes I see at least two other shows a day, on occasions three.

I introduced a gimmick in the *Happy Hour* right from the start, which some thought I should drop when I was refining the show. I am glad I kept it in, as it has developed in a most amusing way. Originally, when I was talking to the audience, I suggested that if anyone gave me any smart responses I would reward them with a packet of Smarties. Now I always reward anyone I actually speak to, and it generates a lot of fun and laughs. I get through about 15 to 20 packets in each performance. This was proving quite expensive, but I have now persuaded Nestlé, who own Smarties, to supply these goods in return for the publicity. I think they should actually sponsor my show, as the product does receive incredible exposure throughout a run of approximately three weeks.

Since starting the *Happy Hour*, I would estimate that I have chatted to about 400 guests, some of them musical but mostly comics. Of those guests, many have been memorable and with some I have built a natural friendship. There is not space in this chapter to mention them all, and in the process of singling some out I will inevitably fail to mention others whom I should. To them, I apologise.

Ross Noble has been one of my most brilliant guests, and we hit it off immediately. He is an exceptionally talented comedian and was a regular on *Just a Minute* for a number of years. He has the most fertile comic mind. He just talks to his audience and from their responses builds a whole comic routine. It is a masterclass in improvisation. Ross's wife, Fran, is Australian, and he was based there for a while, only rarely visiting this country, but when he did come over during the Edinburgh season, on a tour of small venues in Scotland and travelling on his beloved motorbike, he found time to be a guest on my *Happy Hour* even though he had no show in the city to plug. He came on out of friendship, and I was touched, and, of course, he was delightfully funny.

Following Ross's first appearance in my *Happy Hour* in 2001, we blended so well together and created such laughter that the Pleasance decided to mount a one-off show featuring the two of us, which they called *Sneakers and Cravat*. I always wear a cravat in my *Happy Hour* show. I first wore one on television when I was presenting *The All New Alphabet Game* on *Night Network*. I thought I might start a trend, but no one followed. It has become a fixture in my Edinburgh shows. The show with Ross was very successful, and we were keen to take it further. The BBC were interested. Unfortunately, Ross's then manager, who was guiding his career, did not agree. He did not want Ross sharing the limelight with another artist. I felt this was short-sighted. Nowadays, a lot of top comedy performers team up with other comics while retaining their own identity and continuing to appear solo. It was an opportunity lost, and it will probably never surface again. One thing that made our show different was the age gap, two comedy performers coming from different backgrounds and comedy traditions. I sometimes wonder what would have happened to our respective careers if we had allowed the BBC to take up the idea and exploit it.

Another of my favourite comedians in Edinburgh is Jason Byrne. He has been presenting a show on the Fringe for a number of years. He takes a large venue, and it is full every night for four weeks. He is another artist who does not need to come on my show to promote his own. I like to think he does so because he enjoys the conversation and the fun we have together. He is always brilliantly funny, especially when he engages with the audience, picking up on some joke I have generated with them at the beginning. Jason has the most delightful Irish accent and uses the F-word constantly, but in such an unaggressive and natural manner that no one takes offence. After a while, the audience accept it as just another word in his vocabulary. He is circumspect, however, and never uses the word when he guests on my show or when he appears on television.

There was a memorable and hilarious incident when he appeared in the *Happy Hour* in 2006. The musical act 4 Poofs and a Piano, the resident band on *Friday Night with Jonathan Ross*, was engaged as a musical spot in the middle on my show and was scheduled to appear just before Jason. For some reason I forgot this. I have no notes and rely entirely on memory. My PA, Maria, spotted my error and grabbed Jason, who was making his entrance from the back of the venue. During my introduction, she whispered in his ear, 'Tell Nicholas he has forgotten the Poofs.'

Jason made his entrance to thunderous applause, and when he arrived on stage his first words to me were, 'Your PA has given me a message for you. I don't know what it means, but she has asked me to say, "You've forgotten the Poofs."' This received a huge laugh. I suddenly realised what I had done and explained to the audience that I should have introduced a musical group before Jason. At the same time, I was thinking, 'I will bring them on at the end, and they can finish the show.' I announced, 'So we will finish tonight with 4 Poofs and a Funeral.' This received an even bigger laugh.

To make matters worse, Maria then came hurrying up from the back of the auditorium, climbed on stage and quietly told me, 'The Poofs have to leave. They have to go to another gig.' The audience were loving this.

I explained what Maria had said and in my further confusion came out with, 'So there will be no 4 Poofs and a Wedding tonight.' I then turned to Jason and added, 'We have rather messed up your entrance. Would you like to come on again?' He picked up the cue and stepped off the stage, and I said, 'Now a quick return visit by popular request. It is Jason Byrne.' He received even louder applause, and my first question to him was, 'Will you now please stay to the end of the show?'

He replied, 'I'll try, but I had promised to go and watch 4 Poofs and a Piano.' Another big laugh. What a lovely, funny, spontaneous man he is.

The brilliant Canadian entertainer, singer and dancer Phil Nichol is another Fringe regular who has appeared in the *Happy Hour* on a number of occasions. Phil is hugely talented and funny, and it amazes me that he has not become a household name. I find his relative lack of public profile inexplicable and can only put it down to the vagaries of the weird and wonderful profession of show business. Some performers take off and become famous, and others with equal, or even greater, ability do not. Who knows what the magical ingredient is that transforms an artist into a star. To paraphrase John Lennon, if I knew that I would have become a manager and ended up extremely rich.

Michael McIntyre fits firmly into the category of someone who has taken off. He was a guest on my show for the first time six years ago and was full of energy and talent. We had a very funny, animated conversation on stage, so much so that he dropped the microphone. Michael deserves every bit of his success. He always puts so much into his performances. The only thing that worries me about Michael is the amount of physical energy he expends walking back and forth across the stage. I don't know how he is going to be able to keep that up.

One of the great pleasures for me of hosting the *Happy Hour* is when I come across a relatively unknown performer and invite them on to the show. I hope it offers exposure to a different, and broader, audience and acts as something of a step up the show-business ladder. A couple of years ago, I was told about a young comedian, Daniel Sloss, who was described to me as an up-and-coming talent. I went to see him perform, and there were only a dozen or so people there. He was 18 years old, raw, certainly, but entertaining and showing great promise. He guested on the *Happy Hour*, and while we were chatting I encouraged the audience to go and see him. Normally, my guests appear only once in a season. They are all busy with their own shows, and the whole Edinburgh experience can be very tiring. This young chap was different, however. He called Maria and asked whether it would be possible to come on again. Apparently, after his first appearance, his bookings trebled. I was delighted for him and thought it was lovely that he recognised the benefit of appearing with me.

In 2002, I went to see a Liverpudlian comedian who had been recommended to me. He was playing in one of the small venues in the Pleasance Courtyard, in front of no more than 30 people. His name was John Bishop, and at the time he was a businessman trying to find a way to establish himself in show business. He had a strong personality with a great deal of charm, the all-important ingredient.

I knew he would make a good guest, and I was proved correct. He has appeared in the *Happy Hour* every year since, getting funnier and funnier as he has matured as an entertainer and his material has improved. He is now a full-time comedian, appearing regularly on television and guesting on the BBC's prestigious *Live at the Apollo*. I am thrilled for him. I find it very exciting when I see people who were struggling for recognition when I first met them and have since gone on to become successful.

In 2007, John helped me out of a mini professional crisis, and I will always be grateful. It was the final show of the season, and when I arrived at the venue Maria came up to me, looking worried: 'Nicholas, I am terribly sorry. I have slipped up. I went to the pictures this afternoon. I thought everything was set, but I didn't check on the guests. I have never done that before. And I have just heard that one of them can't make it tonight. So you have got only one.'

I told her not to worry, that I could cope and liked a challenge: 'I can always do a bit more of my own stuff. I don't think the audience will mind.' Just then, as the crowd from the previous show were walking out, I saw John Bishop amongst them. 'John,' I said, 'are you free for the next hour and a half?' When he said he was, I asked if he would come on to the show again and have a chat.

'Certainly, it would be a pleasure,' he replied. We took him back into the venue and miked him up, and when he appeared on stage he was wonderful.

Occasionally, I have the situation where an artist's PA or agent is not keen for their client to appear on my show. There is no money on offer, which can cause a problem. This happened with David O'Doherty, the award-winning Irish stand-up comedian and musician. David had apparently said no to our invitation, although I suspected he may not have even heard about it. I went to see his show, and it was brilliant. Afterwards, I chatted to him and told him how much I had enjoyed his performance. I then said, 'David, I'd love you to come on my show. It isn't a hardnosed interview or anything. It is just a chat. We have fun. And if you could bring your keyboard along and play it, that would be marvellous.'

The personal touch worked. He replied, 'Ah, Nicholas,' he said, 'that'll be fine. I'd enjoy that.'

The classic example of this was back in 2002, with the offbeat American comedian Emo Philips. He had agreed to come on the *Happy Hour*, but shortly before the date we received a message that he had pulled out. It seemed that he had recently been upset on a different kind of chat show running at the Fringe, where he felt the host had been aggressive, and did not want to be interviewed by any more British performers. Emo is a complex character, and you have to treat people of that nature with great sensitivity. By sheer chance, shortly after receiving his message I bumped into him outside my venue. 'Emo,' I said, 'I hear you don't want to come on the show.' He explained why, and I told him that my approach was very different. The whole point was to have a lot of laughs. He could talk about whatever he liked. He could pull my leg and just have some fun. Fortunately, he warmed to me and agreed to do it. He was a super guest. He asked me about the show I did, which he called *A Minute Just*. I described it to him, and he suggested we try it out there and then. I gave him a subject, and I kept telling him when he was repeating, hesitating or deviating. The whole thing took off wonderfully well, and the audience loved it. Afterwards, Emo said to me, 'That was one of the most enjoyable 20 minutes I have had in Edinburgh.' It is moments like that which make all the hard work worthwhile.

The list of wonderful guests is long. The brilliant Jo Caulfield has been on my show nearly every year, and I have watched her evolve and grow into one of this country's best comics, with her own radio show. I look forward to seeing Jo again this year. John Hegley has a different style, quiet, gentle and laid-back, with a talent for poetry, which provides a new and interesting angle. It is always a joy to see him. Janey Godley comes from another direction and is always funny. She is very Glaswegian in her humour. She gave me a copy of her autobiography, *Handstands in the Dark*, which detailed her tough childhood. I have great admiration for Janey having come through all she described in her book and still being able to maintain a positive outlook and attitude. She has appeared as a panellist on *Just a Minute* on a few occasions and it is always a joy to see her. Whenever I mention that I will be doing the *Happy Hour* again at the Fringe, she says, 'I couldnae miss that. I've got to come on Uncle Nick's show.'

By far the most polite guest I have had is Reginald D. Hunter, a funny comedian with a great big physique and wonderful deep voice. He is like an old-fashioned southern gentleman. He always refers to me as 'Mr Parsons'. 'You can call me, Nicholas,' I tell him.

'No, no, no. I have respect for age,' he says. 'Where I come from, it is "Mr Parsons". The only other name I will call you is "sir".'

I have been called many things in my career, but never 'sir'. It makes me sound like a schoolmaster.

Most of my guests come alone, but not all of them. Sue Perkins came on one year when she was doing her one-woman show, *Spectacle Wearer of the Year 2006*, and brought her two dogs. I didn't know about this at the time. Maria only told me afterwards when I asked her why she was backstage rather than out in front, as normal. 'I was looking after Sue's dogs,' she said. 'They are very strong. I had them on leads, but when they heard Sue's voice on the stage they kept leaping up, trying to get to her. I was fighting a losing battle.' I had noticed the curtain at the back kept bulging as Sue and I were chatting but had not thought much about it.

It has been quite a challenge in recent years to maintain the standard of guests appearing on the *Happy Hour*, as there are an increasing number of late-night variety shows appearing at the Fringe. The artists from different venues go and perform ten- or fifteen-minute slots, and they receive a fee. Understandably, a lot of artists are keen to appear on these shows, but I am confident that the traditions of the *Happy Hour* and the fact I attract a different type of audience from many other performers will keep us going for a number of years to come. I certainly hope so, as I love the Fringe and I love the show.

All the venues at the Pleasance are different in shape, style and ambience. The Cabaret Bar is at the corner of the main courtyard, and there is no easy entrance from the rear. As I walk into the courtyard, I pass the queue for my show on the left. There are no seat numbers at any venue, so if someone wants to sit near the front they must begin queuing early. I wait near the double doors for the audience from the previous show to traipse out. This means that a lot of my audience see me before I appear on stage, which does take away some of the mystique of show business. I then go in and help the crew of four place the furniture on stage; we test the microphones for my guests and me and make sure my tubes of Smarties are in place. Then the crew let the audience in as I disappear backstage. In no time, the lights are lowered, the music begins, the recorded introduction is played and I burst through some black curtains at the rear of the small stage and off we go.

One night, as I was standing beside the doors waiting to go in, with the head of the queue only a few feet away, a voice from a little way back shouted, 'Hey, pal, this is a queue. Get to the back like everyone else.'

Before I could reply, his female companion said, 'Steady, George, that's Nicholas Parsons.'

He replied, so everyone could hear, 'I don't give a damn who he is. He can still queue like everyone else.'

I said tactfully to him, 'I'm doing a show here in a few minutes.'

He turned to his lady friend and said, 'Have you booked to see Nicholas bloody Parsons? I thought we were seeing that musical show.'

'No, that's tomorrow. It is Nicholas tonight,' she replied.

The queue was already enjoying this thoroughly, and then to make matters worse he shouted, 'You were not my first choice, pal, so you'd better be good. She's one of your fans.'

In my embarrassment, I said, 'I'll see you get some extra Smarties.' At that moment, the audience from the previous show started to exit. I skipped in and began to get ready.

When my show was under way, I found out where this fellow George was sitting, told the audience what had happened outside and had a lot of fun. I also made sure his companion had extra Smarties for putting up with him. When you are engaging and gagging with an audience, it does help to have some characters off whom you can bounce.

There are always surprising experiences in Edinburgh. Three years ago, I moved from the less-than-luxurious flat in Jeffrey Street to a comfortable apartment in a modern block down the Royal Mile. It was a longer walk to the Pleasance, and all uphill, so I booked a taxi every evening to collect me at 4.45 p.m., arriving at the venue at 4.55 p.m. to be inside at 5 p.m. The audience is in at 5.10 p.m., and the show begins at 5.15 p.m. It is all rather tight, but everyone knows what they are doing and it usually runs fairly smoothly. The only worry is whether my guests arrive on time. On one occasion, a group, Five Guys Named Moe, took a taxi and asked for the Pleasance, and the driver took them to another venue run by the same group. It took frantic phone calls to guide them to the correct place. We began the show with the group not in the building, and when it was their turn to walk on stage I explained the situation to the audience and said I would introduce them but could not guarantee they would appear. They didn't, which I managed to turn into a moment of fun that received a big laugh. This is part of the essence of my show, the spontaneity and instant inventiveness. In a professional sense, I am living dangerously. I think it is part of the success of my *Happy Hour*. I did some more of my own comedy, and then said I would try introducing the group again and hoped it would work. They had arrived and came rushing onto the stage from the rear of the auditorium. It created a lot of fun, and the boys received even bigger applause than they would have if they had been there for the first introduction.

One evening, I did not receive my usual call from the cab firm to say the car was outside, so, knowing the tight schedule, I left the flat, hoping to pick up a taxi in the street. I started to walk, uphill. No taxi passed. I arrived at the junction where one turns left to go up to the Pleasance. There was a car waiting for the traffic lights to change, obviously going in my direction. I was now worried that I would not reach my venue in time. I mimed to the driver to lower his passenger window, which he did. 'Could you be very kind?' I said. 'My taxi didn't arrive, and I am due on stage at the Pleasance in about ten minutes. Would you be really generous and give me a lift up the hill? Otherwise I will be late.'

He looked at me intently and said, 'Are you one of those celebrities?'

I said, 'Yes, I suppose you could call me that.'

'Well,' he continued, 'there are too many of you bastards in the city at this time of year,' and sped off.

This was a surprising reaction. He is not typical of the people of Edinburgh, most of whom make you feel extremely welcome and recognise the benefits the Festival offers. I happened to pick the one who did not. The Festival is very positive for the image of the city: it brings in a lot of money, and many individuals make a good income while it is on, and not only those who work in shops, hotels, restaurants and bars. Accommodation is at a premium during August, and some canny Edinburgh folk move out of the city for those four exciting weeks and rent their flats and houses, which provides them with a good return.

One of my most delightful memories of Edinburgh occurred one evening on my way back to my apartment. I set out to walk back to the flat and take a little exercise. As I walked down the Pleasance, the street that leads from the theatre of the same name, I saw a sweet little white-haired old lady about to cross the road. She seemed a little nervous of the traffic, so I offered to guide her across. She was most grateful and thanked me in her precise Edinburgh accent. When we reached the other side, she tripped on the kerb, and said, 'Oh, f***.'

I was stunned and said, 'I don't expect people of your generation to use that word.'

She said, 'Oh, really? I thought that was the word everybody used while the Festival Fringe was on.'

Fortunately, we do not have many incidents when we are forced to ask security to help out, especially in my venue and between 5 p.m and 6 p.m, but there was one occasion that was most surprising. Three women were very drunk. They had obviously been on the booze all day. They were not being aggressive, but their constant interjections were upsetting the audience and making it difficult for me to time my jokes. I asked them to keep quiet. This seemed to egg them on, and in one sense it was quite funny, as they started shouting out remarks like, 'We love you, Nicky. We are your fans. We've been having a party. You should have been there. I want your baby, Nicky Boy. When are we going to meet?' The stage manager slipped outside and brought in security, and they were gently taken outside, but not before some much riper comments were hurled at those escorting them into the Courtyard. They threw back some compliments to me, which amused the audience: 'We're leaving you, Nicky. See you in the bar. I love his little bum.'

The audience heard this, so I said to them, 'She's referring to my nicholarse.' They laughed, and I was able to pick up the show and continue.

Edinburgh is a beautiful city at any time, with its own architectural elegance and charm, but during the Festival it really comes to life. There is an excitement and vivacity in the air. It is infectious, and I have been smitten with it for 20 years, and I hope I will continue to be for many more to come.

REPRISE

I have reached the finale of these memoirs, but what title do I give to this chapter? 'Last Chapter' sounds too final, 'The Ending' even worse. Other variations sound like the words that might be delivered at a funeral or memorial service. I have settled on 'Reprise', because, when I began to write, I realised I was focusing on what working in this profession I love has meant to me, a theme that, I hope, has already weaved its way throughout this book.

Contemplating this finale has made me feel very mortal, with thoughts turning to my eventual demise. I have never shied away from talking about death; it is the one most certain thing after birth. I find, however, that many people are unsettled by it and do not even like to use the word. They talk of someone 'passing away', as if any other mention would hasten their own end. Perhaps it is easier when you have lived through a war and have seen death at close quarters. You know that something unexpected can strike you down at any time. Such fears and anxieties still exist in the unsettled times in which we now live, but they are less potent. What I do know is that the number of years I have left are small in comparison with those that have already passed. This helps me value every day and treasure the happy moments that occur, while fending off the difficult ones.

I have always endeavoured to live life to the full and will continue to do so as long as I am able. I approach all my professional engagements conscientiously, but some are undertaken principally to earn a living while others are performed with joy and pleasure and, if successful, great satisfaction. As I have already explained, I was steered away from expressing myself as an actor when young. The struggles to enter this profession were so challenging that everything I have achieved as a performer is a bonus and offers the same satisfaction as if I was embarking on each job for the first time. It also brings the reassurance and encouragement that everyone craves when they are young and which was missing during the most formative years of my life. Perhaps, on one level, these difficulties acted as a spur for me to continue proving myself. On another level, they also led me subconsciously to construct barriers along the road to establishing myself. Perhaps the fact that the early approval that children find so helpful was lacking meant I was creating ways by which I might fail.

The naive manner in which I handled my part in *Carry on Regardless* is an illustration of an inadvertent attempt to jeopardise my chances of success. My behaviour began to put me under considerable stress, which threatened to become a hindrance to me professionally. My adopted godmother, Joan Ling, was once again very helpful. She suggested that I seek psychiatric help. This was not a fashionable route to take back then if you had emotional problems, unlike today, when there is no stigma attached. It seems nearly every other person you meet is in therapy or having counselling. In the US, they openly talk about seeing a 'shrink'. In the '50s, the only people known to be consulting psychiatrists were severely disturbed individuals, so to do the same for a mild anxiety required a certain courage. It was not something that you openly spoke about, because you ran the risk of being considered very strange or even unbalanced. There is no doubt it helped, and I was able to lay to rest those demons that were unsettling me or, as they say professionally, face up to the dark areas of my personality, which many of us possess and with which most of us can live. How much more at peace with the world you feel when they are not troubling you or making you tense. On advice, I decided that someone should know what I was doing, and I spoke with my father, who, despite being a doctor and a very gentle, caring person, displayed all the prejudices present at that time. He said he really did not want to know. It was my life to lead as I wished, and he would prefer to forget we had ever had the conversation. Also, in no way was I to mention it to my mother, who, he felt, would not understand and would be very unsettled. In that, I am sure he was right, and she probably would have felt that all her anxieties about me entering the disturbing world of show business had been fulfilled.

The help I received has been of lasting benefit. When I married Denise, I told her and she was most understanding. I think actors who are forever delving into their unconscious to be creative accept these things. I also received tremendous support from a settled home and the joy that was brought into my life by my two children, Suzy and Justin. Life has moved on, and now I have the added bonus of adorable grandchildren to whom I am very close and, of course, the love and support of Annie, who makes it possible for me to undertake all the demanding work that comes my way. Annie says I am very tolerant. I just think I am sensible. What is the point of becoming upset about what people do or say? If someone is unpleasant, I ignore it, or them. They have their own problems, so let them find a way to handle them. Why waste energy on negative emotions? Save it for the things that matter. I embrace the positive. Family life also helped me retain my sanity in this crazy world we call show business. I have already stated you need to be a little mad if you wish to become a performer. Perhaps it is more accurate to say that, although I have preserved my sanity, I am not entirely sane or, at least, not entirely conventional. At times I can be a little eccentric and would like to have been more so, but I was confined by my upbringing.

I love talking to small children, connecting with them and seeing how their minds work and react to images and simple humour. All children love play-acting and have a delightful sense of the absurd. They live a great deal of their lives in their own created fantasy world until, as they grow up, conformity piles layers of civilisation on them and they lose much of the spontaneity and sense of fun that I think are so important in life. One of the reasons I was attracted to Edward Lear and his wonderful nonsense was that he was able to enter into the fantasy existence of children and they responded and enjoyed it. Telling bedtime stories, to my children and now my grandchildren, has always been a great pleasure. For them the tales are real, and I love to see the way their minds follow you into the world you are creating, even though it is not always reality.

One of my grandchildren, Lara, who is six, has a vivid imagination and can be very demanding. When I am telling her bedtime stories, after two or three she will suddenly say, 'Papa, now I am going to tell you a story.' She will then launch into complete nonsense, a sequence of non sequiturs, thoughts, phrases and words hung together with very little cohesion. I think it is absolutely wonderful, a young, creative imagination being given free rein. This world of imagination is the one in which actors must live. I believe that performers are more personally in touch with the child within them than most people. It is something we draw on, particularly when it comes to comedy.

I have now written over 120,000 words of memoirs, and although there is a lot more I could have included the information and anecdotes I have written have made me realise what an incredible amount of work I have undertaken over many years. I never think of myself as being old. The years I have lived bear no relation to my age and certainly not to the age I feel. I am a great believer in using my brain as actively and consistently as I can, treating it like another muscle. This helps to keep me sharp and probably feel younger than I am. Actors who are busy professionally continually have to memorise words and speeches, which may be the reason that many of them live to a more advanced age than in other professions. The extent to which I use my brain when hosting *Just a Minute* can be demanding, and the concentration intense. This places my memory under great pressure. How wonderful to think I have a job that I enjoy but which also probably helps to hold back the ageing process.

Just a Minute represents a branch of comedy that is increasingly popular today: improvised or ad-lib comedy, as performed by the Comedy Store Players and others. Paul Merton is one of the Comedy Store Players, and when he tours the country with his Impro Chums, including a regular season at the Edinburgh Festival Fringe, the show is in such demand that it is always packed out. In the early '60s, I devised a new routine to work in cabaret with a friend, the comedy actor Leslie Randall. We asked members of the audience for suggestions of professions, situations, ideas or words that we could then incorporate into an improvised sketch. I received an engagement at a club called

Merrie's, near Portman Square. The plan was to work as a duo to begin with and, if successful, bring in others. Our first reserve was an unknown performer whom I had met at Clement Freud's club, David Frost.

Andrew Merrie was in many ways courageous in allowing us to try something as original as this in his club. Leslie and I had every confidence that we could make it work, but it turned out that the concept was too far ahead of its time. We received a glowing review in *The Stage* from Peter Hepple, and some of the diners at the club did respond to the idea, but most were reluctant to participate in something that was radically different. After a limited run, we sadly decided to abandon it. There was simply not an audience then for that particular style of entertainment. David Frost never actually performed with us, but, soon after, he was launched by Ned Sherrin as the link man in a series that broke new ground in television, *That Was the Week That Was*.

It does not pay to think of an idea too soon or before the public is ready for it. Nowadays, audiences have become more sophisticated as they have been exposed to entertainment of all kinds through the media and elsewhere. Improvised humour is one of the most popular forms and, in my view, produces some of the very best comedy. I think this is owing to the fact that the audience know it is being created on the spur of the moment. They are present at an event in which they play a part, and they respond positively. That has been the ethos of *Just a Minute* from its very first broadcast, and it remains so to this day. I hope it will continue long into the future.

I have seen tremendous changes in my lifetime. The world in which I grew up was utterly different from the world in which we live today. The speed of progress has been so dramatic; on occasions it has affected some of the older generation. They have become bewildered, suffering from what one writer described a few years ago as 'future shock'. They are unable to keep pace with the changes, particularly in the world of technology, where new developments and advances seem to arrive every year. This has made a lot of people long for the pace of life and security that existed when they were younger. This is the reason many of the old films and television shows are still popular. They represent a different era, with simpler attitudes and values, which can be very reassuring and comfortable. This prompts the question: Does entertainment reflect life, or does it help shape it, bringing about social change through its creativity? This latter thought is, I believe, true of the world of comedy.

Humour is classless. That is a statement certainly worth reprising. If something is funny, it will appeal to people across all sections of society, irrespective of their backgrounds and intelligence. It brings people together in what they enjoy and appreciate. As a result, the great comedy shows over the years, particularly in radio and then when television became established, have acted as a catalyst to help create a more egalitarian society than the one that existed when I was young. I have inhabited the world of humorous entertainment for over 70 years, and writing this it is humbling to think that people's attitudes and outlooks may have been affected by the work in which I have been involved with Eric Barker and Arthur Haynes or by other shows, from *Much-Binding-in-the-Marsh* to *Boeing-Boeing* and, of course, *Just a Minute*.

As I reflect on my career, I have come to realise that being an entertainer carries with it an unconscious responsibility. It is not sufficient to be concerned only with performing to the best of your ability, though this is the priority when you are working. Performers should also be aware of the influence their work can have. It is an amazing profession, and I am privileged to be part of it.

From my first performance as Cuckoo the clown when I was four years of age all the way through to my most recent appearance in Edinburgh, I have accepted the challenge of moving audiences to laughter or tears. Perhaps the biggest challenge is to create laughter, which is the best therapy in the world. I will happily continue to do that and enjoy the professional satisfaction that it brings as long as there is an audience to be entertained.

INDEX